For my
Sunshine!

love you,
A

Published by CelebrityPress®, Orlando, FL

CelebrityPress® is a registered trademark

Printed in the United States of America.

ISBN: 978-0-9895187-2-7
LCCN: 2013942729

This publication is designed to provide accurate and authoritative information with regard to the subject matter covered. It is sold with the understanding that the publisher is not engaged in rendering legal, accounting, or other professional advice. If legal advice or other expert assistance is required, the services of a competent professional should be sought. The opinions expressed by the authors in this book are not endorsed by CelebrityPress® and are the sole responsibility of the author rendering the opinion.

Most CelebrityPress® titles are available at special quantity discounts for bulk purchases for sales promotions, premiums, fundraising, and educational use. Special versions or book excerpts can also be created to fit specific needs.

For more information, please write:
CelebrityPress®
520 N. Orlando Ave, #2
Winter Park, FL 32789
or call 1.877.261.4930

Visit us online at: www.CelebrityPressPublishing.com

CELEBRITY PRESS®
Winter Park, Florida

CONTENTS

CHAPTER 1

TAKE ACTION AND NEVER GIVE UP

BY BRIAN TRACY

The world seems to belong to those who reach out and grab it with both hands. It belongs to those who do something, rather than those who just wish and hope and plan and pray, and intend to do something someday, when everything is just right.

Successful people are not necessarily those who make the right decisions all the time. No one can do that, no matter how smart he is. But once successful people have made a decision, they begin moving immediately toward their objectives step-by-step. They begin to get feedback or signals to tell them where they're off course, and when course corrections are necessary. As they take action and move toward their goals, they continually get new information that enables them to adjust their plans in large and small ways. Action is everything.

It is important to understand that life requires a never-ending series of changes, corrections and course adjustments. For example, when an airplane leaves Chicago for Los Angeles, it is off course 99% of the time. This is normal and natural, and to be expected. The pilot makes continual course corrections, a little to the north, a little to the south. The pilot continually adjusts altitude and throttle, and sure enough, several hours later the plane touches down at exactly the time predicted when it first became airborne upon leaving Chicago. The entire journey was a process of adaptations and course adjustments.

What's the reality? The reality is that there are no guarantees in life. Everything you do—even crossing the street—is characterized by uncertainty. You can never be completely sure that any action or behavior is going to bring about the desired result. There is always a risk. And where there is risk, there is fear. And whatever you think about grows in your mind and heart. People who think continually about the risks involved in any undertaking, soon become preoccupied with fears and doubts and anxieties that conspire to hold them back from trying in the first place.

THE CORRIDOR PRINCIPLE

At Babson College, in a 12-year study into the reasons for success, researchers concluded that virtually all success was based on what they called the "corridor principle." They likened achieving success to proceeding down a corridor in life. Each of us stands at the entrance to this corridor, looking into the darkness, seeing the corridor disappearing into the distance. The researchers found in their study that the difference between the successful people and the failures could be summarized by one word: *launch*! Successful people were willing to launch themselves down the corridor of opportunity without any guarantee of what would occur. They were willing to risk uncertainty and overcome the normal fears and doubts that hold the great majority in place.

The remarkable discovery is that as you move down the corridor of life, new doors of opportunity open up on both sides of you. However, you would not have seen those doors if you had not moved into and down the corridor in the first place. These possibilities would not have opened up for you if you had waited for some guarantee before stepping out in faith and taking action.

TAKE THE FIRST STEP

The Confucian saying, "A journey of a thousand leagues begins with a single step," simply means that great accomplishments begin with your willingness to face the inevitable uncertainty of any new enterprise, and step out boldly in the direction of your goal.

Not long ago, a couple came to me with a problem. He was working for a company owned by his family in which he was bitterly unhappy.

It was full of politics, backbiting and negativity, and he was stressed out and hated his job. He wanted to do something else, but had no job offers or potential alternatives to his current position. He asked me for my advice on what to do.

I explained to him that there is a "Vacuum Law of Prosperity" which says that, when you create a vacuum of any kind, nature rushes to fill it. In his case, this meant that as long as he stayed at his current job, there was no way that he could recognize other possibilities, and there was no way that other opportunities could find him. I told him to take a giant leap of faith and just walk away from his current job with no lifeline or safety net. I assured him that if he did, all kinds of opportunities would open up for him that he simply could not see while he was trapped in his current situation.

ACT BOLDLY WITH NO GUARANTEES

He took my advice. He quit his job. The members of his family became very angry and told him that he would be unemployable outside of their business. But he stuck to his guns. He went home, took a few days off and began to think about his experience and his skills, and how they could best be applied to other jobs at other companies.

Within two weeks, without raising a finger, he had two job offers from other companies, both paying substantially more than what he was getting before, and both offering all kinds of opportunities that were vastly superior to the job he had walked away from. As soon as the word had gotten out in the marketplace that he was available, other company owners, having worked with him and his company in the past, were eager to open doors for him. As he moved down the corridor of life, he began to see possibilities that he had been missing completely by limiting himself to where he was.

MAKE YOUR OWN LUCK

If you want to be more successful faster, just do or try more things. Take more action; get busier. Start a little earlier; work a little harder; stay a little later. Put the odds in your favor. According to the Law of Probability, the more things you try, the more likely it is that you will try the one thing that will make all the difference.

Luck is quite predictable. If you want more luck, take more chances. Be more active. Show up more often.

Tom Peters, the best-selling author of *In Search of Excellence* and other business books, found in his study that a key quality of top executives was a "bias for action." Their motto seemed to be, "Ready, aim, fire." Their attitude toward business was summarized in the words, "Do it, fix it, try it." They realized that the future belongs to those who are action-oriented, to those willing to take risks.

STEP OUT IN FAITH

Successful people know, as General Douglas MacArthur once said, "There is no security in life, only opportunity." And the interesting thing is this: If you seek opportunity, you'll end up with all the security you need. However, if you seek security, you'll end up with neither opportunity nor security. The proof of this is all around us, in the downsizing and reconstructing of corporations, where thousands of men and women who sought security are finding themselves unemployed for long periods of time.

Use the "momentum principle of success," which is derived from two physical laws; the Law of Momentum and the Law of Inertia. It applies equally well to everything that you accomplish or fail to accomplish.

In physics, the Law of Momentum states that a body in motion tends to remain in motion unless acted upon by an outside force. The Law of Inertia, on the other hand, states that a body at rest tends to remain at rest unless acted upon by an outside force.

These two laws imply that it may be hard to get started toward your goal, because you have to fight the pull of the comfort zone and the force of inertia. But, once you get into motion toward something that is important to you, it's much easier to continue making progress than it is if you stop somewhere along the way and have to start again.

When you observe successful people, you find that they are very much like the plate spinners in the circus. They get things started. They get the plates spinning. Then, they continually keep them spinning, knowing that if a plate falls off, or something comes to a halt, it's much harder to get it restarted than it is to keep it going in the first place.

GET GOING AND KEEP GOING

Once you have a goal and a plan, get going! Once you start moving toward your goal, don't stop. Do something every day to move yourself closer toward your goal. Don't let the size of the goal, or the amount of time required to accomplish it, discourage you or hold you back from reaching it.

During your planning process, break down the goal into small tasks and activities that you can engage in every day. Create a checklist to follow. You don't have to do a lot, but every day, every week, every month, you should be making progress in the direction of your clearly-defined goals and objectives by completing your predetermined tasks and activities.

THE IRON QUALITY OF SUCCESS

Here is where the rubber meets the road. The single most important quality for success is self-discipline. This is the ability to make yourself do what you should do, when you should do it, whether you feel like it or not.

Let me break down that definition of self-discipline. First, it's the ability to *make yourself* do something. This means that you have to use strength and willpower to jumpstart yourself into motion; to break the power of inertia that holds you back. Second, do what you *should do, when you should do it*. This means that you make a plan, set a schedule, and then do what you say you'll do. You do it when you say you'll do it. You keep your promises to yourself and to others.

The third part of this definition is *whether you feel like it or not*. You see, anyone can do something if he feels like it, if he wants to do it because it makes him happy, if he is well-rested and has lots of time. However, the true test of character is when you do something that you know you must do whether you feel like it or not—especially when you don't like it at all.

In fact, you can tell how badly you really want something, and what you are really made of as a person, by how capable you are of taking action in the direction of your goals and dreams, even when you feel tired and discouraged and disappointed, and you don't seem to be making any progress. Very often, this is the exact time when you will break through to great achievement.

Ralph Waldo Emerson once wrote, "When the night is darkest, the stars come out." Your ability to endure, to continue taking action, step-by-step, in the direction of your dreams, is what will ultimately ensure your success. If you keep on keeping on, nothing can stop you.

PREPARE FOR YOUR SUCCESS

Earl Nightingale once said that if a person does not prepare for his success, when his opportunity finally comes, it will only make him look foolish. You've probably heard it said repeatedly that luck is what happens when *preparedness meets opportunity*. Only when you've paid the price to be ready for your success are you in a position to take advantage of your opportunities when they arise.

The most remarkable factor is this: The very act of preparation attracts to you, like iron filings to a magnet, opportunities to utilize that preparation to make advances in your life. You'll seldom learn anything of value, or prepare yourself in any area, without soon having a chance to use your new knowledge and your new skills to move ahead more rapidly.

There is a series of things that you can do to become ready for success. All of these activities require self-discipline and a good deal of faith. They require self-discipline because the most normal and natural thing for people to do is to try to get by without preparation. Instead of taking the time and making the effort to be ready for their chance when it comes, they fool around, play on their computer, become preoccupied with social media, and just go around in circles of continual distraction, accomplishing little or nothing.

BELIEVE IN YOURSELF

Preparation also requires a good deal of faith; you have no proof beforehand to demonstrate that the preparation will pay off. You simply have to believe, deep within yourself, that everything you do of a constructive nature will come back to you in some way. You have to know that no good effort is ever wasted. You have to be willing to sow for a long time before you reap the rewards, knowing that if you do sow in quality and quantity, the reaping will come about inevitably with the force of the law of nature.

Look at your work. Be honest and objective about your strengths and weaknesses. What are you good at? What are you poor at? What is your major area of weakness? What must you absolutely, positively be excellent at in order to move to the top of your field? What one weakness could possibly be holding you back from using all your other skills?

In preparing for success, one of the very best questions that you can ask yourself repeatedly is, *"What can I—and only I—do that, if done well, will make a real difference in my career?"* Usually there are only one, or perhaps two answers to that question. It is critical to possess the ability to honestly appraise yourself, and to identify the particular skill area that may be holding you back.

PREPARE FOR A GREAT DAY

In the period of time before work, another thing that highly successful people do is plan and prepare for their entire day. They review all of the tasks and responsibilities that they have for the coming hours. They carefully make a prioritized list of all their activities. They decide which things are most important to do, which are secondary in importance, and which things should not be done at all unless all the other things are finished. They then discipline themselves to start working on their most important tasks, and stay with them during the day until they're complete.

PRACTICE POSITIVE SELF-TALK

To be at your peak performance level, you should also talk to yourself in a positive way. The way you talk to yourself largely determines your emotions; how you feel about yourself on a minute-to-minute basis. If you don't deliberately and consciously think about what you want, and talk to yourself in a positive way, your mind will tend to slip toward your worries and your concerns. Negative thinking dulls your personality and your enthusiasm, which is vitally important to your success with people.

DEVELOP A HARDY PERSONALITY

Use every setback or disappointment as a spur to greater effort. Decide that nothing will ever get you down. Decide that you will bounce back instead of break apart. Develop a resilient or hardy personality. Become the kind of person who is always cheerful, no matter what happens on the outside. Develop an attitude of gratitude, and give thanks for everything that happens to you, knowing that every step forward is a step toward achieving something bigger and better than your current situation. In this way, you become a far more resourceful and effective person. Preparing mentally, you become almost unstoppable.

KEEP LEARNING

Remember, we live in a knowledge-based society, and knowledge in every field is increasing more rapidly than ever before. Some experts say that the total store of knowledge and information will be doubling every 72 hours by 2020. This means that you must continue learning in your field just to stay even, never mind getting ahead. You're already "maxxed out" at your current level of knowledge and skill. You've reached the ceiling in your career with your current talents and abilities. You must continue learning to stay ahead of the curve.

Some words of Abraham Lincoln had a great influence on my life when I was 15. It was a statement he made when he was a young lawyer in Springfield, Illinois. He said, "I will study and prepare myself, and someday my chance will come." And so it did.

If you study and prepare yourself, your chance will come as well. There is nothing that you cannot accomplish if you invest the effort to get yourself ready for the success that you desire. Nothing can stop you but your own lack of preparation.

Let me end this chapter with this beautiful poem by Henry Wadsworth Longfellow:

> *"Those heights by great men won and kept;*
> *were not achieved by sudden flight;*
> *But they, while their companions slept,*
> *were toiling upward in the night"*

Your possibilities are endless, your potential is unlimited, and your future opens up before you when you prepare yourself for the success that must inevitably be yours.

About Brian

Brian Tracy is Chairman and CEO of Brian Tracy International, a company specializing in the training and development of individuals and organizations. Brian's goal is to help people achieve their personal and business goals faster and easier than they ever imagined.

Brian Tracy has consulted for more than 1,000 companies and addressed more than 5,000,000 people in 5,000 talks and seminars throughout the US, Canada and 55 other countries worldwide. As a Keynote speaker and seminar leader, he addresses more than 250,000 people each year.

For more information on Brian Tracy programs, go to: www.briantracy.com

CHAPTER 2

REBUILDING THE FOUNDATION:
Reaching the "American Dream" by Going Back to Basics

BY ALY N. BENITEZ, ESQ.

At the age of 9, I attended my class Halloween party dressed as a "business woman." I, of course, had no idea what a business woman was - but I knew from a very early age that I wanted to be one. This was my dream.

Luckily, my parents never pushed me towards any certain career. They never told me I had to be a doctor or a scientist. They never laughed at me when, at 12 years old, I gave them an invoice for the breakfast I prepared. They simply gave me one piece of advice: *"Whatever you choose, enjoy what you do. If you enjoy your work, you will be better at it and live a happier life."* This is a simple concept that we have all heard before - but it's one that I hope resonates with you.

I've built a career and I am living my dream by remaining consciously focused on basic principles. These principles are straightforward and you've all heard them before. But what I have found is that by remaining focused on simple things like being passionate about what you do and not being scared of failure, success will come to you.

So, what is your "dream"? How can you achieve that dream when the economy is floundering and unemployment is at an all-time high?

I'm not going to give you a twelve-step program to success. I won't tell you it's going to be easy, or *"If you think it, it will happen."* I'm simply going to give you my story and a set of basic but fundamental principles that I hope will help along the way.

THE "AMERICAN DREAM"

The American Dream is the country's most important asset— more valuable than its extraordinary natural resources, deep financial capacity, or unparalleled workforce.
~ Nitin Nohria, Dean of Harvard Business School.

At the center of American ideology rests a promise: that anyone can succeed through hard work in the pursuit of happiness. Today, Americans seek not only job security and a steady income, but also the ability to create our own opportunities - to be our own boss. **Entrepreneurship is the new "American Dream".**

If you are one of the many Americans who crave the personal autonomy of being your own boss, but do not know how to start your own business during a sluggish economy, then this chapter is for you.

For those chasing this dream, there are many obstacles. According to data from the Census Bureau's *Business Database Census*, over 50% of new employer businesses do not make it past the first 5 years. In 2009, during the recession, more than 550,000 businesses opened while more than 660,000 closed and over 60,000 filed for bankruptcy.[1]

These statistics look bleak, but do not let them discourage you! Within this chapter, I have outlined basic principles that I believe are fundamental to creating a successful business. On paper, they seem straightforward. But what I've come to learn is that so often we ignore the most basic principles. We create our own roadblocks. Let's go back to basics and remember that the foundation is the most important element in construction.

---

1 U.S. Small Business Administration - http://web.sba.gov/faqs/faqindex.cfm?areaID=24.

PRINCIPLE 1: DON'T WAIT FOR PERMISSION!

Are you thinking of starting a company, but are discouraged because of the lagging economy and daunting barriers to entry? Understandable! But trust me when I say that a down economy might actually be an advantage for you. If you wait for the perfect time to start a business, you miss out on these **advantages of starting a business in a down economy**.

First, a struggling economy means cheaper labor. When people are struggling financially they take the work they can get - often at a fraction of the price. For example, you need a web designer but cannot pay big firm prices. Instead, put a posting up for a web designer online or at a local coffee shop – you may be surprised at the response. Instead of paying $1,000.00-$1,500.00 for site work, you may get a qualified designer charging $300.00! Use this to your advantage.

Not everyone has millions of dollars at their disposal. This means as a business owner you must get creative! Save money by leveraging your resources. For example, you are an accountant and want to develop a smart phone application. You can't afford the $10,000.00 price tag for app development. Trade the app development for accounting services. The money saved by leveraging resources can make or break your business, especially when money is tight and work is scarce. Most people are more than happy to trade services. Odds are, they need something but don't want to spend the money right now to do it.

In addition to bartering, go online and take advantage of the free resources available. In 2006, my dear friend Julie was diagnosed with an aggressive form of cancer. Her prognosis was not good and in order to pay her medical bills she lost everything - her home, savings and investment properties. After watching her battle, I vowed to help. In an attempt to ease the burden, I started a non-profit organization to raise money and help defray her costs. I had never started a non-profit, knew nothing about state and federal filings or what was required. For me, this was certainly not the right time to take on this challenge – I was fresh out of law school, the economy was circling the drain and I had no clue what I was doing. This didn't stop me. I went online and found great resources with information on forming a 501(c)(3) non-profit. From sites like the *Council of Non-Profits* (http://www.councilofnonprofits. org) to blogs written by non-profit founders, the information was at my fingertips and I took advantage of this.

The *Grace Alexander Foundation, Inc.* incorporated on December 4, 2007. Julie passed on April 22, 2008. After her passing the foundation presented a check to Julie's family, which helped relieve some of the financial pressure. Since then, the foundation has donated thousands of dollars and is now focused on providing financial support for children battling cancer in the Central Florida area. None of this would have been possible if I had not taken advantage of the resources available. It takes time to do the research, but if you're saving money and accomplishing a goal, then your time is well spent.

There's no perfect time to start, don't wait for permission! Cheap labor, bartering, and taking advantage of free resources should give you confidence when starting a new business during a down economy. Of course, none of this will matter if you do not believe in your business.

PRINCIPLE 2: PASSION PAYS

Passion is fundamental to success, especially during a sluggish economy. I know, you've heard this a thousand times. But I'll say it again, because it's important. If you do not enjoy what you do, or if you do not believe in your business - **DO NOT DO IT.** In my view, you're only wasting your time, money and resources. Even worse, you're wasting someone else's time, money and resources.

Recently, I've started a company called *Allied Pest Solutions* that is developing a device to prevent rodents from accessing residential and commercial properties. As an attorney and real estate professional, I certainly never imagined I would get into the pest control industry. But after purchasing my home in 2011, I noticed that rats were using power lines to get onto my roof, chew siding and even get into my attic. I thought for sure there would be some device available to place on the lines and block access. After extensive research I discovered nothing like this existed. So I hired my friend, an engineer, to design a prototype. After installing the prototype on my line, I realized that we had something here. Not only did it block the rodents from accessing my roof, it was aesthetically pleasing, safe for the lines and easy to install.

Our product, "Rodent Blocker" is now patent-pending and we are working with an American manufacturing company who is producing our first market production. Our goal is to partner with power and cable companies across the nation, putting Rodent Blockers on all of their lines. In the end, this will give property owners peace of mind and bring additional revenue to the power and cable companies.

Do I love rodents? Absolutely not. Am I passionate about raccoons? Doubtful. But I believe in my product, and that provides the necessary passion to push through obstacles such as establishing relationships with power companies. My belief in this product has kept me motivated.

Simple things like enjoying what you do and believing in a product will provide the necessary motivation to push through barriers that prevent so many from pursuing their dream. Passion leads to self-motivation. Self-motivation leads to success. Success leads you closer to achieving your dream. I don't expect to make millions on Rodent Blocker, but I see a need for the product and am excited to be the one to bring it to market. Having passion may seem like a basic principle, but so many people ignore their passion to chase the money. This leads us to Principle 3.

PRINCIPLE 3: MONEY ISN'T EVERYTHING

If you define money alone as success and that is your dream, you're reading the wrong chapter! When thinking about going to law school, I asked several law students why they chose that path. Often, the response was this: *"Because I want to be rich."* They believed a law degree equaled big bucks and powerful positions. They were chasing the money. Unfortunately, most law students quickly find out that the job market is saturated and the starting salary is sometimes less than that of teachers.

This, of course, is not true for everyone. Some attorneys enter the field because they simply love litigating or fighting for children's rights. For those people, money was not the motivating factor (and I'd be willing to bet they are making quite a profitable living doing what they love).

In my final year of law school, not knowing what I wanted to do after graduation, I applied for Air Force JAG. This is a prestigious position, as only 10% of applicants are accepted. The benefits were great, pay was surprisingly higher than many first year attorneys make and there was a pension at the end of the rainbow. This meant job security and a steady income. After months of waiting, I received a phone call from the pentagon: *"I am pleased to inform you that you have been selected as a United States Air Force Judge Advocate General."* I was thrilled and, honestly, stunned. The position offered stability, good pay, and the prestige of JAG! So I did what any recent law school graduate in a tough market would do.... I turned it down. Wait? Why?!

Ultimately, I followed my instincts and stayed true to my dream. I never envisioned a life in the military but was grateful for the opportunity. Instead, I turned down a sure thing for the prospect of building my own company and ultimately achieving my dream of being a "business woman" *(at this point, I had a better understanding of what this meant)*. I stuck to basics and followed my passion. Today, I'm thankful I chose this path and took that risk.

PRINCIPLE 4: UNDERSTAND RISKS, AND TAKE THEM

Risk is not a four-letter word. Well, ok, it is – but not a bad one. Don't be scared of risk, be scared of what you may never achieve if you hadn't taken that risk. ***Remember, the risks you don't take can be more harmful than those you do take.***

In July 2008, I took a risk and started a legal consulting business, *Sidebar Consulting, P.L.* Friends and family laughed, as I was a 27-year-old kid and only one year out of law school. What could I possibly offer as a consultant? I took this risk because I believed I could help other law firms save money. After researching the market, I found a niche in personal injury law. Injury cases are almost always billed on a contingency basis, which means attorneys cannot bill the client per hour. By offering to conduct initial interviews and signing up new injury clients, I saved attorneys hundreds of dollars an hour in billable time.

To market this service, I sent letters and brochures detailing my services and competitive pricing to local personal injury firms. After weeks with no calls, I remained persistent. Finally, after a few months, I received a phone call from a "big fish." This well known attorney called me and asked if I'd be willing to come in for a formal interview. I was thrilled, and met with him the following week. After sitting down he looked at me and said, *"Well, I know nothing about you, but I like you. You're persistent as hell!"* The attorney tested my knowledge in personal injury law and agreed to give me a shot. From there, I secured several other accounts and soon was making an additional $200-500 per day in addition to my salary as an attorney.

This never would have happened if I hadn't taken the risk to start

Sidebar, and the business never would have taken off if I had accepted the initial rejection. My failure to get a call back within the first few months did not deter me.

PRINCIPLE 5: FAILURE IS GOOD

Failure is good. Failing at something gives us insight into what we are doing wrong and how to approach future obstacles. These lessons stay with you and help you avoid the same pitfalls in the future. Again, *Sidebar* would not exist had I thrown in the towel after my letters went unanswered. Since that first meeting, *Sidebar* has expanded from helping local attorneys to now providing guidance and drafting legal documents for companies across the country.

Do not be discouraged by a failed attempt - at least you had the courage to make an attempt. Learn from your failures and move forward.

PRINCIPLE 6: REPUTATION IS EVERYTHING!

This one will be short. If there is only one sentence you remember from this chapter, I hope it is this: Reputations take years to build and seconds to lose. When faced with a situation where your integrity is tested, remember that phrase, and think about people like O.J. Simpson, Bernard "Bernie" Madoff, and Jerry Sandusky!

And that's it. I can't prove any of this and it's not scientific, but I hope re-examining these basic principles will help you reach your American Dream. There's never a perfect time to start a business. Make the decision to take that first step and use the down economy to your advantage. But make sure before taking that step, you believe in your business or product. Passion is not an option. You are going to be married to the business – how sad if you don't enjoy it.

Remember, money isn't everything and don't be afraid to take risks. When taking these risks, don't be afraid to fail! Learn from your failures and move forward. Finally, protect your reputation by conducting business with colleagues, employees, customers and competitors with integrity. Your reputation doesn't cost you a thing, yet it is the most valuable thing you possess!

I wish you the best of luck in whatever venture you pursue. Please feel free to contact me any time, whether to ask a question or to tell a great success story – I'd love to hear both!

About Aly

Aly Benitez is a business and real estate attorney in Orlando, Florida. Aly provides legal and real estate services to individuals, businesses owners, athletes, musicians and investors from around the world. Aly is also a licensed Realtor and serial entrepreneur. In addition to her law practice, Aly is currently developing a patented device called "Rodent Blocker" and has founded several successful companies including *Sidebar Consulting, P.L., Allied Pest Solutions, Inc.* and *Grace Alexander Foundation, Inc.*

Aly will be seen this fall on ABC, NBC, CBS and Fox affiliates as one of America's Premier Experts in law and business. Aly is consistently named one of Florida's top professionals and received the Orlando Business Journal's prestigious *40 Under 40* award, a recognition that spotlights the region's top 40 business and civic leaders under the age of 40. In 2010, Aly received the *Certificate of Special Congressional Recognition*, Presented by Congressman Alan Grayson and she also serves on the City of Orlando's Historical Preservation Board.

With a personal interest in philanthropy, Aly actively supports numerous charities. In 2007, Aly founded a 501(c)(3) non-profit organization, the *Grace Alexander Foundation, Inc.*, which raises money for cancer patients who cannot afford health care costs.

Aly is a member of the Florida Bar and obtained her Juris Doctorate and Masters in Business Administration from Stetson University. Prior to this, Aly was a scholarship athlete at the University of Virginia, where she majored in American Politics and played Women's Soccer. Aly also played semi-professional soccer for the *Tampa Bay Extreme*.

Contact Aly at: Aly@BenitezLawGroup.com

For more information on Aly's law practice and her speaking engagements, visit: www.BenitezLawGroup.com and: www.AlyBenitez.com

CHAPTER 3

THE TORTOISE ALWAYS WINS

BY COREY TAYLOR

It felt like a dark and stormy night, volcanoes, floods, the whole bit. There I was, broke, in major debt and exhausted. If you've had financial distress then you know. I was essentially in shock from the business mountain I'd just fallen from. I couldn't stop asking myself, "How did I get here?" In the search for an answer I had come across Dave Ramsey. Dave had asked a Billionaire the number 1 secret to success. He was on the edge of his seat for the answer, notepad and pen in hand, big smile, ready to unlock the complex maze of wisdom. After all, to be successful you have to know what successful people do, and successful people are always super sophisticated. The Billionaire says, "The tortoise always wins." He wasn't kidding, and it wasn't so sophisticated after all. It might sound silly at first, but you're about to learn how this simple truth from a children's story changed my life and will change yours too. So let's roll back to the beginning, way before the dark and stormy night part. I need to share my experience with you entrepreneurs out there so you can understand why it is so important to become the Tortoise (aka winner) and not the Hare (aka loser).

From a very young age, I got spoiled by success. I had done well enough in South Florida high school academics and sports that I got into the Naval Academy in 93. It was physically and academically challenging being surrounded by a bunch of other competitive men and women trying to outdo each other. The summer trainings for midshipmen were an amazing experience. Riding in submarines underwater for weeks, flying planes and helicopters, running around in the woods with M-16s, and driving ships up the east coast were just a few of the unforgettable summers to learn what you're good at. Although, I do get chills even now when I remember my 2nd year with record low temperatures for Maryland, when the bay froze over. For a Florida boy that was no fun! USNA was a place that demanded performance and I learned to work hard and do well. When the time came to graduate, I took the Marine Corps option that a handful of guys get to choose through the screening process.

Some of you have heard the phrase "If it doesn't kill you, it only makes you stronger." This was the informal Marine Corps mantra, so needless to say, I got stronger. By the time you get out of The Basic School that all Marine Officers go through, plus the Occupational School for one's particular specialty, you feel like you can conquer anything. I suppose that's the whole point of the process, and it sure does work. By the time you get some salt under your belt in the fleet, you'd take on an inbound comet if called to do so. The Corps is an extremely competitive environment that grows confidence and ability no matter what your job is. I had some superb commanders, and the honor of serving with some great guys. It felt good, significant even, to be the guys at the end of the red phone when something goes wrong and the USA needed some butt-kicking action on call. The job isn't idle, so I was very busy, but it was about this time in my young Corps career, several years into my tour, I just couldn't ignore the entrepreneur's itch. I call it an "itch" now, but at the time I didn't know what it was. I would describe it as a strong urge to have some business venture of my own, and I felt less need to be part of an organization or an employee. Maybe I just got tired of authority and wanted to be the boss, who knows, but it wouldn't go away. I soon came across the Rich Dad Poor Dad book like millions of other people, and I was hooked on doing some kind of business. I dreamed of being a real estate investor who could control my own schedule and make the kind of money I thought I was ready for. You know how excited you get when going into something new and adventurous? Thus began my race to business success. With no knowledge of Tortoise vs. Hare as it relates to business and life, I jumped across the starting line as a fluffy, full-fledged, over-confident, Hare. After all, Marines don't fail, and risks must be taken, reaching the mountaintop was a certainty in my mind.

So I'm bouncing down the road and learned enough to pick up a few rentals, but I'm part-time. I still had a day job after all, and I had a lot to learn so I kept reading and buying courses like crazy. You know, things like entity structures, house buying, house fixing, house selling, bookkeeping, and I discovered the no money down strategies everyone hears about. I was at Quantico by now (2002), and the work schedule isn't like the fleet, so I had more time after hours to feed my new business education addiction. The good thing about me is I take action, so I was fully into the marketing, finding private lenders, meeting homeowners, and we had some awesome successes. My wife and I were a good team, and we were making more in real estate part time than my Corps salary. In 2004 my daughter was born, real estate fix and flips were doing well, and we liked Virginia, so I decided not to continue my Marine Corps career and got out to do real estate investing full time. A transformation occurred. Now I wasn't just a Hare, I became Super Marine Hare with a lot more time on my hands. Think how much faster I could go!

Now I was living the entrepreneur's dream. I got up when I wanted, we traveled when we wanted, I played golf when I wanted (sorry, Dear), and I ran my own show that was growing with my full time efforts. I found a great partner so my wife could do other things she enjoyed. We did hundreds of deals. Life was awesome. We made fantastic money and gave a lot of it away in our community, which is what we really enjoyed doing to help other people.

If you've been sleep-reading, here's where you should PAY CLOSE ATTENTION. At this point in my life is when I could have really used another piece of advice I found later from a very smart guy. Confucius said: "The man who chases many rabbits catches none." Did you get that? I don't care how smart, or process-driven, or what a great outsourcer you are, you can only manage to grow so many things at once. Not knowing this meant I chased almost every promising opportunity that came by me. Alarmingly, I didn't even use my Marine training to fully assess risk vs. potential gain. Don't ask me why, I was an idiot. Basically, I was out of my mind because I hadn't yet felt the sting of failure. Call it laziness, irresponsibility, whatever, I agree with about any term you use. But no one was around to tell me otherwise, so I got involved in five or six different ventures of various kinds that pulled me six ways to Sunday. Some good, some not, but either way, I was overextending my time and money. But chasing rabbits was fun, forgetting that I have to catch them to eat. I also didn't realize I was chasing them to the edge of a cliff. A cliff created by debt that kept getting taller and taller without me looking to see how far the fall was.

I was managing debt well for my personal things, but on the business side, many of the real estate investment educators teach debt is "leverage" and the more you leverage debt to get assets the more wealthy you become. Even writing that sentence now makes me want to laugh and cry at the same time, but that's what we all hear from the business culture. Well, my partners and I took on a lot of what we thought was "safe" debt to acquire properties. I won't bore you with details you've heard a hundred times by now. We had the wrong model at the wrong time. We all know the financial markets changed, and our "safe" debt became "sour" debt and all of a sudden, it's free-fall. I didn't even know I was near the cliff, and all of a sudden I was falling from it. Have you ever had that feeling of thinking you're doing something right, and when it goes terribly wrong you're in complete disarray? That's how I was feeling. How did Goldman-Sachs not tell me ahead of time that sub-prime was going away? How is it possible for house values to drop 40%? Why did I listen to the young guys saying there was no bubble instead of the old guys who said they've seen it before? The answer is that I was a Hare, worse, a Super Marine Hare, not the Tortoise. I was the big-shot boss, I only heard what I wanted to hear to "grow" faster than my peers. I wanted levels of achievement that my business acumen wasn't ready to achieve. And now I didn't know what to think or do. Do I quit and do something else? Do I keep doing more of what I thought I was good at? Am I even good at that after all? I had made a lot of promises I couldn't keep anymore, and I had zero experience in dealing with failure. Oh yeah, and two kids chirping for food by now. I will never publish that Marines are afraid of anything, but I'll admit to you personally that fear was sitting on my shoulder whispering sweet nothings.

The next few years were ugly. I thought I knew God before, Ha! Nothing like total failure to make you remember who's in charge. Imagine me reaching out of this book to shake you by the shoulders to get your attention. If you're in this spot now, keep reading, the answers are here. If you're not in this spot and I find out you got in a spot after reading this, I'm driving to your house to shake you again. You don't understand how terrible it can be if you don't manage risk appropriately. I had a lot of very difficult discussions with lenders, friends who were lenders, contractors, and professional associates. The list was long and they all wanted their pound of flesh. Can you blame them? You see, Hares don't just cause their own pain, they cause pain for others too.

Our culture measures our significance with success, especially men, and especially earnings. So to go from millionaire to broke is not an easy thing to swallow. This mess was a real blow to my pride. I learned a lot about myself, my partners, and my priorities. The thing is, some mistakes you make can't be fixed overnight. When you don't measure risk, you don't know if you're making a 1 month, 1 year, or 10 year mistake if it goes bad. Is this sounding a little bit like the Hare? Dashing along too fast, making reckless assumptions, foolish over-confidence? You bet. This is often what entrepreneurs think they SHOULD be doing, but it's not. For every reckless entrepreneur success story, I'll give you three that never made it to the finish line. I had taken "failing forward" to a whole new level. Honestly, one of the biggest blows was that we couldn't give anymore. That was a huge one for my wife, and my decisions had taken that away from her for a long time. You married guys and gals, remember your spouse has to live with your decisions and they don't like Hares. All this was on my mind that dark and stormy night when this burden was a crushing weight on my shoulders.

I had to figure out what to do to fix this gargantuan problem. A friend gave us a Dave Ramsey book, which explained financial true North, and I soon began facilitating his Financial Peace course at our church. I simply felt compelled to prevent this from happening to as many people as I could. It was in that course where Dave explained his Billionaire revelation. The Tortoise always wins, and all my previous actions became clear, High-Definition clear, that I'd been a Hare. Now what? I wasn't even sure how to be a tortoise, a real winner, but I was determined to find wisdom.

By following the steps I'm about to share with you, I was able to get sound counsel from grey haired guys that helped put me in place, re-tool my real estate business, focus on the right priorities, and get back on track. Real success feels good. There are still scars from the mistakes made, and some pain I inflicted on others will take a little longer to heal as my colleagues get made whole. But it felt really good to come out of the storm a better man than when I went in, and with a business that was growing consistently and could be relied upon to WIN.

For those with the entrepreneur's itch, or even seasoned pros out there, let me share seven points of wisdom to become a WINNER – who people will honor and respect. Make note and post them on your corkboard or fridge:

1. Accept and internalize that the Tortoise is the winner, the Hare is the loser!

2. Figure out what big thing you're supposed to accomplish in the world (not making money). Ours is giving through our church to various ministries and facilitating Financial Peace. Kids need help, mothers need help, and disabled people need help. Making money is the means to an end, figure out your purpose UP FRONT. You'll be much more motivated.

3. You must seek sound business counsel consistently. I recommend CBMC, Connecting Businessmen to Christ. God knows a lot about business, He proved it in Proverbs. Get people around you that won't hesitate to tell you why you're wrong.

4. Acknowledge debt is a type of potent poison, not "leverage." If you want to use it, then:
(a) it must be secured on something twice the value of the debt and
(b) get rid of it before it kills you when you least expect it.

5. "The man who chases many rabbits catches none." Don't go after every shiny opportunity. You have to choose the prize tomato. Only 1 or 2 opportunities are worth your time, money, and attention. Choosing is tough for those of you who think you can do it all. You can't, sorry to break that news to you. So pick one, get it working and automated, then you can grow the next.

6. Work in your strengths, when it seems easy and comes naturally, monetize that strength and it won't feel like work. Ask others what your strengths are, you likely don't know. Everyone discounts their strength because it feels easy.

7. Focus on relationships, both personal and business. At the end of the day, that's what matters most. Your significance does not come from the business you build, it comes from the people you impact and make better as a result of your help or shared experience. If I had not had a solid relationship with my wife,

it's difficult to imagine how much harder it would have been to get through those rough times together. You need shelter if the storm comes.

There is no other way to guarantee success. There is nothing new under the sun, and this decade is no different than 1000 years ago, so don't kid yourself. You can't count on luck, rely on proven wisdom to get you to your goal and make an impact in the world around you.

Maybe you're someone who's in a spot now that seems daunting, you've been the Hare in life or business and living the regrets of those consequences. Let me assure you the storm will pass if you stand tall and keep moving forward. One of my favorite quotations to get through my storm was this:

> *Success is not final, failure is not fatal:*
> *it is the courage to continue that counts.*
> ~ Winston Churchill

About Corey

Corey Taylor is an active Real Estate Entrepreneur, financial counselor, and investment trainer with a highly successful Investing Course called Elite Tax Sale Training. With his experience from the US Naval Academy and service in the US Marine Corps, he bought every real estate course under the sun and took action. Having built an investment company part-time, he got out of the Marine Corps in late 2004 and became a full-time investor. Within a few years he had over 100 transactions worth of experience in rehabs, wholesales, short sales, lease options, owner financing, note-selling, self-directed IRAs, and managing millions in private money.

Then Corey admits failing to stay on top of his business during the Real Estate downturn and suffered his first taste of failure. It didn't taste good. He got back up, adjusted his business with the fresh sting of painful lessons and went back to work. He discovered with his Partner Tom how Tax Sales provide both discounted property, as well as huge, secured returns on capital, and that's where he has focused his efforts ever since. They founded Fortris LLC, a company that makes incredible returns by purchasing liens and deeds after the auction process, called assignment purchasing. Fortris training programs teach others how to use the tax sale process to help communities recover financially and make a safe, high interest return, or own properties for pennies on the dollar without harming homeowners. It can be done very part-time, or full time, either way it fits easily into someone's work schedule. These strategies are perfect for the busy professional who wants to earn more reliable returns while still focusing on what they do best.

Corey's full time activity is working the Tax Sale Investment Strategies in Fortris and speaking around the country on its lucrative and secure benefits anyone can enjoy. Corey also voluntarily facilitates hundreds of people through Dave Ramsey's Financial Peace University every year and advocates everyone seek true financial wisdom. Corey's wonderful wife is Andrea, and they have 2 young children.

To learn more about Corey Taylor, whether for business or financial coaching, visit: www.TaxSaleTraining.com/GrowMoney or call toll-free: 1-800-704-9528.

www.TaxSaleTraining.com/GrowMoney

CHAPTER 4

LIVING WITH UNBRIDLED PASSION

BY CYNDI MCCAY

YOU ALREADY HAVE WHAT IT TAKES!

I'm a Licensed Clinical Social Worker and Certified Life Coach. I help people uncover who they are and what they want, and how they will get where they want to go. I come from a varied background and therefore have a variety of experiences on which to draw. I've been a medic, reserve police officer, a child-victim advocate in the prosecutor's office, and I spent many years in manufacturing businesses at many levels; foreman, scheduler, sales manager, and corporate training manager.

You are an individual--unique and distinctive. There is no one on the planet that has the exact same set of gifts, talents, and passions that you do. There is no one else who has had the same set of experiences, skills, capabilities, and understandings as you do. It is important because you have a contribution to make to the world that can't be made by anyone else.

You already have what it takes to be successful...but you have to look for it—uncover it—if you don't know what that is yet. For most of us, finding our purpose is a lifelong pursuit and one that continually evolves.

There are foundational characteristics that are needed for life success; Attitude, focus, integrity, perseverance, self-discipline, etc. In Dan Miller's book, *No More Mondays*, he lists five predictors of success: Passion, Determination, Talent, Self-discipline, and Faith. The basic building blocks of success have been written about by a lot of brilliant people and it seems every writer has a slightly different set of requirements.

Bob Buford, author of *Halftime*, stated that in the first part of our life we pursue "success," usually evidenced by material wealth. During the second half of our lives, we transition from "success" to "significance." This is a change in perspective that, as Buford explains, "What you do best for God will rise out of that core being He has created within you." In other words, what gives meaning to your life and provides service to others.

My faith is an integral part in how I define success in my life. It is the vessel that shapes my core values that guide me. My core values provide a compass that prevents me from stepping over boundaries I must not cross in pursuit of my dreams and goals. I believe God leads me in the direction I'll be most useful and most fulfilled going, by my feelings of interest, attraction, and passion. He has instilled those feelings in me to connect my gifts and talents to my desires.

OLYMPIC LESSONS

Back in 1982-83, I was at the Olympic Training Center (OTC) preparing for the 1984 Olympics in Women's Judo. I hadn't started judo (or even knew it existed) until my sophomore year of college in 1978. While I never got the chance to compete in the Olympics (Women's Judo was removed as a selective in 1984 and replaced with Ping-Pong), I learned a lot of lessons I could apply to life.

One of the more important things I learned at the OTC was at that level of competition, almost everyone was at the same physical and technical ability. What made the difference in competition was a competitor's mental edge. Ninety percent of winning is your preparation--being physically ready—strength, flexibility, and technical ability. Practice. Practice. Practice. You know, the things that every dedicated athlete does. The last 10% is all about the mental game—having confidence in your prep and belief in your self and your abilities.

> *"Whether you believe you can or believe you can't, you're right."*
> ~ Henry Ford

Our coaches taught us to mentally rehearse our techniques and to picture doing them perfectly. It was a powerful precursor to performing them well in practice and tournaments. You can use the same idea for any of the things you plan to say or do. It's a critical piece of preparing yourself for any endeavor. Always picture it going perfectly. If during your mental rehearsal you find a flaw or your mind comes up with a scenario you aren't prepared for, come up with a plan and run it again. Correct any deviations from perfection no matter how minor they might be. You'll be amazed at how well it will go in actuality from your rehearsal.

TAKE ACTION

Being successful requires action. Most people dream about things. They want life to be a certain way. But they either don't know how to get there, or they are afraid, or not willing to do the work to get there. Dreams come to fruition when you take action to get there. How do you climb a mountain? Taking one small step after the other does it.

When you add all those little steps together it equals the completion of the task. Do the following:

1. Define your goal.

2. Write it down. Envision it as clearly as possible. **Clarity** is key.

3. Then break your goal into small steps--as small and finite as possible. After you have written all the steps you can think of, go back and, under each step,

4. Write all the obstacles you can think of that could keep you from accomplishing that step.

5. Then, write how you will overcome each obstacle. That's your plan! Wait though! There is one more **critical** step to make it happen.

6. **Set a date** to accomplish your plan. This is another key point. Go back and fill in dates for each of the steps. Look at it critically and decide what is realistic for you, given your other responsibilities, and yet reflects the exigency of your passion. You can always change the dates as the need arises but a date propels you to action. Think back to high school or college when you had a paper due. Some of you started when the paper

was assigned. The majority of us started the night before. Why? Because that was when we *had* to—unless we weren't turning it in at all. A goal isn't about whether you start right away or at the last minute; it's that you get it done.

Now, what if you just don't know what your passions are? Here's just one way…

FIND *YOUR* PASSION THROUGH PLAY

It has taken years for me to uncover what my own unique gifts, talents, and passions are—and it's an ongoing pursuit. I love to ride horses, hike, snow- and water-ski, make pottery, paint, boat, read, write, jog, bike, camp, and I could go on about hobbies for longer than you would care to hear. I go by the old adage that "you don't know until you try," whether you'll like something or not (notice I didn't say anything about being "good" at it). By trying a lot of different interests however, I have found things I never would have known I am good at, or that I like and enjoy. Plus, it's so important to give your mind and body down-time. When you do, you give yourself the gift of de-stressing—which *allows you to be more creative.*

In fact, play is so important that there has been a rash of attention given to it in recent years. One of the books written about it is *Play*, by Stuart Brown, M.D. He states that play is so important to our development and survival that it is a necessary part of our biological drive! Play as a child is a rehearsal for the challenges and ambiguities of life and surprisingly but most importantly, socializing. When kittens are deprived from play fighting they grow up to be able to hunt just fine. However, what they never learn to do is socialize successfully (Play, pg.32).

Brown actually first learned about the importance of play from research he performed as part of a task force studying the Charles J. Whitman Texas Tower Massacre case. What he found was astounding. Lack of play is the common denominator in a carefully studied group of homicidal young males.

"The committee concluded that lack of play was a key factor in Whitman's homicidal actions – if he had experienced regular moments of spontaneous play during his life, they believed he would have

developed the skill, flexibility, and strength to cope with the stressful situations without violence.

Dr. Brown's subsequent research of other violent individuals concludes that play can act as a powerful deterrent, even an antidote to prevent violence. Play is a powerful catalyst for positive socialization."
~ The Institute for Play – Vision

In play, we can imagine and experience situations and possibilities that never existed before. We make new cognitive connections. New cognitive connections equal neuron (brain cell) growth and that literally means new connections being made in the brain. Find the play that feeds your soul, and build an environment around you that makes staying play-nourished a priority. Experiment with incorporating a more playful approach to your work. According to Brown:

"Without some sense of fun or play, people usually can't make themselves stick to any discipline long enough to master it."

FIND YOUR INTERNAL COMPASS

An issue I consistently see in my practice—both counseling and coaching—is that people lose sight of their passions. It's understandable. We grow up being taught to follow directions. We learn to want to please people—it not only feels good but we stay out of trouble that way! But in doing that, we get disconnected from our authentic self; one of many ways people fall into depression. A person might have wanted to be an actor, but their parents wanted them to go into a more "secure" field like business. They convinced themselves that their parents (or some other person important to them) knew better than they did themselves. They ignore the feeling in their belly—their own sense of themselves—that is telling them that being in business would be a chore to go to every day.

We start to put aside the things that we enjoyed and found fulfilling. If we weren't lucky enough to have parents who encouraged finding our passions, then we lose sight of those things. As we grow up, we don't even remember what our dreams were, what our passions were, or sometimes, even how to have fun.

If you are having difficulty finding things you are passionate about, try taking a less direct path of pursuit. I have a deck of several hundred "hobby" cards I use with clients (you can find lists of hobbies on the web). I have them sort them into three piles. Those they like, don't like, and would like to try. Then, they must commit themselves to trying their top one or two.

Self-discipline is a necessity, but as a therapist, I know there are many things that get in the way and cause procrastination: Fear of failure; fear of not being perfect; the inability to envision how to start; getting organized; attention deficit disorder; depression; etc. So, if you are finding yourself consistently putting off tasks, not completing tasks, or possibly even sabotaging yourself, there's a reason for it. A life coach or therapist can be your best friend to help you figure it out and overcome it.

STAY TRUE TO YOU

Develop the capacity to ignore others who say it can't be done. According to Tim Ferriss, author of *The Four Hour Work Week*, the best people in almost any field are almost always the people who get the most criticism." Ferriss jokes he has haters "in about 35 languages."

When things come easy to you, you may be misled to believe it's easy for everyone. Most likely, it isn't. Mistakenly, you don't put much value on your own gifts or talents because it comes so naturally to you, or evolved over time to get easy for you from lots of practice.

> *"Every expert at anything, was once a beginner."*
> ~ Helen Hayes, actress

What was impossible yesterday is possible today. Shift your mind. Open the box and climb out. We are unfortunately too good at talking ourselves out of being able to accomplish our goals and dreams. We tell ourselves we won't have enough time, energy, money, knowledge, etc. Focus on what you can do, not what you can't. Do what you can and God will do the rest!

Many clients have been paralyzed by believing they *have* to find their life pursuit in their first (or next) position. That's huge pressure to put on one's self to decide something when you don't even have all the facts yet about who you are. You never have ALL the facts! We're always (hopefully) evolving. Everything you choose to do gives you information about who you are, what you like, don't like, that for which you have talent, etc. Your next job is just another step. Everything you do—when you choose to do it to the best of your ability—contributes to your future and your life purpose.

I haven't had a job or experience yet that hasn't ultimately contributed something useful to my life purpose and/or helped me to help someone else. Painful moments have taught me some of the best life lessons.

Interestingly enough, many of those painful moments came from NOT listening to my gut instincts and intuition. Instead, I listened to another person that said or intimated they knew better than I did about what I "should" do.

> Should: used to indicate obligation, duty or correctness, typically when *criticizing* someone's actions (dictionary.com)

"Should" is a word that is a big red flag telling me that I'm supposed to meet someone else's expectation or standard that I haven't bought in to; not my own. I wanted to be able to be what they wanted or meet their expectation. I didn't want to disappoint them or feel inadequate or lacking in myself. "Should" is a useful word in certain situations, but not when a client (or myself) is using it to beat up on themselves. It becomes insinuated in your speech and negatively impacts your self-esteem.

Have you ever noticed the implied meaning? It's easier to recognize when *you* say it. "I should be happy…but I'm not." It's more difficult, unless you're listening for it, when someone *else* says it—"You should be happy (ok with, done with) about that." The implication being that you (your performance, your decision, etc.) is not measuring up to their expected result.

STRETCH YOURSELF

Most of us live in our comfort zone. It's a restful place and a desired place but paradoxically, it isn't a place that creates happiness for us. If we live there too much, it is also a stagnant place. When we take risks, small or big, we create growth, fun, and most importantly, excitement! Everyone has a different tolerance for taking risks based on their history and experiences. Step out of your comfort zone. Reach out to a new adventure in relationships, business, or outdoor adventure. Set the goals and take action to create the life you've always wanted to live!

> *"Our deepest fear is not that we are inadequate. Our deepest fear is that we are powerful beyond measure. It is our light, not our darkness that most frightens us. We ask ourselves, Who am I to be brilliant, gorgeous, talented, fabulous? Actually, who are you not to be? You are a child of God. Your playing small does not serve the world. There is nothing enlightened about shrinking so that other people won't feel insecure around you. We are all meant to shine, as children do. We were born to make manifest the glory of God that is within us. It's not just in some of us; it's in everyone. And as we let our own light shine, we unconsciously give other people permission to do the same. As we are liberated from our own fear, our presence automatically liberates others."*

> *A Return To Love: Reflections on the*
> *Principles of A Course in Miracles*
> ~ Marianne Williamson

About Cyndi

Cyndi McCay is a Licensed Clinical Social Worker and Certified Life Coach. After completing a BA in Psychology, she spent almost 20 years in the manufacturing business. Feeling called to a new direction, Cyndi pursued and received a Master's in Social Work, also from Indiana University. From here, she pursued her passion as a counselor and later also became certified as a life coach.

Cyndi currently works in an elementary school as a School Social Worker and maintains a private practice as a Therapist and a Coach. She has worked with a variety of mental health and life issues but especially enjoys working with anyone who is seeking to take their life to the next level, or uncover their gifts, talent, passions, or life purpose.

Her home is in Indiana on a working farm. She lives with her husband, son, horses, dogs, and cats. Of her many interests, her passions are horseback riding, hiking, and reading.

For more information about Cyndi, please see her website: cyndimccaycoaching.com

CHAPTER 5

RELEASING THE ATHLETE INSIDE YOU

BY CHRISTINA CHITWOOD

I'm standing on the ice in an arena packed with thousands of people. It's the 2010 World Figure Skating Championships in Turin, Italy, and I hear my name announced: "Representing Great Britain, please welcome Christina Chitwood…"

Five years earlier:
At age 15, I'm completing my second college course with straight A's and my senior year of homeschool high school in Colorado Springs, Colorado. It's been a couple of months since I arrived back from my trip to the UK and found the ideal ice-dance partner for me. This may sound like an easy feat, but finding an ideal ice-dance partner who's the right match physically, athletically, and talent-wise is similar to finding the ideal husband or wife. There wasn't the right match for me in the U.S. or even Canada at the time, so I decided to broaden my horizons when I was contacted by a potential partner from Scotland. It was at this point in my life that I decided to begin going "against the grain" to follow my path to success in ice dancing and beyond.

Fast forward a few months:
I've moved to Sheffield, England, to pursue success in my ice-dance career and obtain my university degree. This was a very difficult decision to make as it meant living across the ocean from my loving family at only age 16 and placing my faith in the future.

Leap forward a year:
Success is looking far in the distance as the politics of ice dancing in another country are hard to overcome. On the other hand, my studies are fantastic and I'm at the top of my class as I complete my first year of college. I'm closer to my mom than ever as she moved to England for a year and a half especially to be with me and get her master's degree in the process. For my parents, who've been happily married over 30 years, this is a huge sacrifice.

Skip forward two years:
I've graduated from Sheffield Hallam University at age 19 with my BA in Performance and Professional Practice with First Class Honours. I've had a fairytale wedding at Hazlewood Castle to the man of my dreams and British husband, Tom Parkin. Tom is not involved in ice skating whatsoever. My ice-dance partner, Mark, and I have won two national- and two international medals, and I've started two businesses. My ice dancing and off-ice workouts led to a passion for fitness and working in the fitness industry. One business I've started is a unique performance-coaching business for skaters (a position that I created using research from my dissertation). Also, I have a busy personal-training business where I'm training clients at night and doing my ice-dance training morning and afternoon.

Jump ahead half a year:
I've been traveling and competing internationally every few weeks. The highlight is traveling to and winning the 19th Paektusan Prize International Figure Skating Festival in North Korea. Visiting and competing in North Korea is a unique opportunity I never would have dreamed of actually happening.

Fast forward to March 2010:
I'm experiencing my dream and the successful completion of a goal I've worked toward for 14 years. I'm competing at the World Figure Skating Championships and celebrating my 20th birthday with my birthday buddy and ice-dance partner, Mark. This is a goal we've worked toward for so long...to be able to share our March 21st birthdays competing at the World Championships.

After fulfilling my dream of competing at the World Championships, I toured the UK as a professional show skater. After I finished performing as a show skater, my husband and I wanted to find a way to settle down in San Diego, California.

Fast forward a few years:
My husband and I live in San Diego, where I am a fitness specialist and consultant, founder and author of three blogs and a website, contributing author at another blog, motivational speaker, and ice-skating coach. I'm in the process of creating multiple fitness products and training aids. Life is full of opportunities, and I'm loving living my life fully.

YOUR INNER ATHLETE

The athlete inside desires to excel and push beyond self-imposed limits. A true athlete sees challenges as hurdles to leap rather than walls blocking his or her way.

You may already feel tapped into your inner athlete, and perhaps you are completing intense workouts, competing in marathons, or part of a sports team. You just have to seek your inner athlete and discover the endless possibilities available.

In this chapter, I'm going to assist you in releasing the athlete inside you through fitness, goal setting, positive lifestyle, and healthy nutrition.

RELEASING YOUR INNER ATHLETE THROUGH FITNESS

Creating Increased Energy through Fitness
Working out regularly helps increase energy, concentration, and productivity in daily life. I like to start my day with a workout (strength training and/or cardio with stretching). This helps me feel great throughout the day.

When I was training four hours a day on the ice, I worked out off the ice in the late afternoon or evening, as it felt better to work out after training. I recommend working out five to six days per week to achieve the full benefits of working out. If this sounds extreme, unlock your athletic intensity.

Unlocking Your Athletic Intensity
Athletes tend to work out harder than the general population, which is why athletes are some of the strongest, fastest, and fittest human beings. You have this potential, too. Unlocking your athletic intensity to go

above and beyond the normal in your workouts can be achieved through the following:

1. **Set an intense fitness goal.** Picture the intense goal you've dreamed of achieving but have been avoiding. Set your intense long-term goal and break it down into shorter-term intense goals.

2. **Design a plan to achieve your intense goal.** Learn from previous experience to build your plan. For example, when cutting sugar out of my diet, I knew I wouldn't be as successful if I still had honey and agave nectar. So, I learned from past experience to cut out all types of sugar.

3. **Create an accountability circle to add intensity.** Accountability produces success. Athletes have coaches and teammates to help keep them accountable. Success is more likely by creating a close circle of people who help keep you accountable.

4. **Track your results to inspire intensity.** Track your results monthly.

5. **Picture your goal at every workout to push you to a higher intensity than ever before.** At the most challenging points in your workout, visualize your goal to help you realize that short-term sacrifice equals long-term gain. Listen to your body, so you know when to push harder and when to ease back.

Making Fitness Fun

You will typically live longer and have a healthier and happier life through regular workouts, so make your workout fun. If you're enjoying your workout, you will be more involved and push harder. You may even start to look forward to your workouts.

Workouts don't have to just be in the gym or running outdoors. The options are endless now. If you love golf, you can incorporate this into your workout schedule (but try to walk with a push cart instead of taking a driving cart). Any sport or activity that increases your heart rate is giving you a workout. Figure out which activities you enjoy, and start incorporating them into your weekly workout plan.

Your Body Has Its Own Goals

Your body wants to achieve certain goals. Your body may make you feel uneasy until you develop the goals it has for you. Your body wants to become strong, fast, graceful, and fluid. Your body speaks to you.

Maybe you've always had an inner desire to run in a race, or take a dance class, or be in a bodybuilding competition. However, every time you've felt this desire, you've dismissed the idea as silly or felt unable to achieve it. While keeping your body's larger goal in mind, break the larger goal down in size to many smaller goals and even micro-goals. Your body wants great things for you.

Using Food as Fuel

Once you begin this journey of exercise, it is common for your body to crave what it needs rather than what your taste buds want. You will make smarter food choices. Once you get into the state-of-mind of eating what you need instead of what you want, you are eating like an athlete. Remember, food is fuel. When you put healthy food into your body, it fuels you throughout your day. When eating healthily, you will feel energized and ready to take on the world.

The Athlete Inside Is Imprisoned by Bad Bodily Experiences

It's very common for your inner athletc to be suppressed by negative bodily experiences or memories. This can vary from a bad experience or humiliation with sports, a childhood memory of being teased about your body, a past sports injury, or any type of injury such as breaking an arm after falling off the jungle gym as a youngster. These types of negative bodily experiences can happen at a young age or older but are carried with you throughout your adult life.

When I was 17, I was told by an authority figure in ice skating that I needed to lose weight. Later, my skating partner and coach made similar comments. Although my skating partner and coach were generally supportive of me, I felt like my body was under intense scrutiny most days. I was shocked. This eroded my self-confidence and made me question myself over the next few years.

In ice dancing, your body has to be on the edge of super skinny while remaining healthy. I began adding additional workout days into my six-days-per-week, four-hours-per-day on-ice training schedule and went on a healthy diet of no dairy and no desserts until I achieved my bodyweight goal. After this, even when I knew I looked good and was at a healthy weight for an ice dancer, I would feel like covering up with layers of clothing and wearing all black.

Only through consistent workouts, healthy nutrition, support of my husband and family, discussing my feelings, and incorporating positive thinking and affirmations was I able to come through this period in my life stronger than ever. Now, I am thankful to have had these experiences as I am better able to help and empathize with people's bodyweight issues and other problems.

Transforming Negative Experiences

Negative experiences and memories have a seed of transformation inside them. These soul seeds want these experiences to be understood, processed, and used to make you stronger and help others with similar struggles. Your soul's perspective gives these experiences meaning. These transformational soul seeds can be accessed through the following:

1. In a meditative state, while keeping the negative experience in mind, wait until your soul communicates with you through an image or words that will be the beginning of a larger understanding of this negative experience.

2. In a meditative state, remembering your negative experience, ask your soul to give you its perspective on this experience. Continue a written or verbal dialogue with your soul on this experience and other issues.

Choose the Positive

You can develop new bodily experiences and live the bodily process completely if you let go of past negative bodily experiences. Enter your positive life process, and flow with the river of momentum. Once you start living your new positive life, more and more amazing experiences will come to you.

Surround yourself with positive people and relationships. Involve these people in your activities involving exercise. These positive experiences will begin to replace any negative experiences you had with people involving sports and exercise.

SETTING GOALS LIKE AN ELITE ATHLETE

Setting goals, working toward them, and achieving them are the elite athlete's greatest secrets to success. You can behave like an elite athlete. Let your goals motivate you and keep you strong when you go through low points.

The daily training for ice dancing wasn't the enjoyable part for me. What

I loved most was performing at competitions and shows. To perform well at these important events, I had to push through my daily training and do my best no matter what. Having goals that I wanted to achieve, such as competing internationally and at the World Championships, inspired me and led me to success.

Setting Your Goals

The more often you set goals and review them, the quicker you achieve them. Imagine your ideal life and biggest goals, and then break them down into smaller goals. Start with your 10-year and 5-year goals. Then break these into yearly, quarterly, monthly, weekly, and daily goals. It's very important to write your goals down.

I use SMART goals for myself and my clients:

Specific

Measurable

Appropriate

Realistic

Time-Bound

Reviewing Your Goals

Did you achieve what you set out to achieve? How can you improve for next time? How could you prepare better? A good time to review your goals is weekly, monthly, and after big life events. Revise your goals when necessary.

Your Personal Map

After traveling to a number of countries, travel has become one of my favorite things in life. So, to make goals clear, visual, and more exciting for me, I created my personal map. You can create your personal map on a world map, map of your country, or blank poster board. It may be a list of goals, a mind map of goals, a dream board of goals, a Pinterest board of goals, or a combination of these methods. You may use pictures, quotes, color - anything that puts your goals in writing and makes it visual for you will work. The key is making it meaningful and personal to you.

First, add your 5-year goals and 10-year goals to your map. I like to find pictures that represent these for me and type my long-term goals onto the pictures. Do the same with your shorter-term goals. As your goals change, you can update your map or even make a new one. One of the most exciting things about life is the unexpected twists and turns.

THE PROCESS OF RELEASING THE ATHLETE INSIDE YOU

1. Discover your body's goals.

2. Transform your negative bodily experiences, thus releasing the athlete inside.

3. Nourish your released inner athlete by eating and training like an elite athlete.

4. Set your goals like an elite athlete.

5. Go against the grain, and discover freedom and success.

GOING AGAINST THE GRAIN

Going against the grain is the path for the individual. An individual has his or her unique way of approaching life. It's not following the collective way or group way, which leads to mediocrity. Instead of accepting consensus reality, the individual is an innovator of the future. This means that being your unique self is the key to success in business ...and in life.

About Christina

Christina Chitwood, A.K.A. Christina Chitwood-Parkin, and her husband, Tom Parkin, live and work in San Diego, California.

Christina has been seen on BBC and ITV television in England as well as in The Star, Yorkshire Post, The Herald Scotland, Sheffield Telegraph, and Oxford Journal. Christina has been heard on BBC Radio Sheffield and other stations. Christina is a popular media choice for television and radio interviews, sharing her experience from living abroad, representing Great Britain as a World-level ice dancer, and running multiple businesses.

Christina is a fitness expert and consultant. Her fitness system is based on developing the long, lean, strong, and healthy body of a dancer and releasing the athlete in everyone. Her brand Fit Body Full Life also specializes in producing strong and graceful women and flexible and iron men.

Christina is the founder and author of websites ChristinaChitwood.com, FitBodyFullLife. com, and ChristinaChitwoodPerformance.com. She is also a contributing author at ChitwoodSkating.com.

Christina developed a love of sports and fitness at a very young age, becoming a 3-time NASTAR national ski-racing champion and Junior Olympic karate gold medalist.

As a figure skater, Christina became a quadruple gold USFSA test medalist by age 12 and a quintuple gold test medalist by 16. She competed at the World level, and was a 3-time international medalist and 2-time British national medalist in ice dance, all by the age of 20. Christina also toured the UK as a professional ice dancer in shows. She is a professional ice dancer, ice skating coach, choreographer, and motivational speaker.

As an international ice-dancing star, Christina is a headlining performer in the Learn To Dance On Ice DVD and starred in the promotional film for the European Figure Skating Championships 2012.

Christina has been featured in the following books: Spiritual Steps on the Road to Success: Gaining the Goal Without Losing Your Soul and Figure Skaters' Favorites: A Collection of Recipes from Figure Skaters Around the World.

At age 19, Christina graduated from Sheffield Hallam University in England with a BA (Hons) Degree in Performance and Professional Practice with First Class Honours. She was on the Elite Hallam Athletic Squad at Sheffield Hallam University. Christina also received the Creative Spark Award for Outstanding Work in the Creative Disciplines from Sheffield Hallam University, as well as Outstanding Achievement Award and Most Outstanding Work Award from Rotherham College.

Following her passion for fitness and love of lifelong learning, Christina's completed these fitness certifications and training courses: Stott Pilates Certified Instructor Level 1 in Matwork, Reformer, Cadillac, Stability Chair, and Barrels, NASM Personal Training Certification, Total Barre, Kettlebell Training, Sports Conditioning, Power Plate Core Fundamentals, Power Plate Post Natal Training, Pre- and Post-Natal Fitness, NASM Youth Fitness Course, Zumba Basics 1 and 2, Zumba Gold, Zumba Toning, Aqua Zumba, and Zumbatomic.

Christina has experience working as a dancer, actor, model, announcer, and presenter.

To learn more about fitness specialist, consultant, and motivational speaker Christina Chitwood, visit ChristinaChitwood.com or FitBodyFullLife.com.

CHAPTER 6

MY DAY

BY ARHAM FARAAZ

It was 1999; the Millennium was closing. Saturday morning, 6:59 AM, the alarm rings Tong-Tong-Tong. It sounded like the church bell has been struck with a sledgehammer. The vibrations were so intense that both Tom and Jerry would vibrate for a complete episode inside the bell. This vicarious feeling shook Addy from his sleep, our boy in this story. Feeling restless, Addy takes his fist and bangs the alarm with it: "Tong for the last time today."

Wrapping himself in the blanket, taking the first **STEP** in his **DREAM** world, he starts climbing the ladder to **ACHIEVE** his dreams. Then, suddenly he finds his leg stuck in the ladder, or it felt like someone was pulling him down, and not letting him achieve his **GOAL** at the top of the ladder. "Leave me, let me **reach higher in LIFE**," cried out Addy. "For that you will need to wake up, son," was the sweet response from his mom.

Addy replies, "Oh no, not again mom! Today is Saturday, please let me sleep." "Addy, its quarter past seven, you will be late and miss your bus, I do not want my son to be late for college or the bus." This did not matter to the boy, he was back in his bed enjoying the sleep, didn't feel like going to college on that day.

"Addy, your breakfast is ready, are you awake, dear?" There was no response. "Addy" called out mom, "Last night you told me that there are no classes today, don't you want to go today to meet your friends?" Ah, no classes, he flipped himself from the bed like a Rock star, and rushed to the washroom like a horse, **repeating** the chants *"My Day, My Day, My Day*. No classes, today is My Day at college." But, the boy was late, the room was already occupied by his elder brother.

THUD-THUD-THUD was the bang on the wooden door, "Come out bro, I am getting late for college," shouted Addy. Out came a voice, "You lazy bum, wait for some time, why did you wake up late? Now do not disturb me, I am busy." Addy replied, "I need to go to the college as early as possible, mom doesn't want me to be late and you want me to be late, please come out soon." No response this time. "Bro, I have my Physics practical examination in the morning, I can't be late". Addy's brother knew Addy pretty well, he responded, "Good for you, but you see, I am in biology practicals now, do not disturb." Addy called to his mom furiously, "Mom, do you want me to fail?" "No, I **DO NOT** want my son to **FAIL**," came the response. In the meantime, the door opened and the big brother walked out, giving a look in Addy's eye. Addy jumped in and closed the door. Bro asked mom, "Does he really have practical exams today?" Mom replied, "Naah."

Out came Addy in time, repeating his slogan, "My Day-My Day-My Day, no classes at college, today is My Day." Addy's brother looks at him and says, "you will **LEARN** a lesson today, without going to class. And this will be a good one." "Just chill bro", replied Addy. "It is all yours, please go back to the washroom, do not disturb me in my breakfast time." Addy gulped the breakfast in the excitement to go meet his friends and enjoying the day at college. He gets ready, puts on his canvas shoes, and the footloose bag and leaves for college with a humble bye to mom. Mom says, "I hope he **LEARNS** something today, to **help himself** stand up in life."

My Day-My Day-My Day, the chant continues, as Addy heads towards the bus stop. The bus on route number 119 starts, Addy see the bus moving at a distance of 100m from him, he shouts, "Wait, wait, wait, please wait, I don't want to be late for college today." Hardly anyone could hear him in the bus at such a distance. Addy starts running, but in vain. The bus is equally fast, the distance is not closing. Addy, had learnt about **choosing alternatives** in life, so he decides to take the muddy and bushy bypass road to catch the bus, he runs as fast as possible, as though he was in the final race of a competition. He jumps over the narrow ditches, accepts all the **ups and downs**, ducks below the branches, and finally makes it, before the bus could reach the next stop, but at the cost of some minor bruises.

"Yes, My Day," says the young lad. "I am the fastest man on planet, thanks to Johnson for inspiring me."

He enters the bus, sees some charming faces and regrets the fact that they are in the front portion of the bus and he is in the back. The bus reaches the college, he meets his friends. "Hey guys, wassup? How are you all?" All of them were in the first year of college. There were high fives and butt fights – the usual way of greeting one another. "Guys! Let us party today, no classes, just a gathering for couple of hours." The boys went into the auditorium filled with 600+ boys, Addy pulled all his friends into row number 29, the penultimate row, everyone loves to be seated in LAST but aims to come first, Addy was one such character.

There was a silence, as Father (Fr.) Henry walked in to address the students. "Good Moring students," said the father. "Today we all have gathered to **learn** something." Addy's ears popped, recollecting his brother's words, that he will learn something today. Fr. continued, "We all will have to do something good for society and today is the first step; all of you are 16+ and I believe it is time you all need to **start THINKING** about the society's welfare **today, lets us DO IT NOW."** **"Your today will make your tomorrow**, so I want each and every one of you to **write down your goal**, one sentence, on how **you will improve this society** we live in." Little did Addy believe how true these words will be for him.

Addy was thinking, okay now this is tough, but not impossible, he started to think what he has to write. Father then added, "That is **not** the final task for today. You need to come on the **stage** and **READ** that to everyone." Some students were excited, some were nervous, some were like, OK, what is new in this, but the world below Addy's feet just split apart, and he was falling into a deep abyss, into the cold and pressure-filled zone. Addy had never been on stage in his 10 years of schooling, and this was the **greatest fear** he had, as good as death for him. No, No, No, Father, please don't call me on stage. Addy cried out to himself in his HEART, he prayed that he would never get an opportunity to speak on the stage today. He was getting cold, he could not hold his pen properly and write due to the fear. His friend saw that something was wrong. What is wrong dude? Write down your line that we have to go and read. Addy replied, "B-B-B-But, I am so tensed and nervous, I don't want to go on stage, I have never been on STAGE in my life, it kills me, I get cold, my tongue gets tied, and I look like I am paralyzed." His friend replied, "Dude, when you can talk so much here, you can read out your line as well, very easily. And I will give you a hint, memorize it buddy, just go and read it out. It's as SIMPLE as that." Addy replied, **"NOT MY DAY!"**

Students started reading their lines. Some were novel, some were repetitive but they all showed the guts to stand up and speak their **thoughts**, meanwhile Addy had written his line, but was feeling smaller, since he lacked the courage. He wished "hope there were 290 rows and I would never get my chance today." But life has a different reality; then came his turn as they were approaching the steps. It flashed by Addy, "let me fall down the steps and then in an emergency I can go home." Addy tried a self-fall, but why do we have FRIENDS? To hold us in difficult times, his friend held him, "Easy dude, you will fall" were the words. Addy was like, it can't get worse, **NOT My DAY were his last words** before he stood before the microphone.

It was now "Cold Addy's" turn. He stood before the mike with a dry throat, fixed tongue, he made all the effort to tell his name, but all in vain. It looked like Addy had nailed his lips together, they wouldn't open, his hands had the paper in it, and were shivering, he was sweating profusely, the entire crowd of 600 students remained silent seeing Addy's helplessness. "Come on Son, tell us your name" shouted Father Henry, **listening** to this, Addy forced himself to speak out, "M- m-my name is…Addy", this bought a commendable applause from the other students, Addy felt that he had just won an Oscar. And he presumed that he was done, but no, he still had to read his lines. "Son read your line," said Father. Addy again built up all his courage and spoke, **"W-w-we … ssh-sh-hu should all work together for the welfare of society. Thank You."** There was a second round of Applause. **'NOT My Day'** were the words in his heart….

He felt he was a loser, embarrassed, ashamed and guilty. He went back to his seat and did not speak up. Father came on the stage once again and gave another opportunity for anyone who wanted to speak once more, Addy thought as though it was done only for him to come on the stage and do it. Many students who had already spoken their lines went and read out once again, but Addy did not have the guts to go and stand on that stage. It looked to him as though he feared it more than his death. Never again did he meet Father Henry and see him, but he remembers his face and the day vividly.

Addy went back home and never spoke about what happened on that day to anyone. Life continued in this mundane manner on many such occasions. Addy was vegetating, making no efforts to address this issue. He was now an engineer, and all his practical events were a similar story, he was tongue-tied when addressing a gathering or speaking to a stranger. **Only one person could help Addy and it was "himself"** but Addy did not **BELIEVE** that he could help himself.

Past his engineering Addy had dreams of making it into an elite college in his country; he had joined a coaching center to learn some skills on Aptitude to crack the examination. One day, he was called to speak on a topic known very well to him, and you know the rest of the story … **NOT My DAY**.

But, this day when he failed to speak he walked back to his seat, and told to himself. "I should be ashamed of myself, 16 years of education in the best institutions of the country and I am not able to **speak out my thoughts,** I pity my parents." Somewhere from inside a voice came, **"fix this issue now, it is never too late."** He headed towards his father's office instead of his home. He mentioned all the issues on stage starting from the retreat 6 years ago. His dad told him, "Good job boy, in telling this to me." Daddy motivated Addy and gave him a secret formula for his Aid. Addy was very confident having with him the **secret formula**, and he went home.

The next morning Addy woke up as usual, there was nothing new about it, except for the fact that he started to speak to himself in front of the mirror in the washroom. He had learnt a mantra from his mother, **"I will persist-I will succeed."** He also **believed and trusted consistent daily small improvements**. Practicing this and a few more nuances from experts for a few months he saw some changes in his fear, his fears were slowly drifting away from the shore of his heart.

And then one fine day, the boy was supposed to present on a topic on Software Management at an educational institution in front of 50+

people, some Managers, some peers, & some directors, all experts on the topic on which he spoke. Addy took a deep breath and told himself, **"Addy, it is your day today,"** and ensured that he did a great job – twenty minutes of clear, engaged presentation. The presentation was so good that he was congratulated by everyone including the Director. **Addy was in seventh heaven** and repeated the words to himself, **MY DAY-MY DAY-MY DAY**. He repeated this feat many time over the next 3 years in the institution, and in his office where he worked as a Software Source Code deployer at companies like Oracle and Dell.

Seeing his potential within himself, he decided to start a national initiative. He named it **L.E.A.D. – Learn.Excel.Achieve.Drive** in 2012 in INDIA. He decided to help college graduates to develop Individual Leadership skills to be best in their education and work. He trained people using his many years of experience in IT industry and his passion for leadership, and not forget thinking about the line he spoke 13 years ago – **"We should all work together for the welfare of society."** And in this initiative he trained and motivated 2000+ people on LEADership qualities to **help themselves reach higher in LIFE**. For his initiative, he **won** the **National Competition** as one of the best **Social Impact** projects on Education in the competition held on sparktherise.com. It was sponsored by Mahindra & Mahindra group. Addy believes in **impact**, so he trained the people on LEADership without charging them.

Going **"Against the Grain,"** Addy has quit his IT job to pursue his **DREAM**, and believes in burning bridges to go forward in life. These days he has started a new profession, a skill he didn't use, a passion that was not fulfilled in the IT job for many years. **He inspires, motivates & guides corporate employees, students and individuals on LEADership and Success**, and every time he is on stage, there is one line on his lips: **My Day-My Day-My Day.** He loves this part of his life.

It reminds him of the wish his brother and mother made that he Learn something in life. He has now *Excelled* by training 2000+ individuals, *Achieved* the status of a National Winner in India, for a **Social Impact Project** on educating students on LEADership and now *Drives* this initiative across the country and will take it globally. He has learnt to make a difference.

He has also shared the **secret formula** given by his dad that helped him overcome his fears, it is called **HOPE**. He believes that, **"Your greatest weakness can become your greatest strength, if you act upon it with hope."**

Addy also shared his belief that he learnt from Napoleon Hill, "What a man's mind can conceive and believe, he will achieve it."

I would like to end this story with a fact: "Today the world knows him as the author of this short story, **My Day, Arham Faraaz**."

About Arham

Arham Faraaz is a LEADership Coach and a Motivational Speaker; he trains people and organizations on excelling in tough times by utilizing their individual leadership skills – what he calls "Succeed without a Title." He is a young, dynamic public speaker on LEADership. He was in the IT industry for many years as a Successful Software Release Engineer, working at organizations like Oracle and Dell. During his tenure in the IT industry, he analyzed human behavior and discovered the importance and methods of individual LEADership skills which help people reach higher in life. He has great relationships with his colleagues, guided them on LEADership, success and motivation, and helped them excel in their jobs. In doing so he realized his true passion to help people live great lives. Going "Against the grain" he resigned from his successful IT job to go forward in his passion and founded the Arham Faraaz LEADership Academy, a respected training firm that specializes in developing the leadership and improving performance of individuals and organizations in changing times. It gives him great meaning in guiding his clients on LEADership and excellence.

At 29 years of age, Arham is also a Social Entrepreneur and a National Winner for his initiative L.E.A.D as one of the best "Social Impact Projects" in India on Education, a project to bridge the gap between college and corporate life. He has trained 2000+ people on LEADership in this initiative in less than 150 days in 2012 /13 through his own funding. He has done his Bachelors in Engineering, and has also done his vocational training on "Project Management" from 2007 to 2010 at the Indian Institute of Science, Bangalore.

Arham is a great relationship builder; you can reach him at:

www.arhamfaraaz.com and +91 9611299211

email : arham.faraaz@arhamfaraaz.com—just to tell him "Hi!"

visit www.arhamfaraaz.com

CHAPTER 7

DOWN AND OUT AT 53! I CAME BACK AND YOU CAN TOO!

BY DAVID SMITH

> *"You have to crack-up to let in the light"*
> -· Lara Owen

I died. I must have, or the nice lady wouldn't be talking about the division of my estate - something about a dividend…huh? Wait a minute! What estate? I was about to declare bankruptcy. It *all* goes!

I was in shock. How in the world could this be happening to me? I was floating, barely in my body. I worked very hard all my life – over 35 years in business making a good living. I had taken care of many clients over the years in the financial industry from banking, business consulting, budgeting and management, to sales. There had been few complaints from customers or employers.

I liked people. People liked me. I was kind. I was good with money. I paid attention to the details. I had been treasurer for my church for over 15 years. I was happily married for over 30 years, with two lovely children. I was a good husband, father, and provider.

I was a good person.

And yet, here I was having a near-death experience. There was no light and warmth ahead in a tunnel. I had only a sense of numbness, a disembodied drifting. I was aloft and apart from it all. As I looked down from the heavens, or was it a perch in hell, I saw myself, my life, the equity in our home and my self-worth all melt away

REALLY, HOW *DID* THIS HAPPEN?

Well, my consulting business, which once was thriving, had started to dry up, little by little. Clients began to drift away - perhaps they could no longer afford my services, maybe I had lost my touch, maybe there were cheaper or better alternative providers? Maybe business was tough all over?

I couldn't tell. One thing I did know, I was in over my head. I couldn't pay all the bills and my debt load was gaining on me. In fact, I was buried. Back in our early 30's, my wife and I had paid off the mortgage on our first house and our two new cars. We were debt-free. We were awesome! Then, through a series of ill-timed real estate moves, we managed to lose money and somehow go unconscious, not fully realizing where we were heading.

How is it that our mortgage grew larger every few years? Well, the washing machine quit, the roof needed replacing, the car broke down, and stuff wore out. We were living beyond our means and did not see it.

Meanwhile life happened.

My mother developed early dementia and could not support herself. We paid some of her bills for a while but then we had mom move in with us. She stayed for the next 8 years until we couldn't cope. She moved to an independent living facility for 4 years; all the while we paid for some of her expenses. All this cost us considerably both financially and emotionally. Our stress levels went through the roof. We made poor choices. Rather than clarity there was fog and denial. I could no longer see clearly. Life was a blur. I was no longer grounded. I had become rooted in fantasy.

The Pain of Salvation
Then one day, in desperation, I confided in a close trusted friend. He told me the truth "You're done. Go to KPMG Bankruptcy trustees. They will help you." Then he, a successful entrepreneur and businessman,

said to me, "I know about this because I had to go there as well." He hadn't said a word about it before, yet we were good friends. The worst part of bankruptcy is the sense of shame and feeling of failure; of being a "loser." So one keeps quiet, isolated, hidden away in pain.

In the financial industry, declaring personal bankruptcy is not helpful to one's business reputation. You are supposed to know better. You are expected to be a model of sound fiscal management. I had *been* that person.

Many things came to an end. My business, my job, my reputation, my self-esteem, self-confidence and sense of being anything worthwhile. My light inside was almost out. Was I a waste of space? My life was for naught. I had failed my family and myself. I realized that I was worth more dead than alive due to my life insurance. It occurred to me I could just get in my car and drive off the side of the road. At least my family would have money to begin again.

While these feelings of hopelessness arose in me, I realized that others were going bankrupt as well. I recall several stories of a number of people around the world committing suicide because of business failure and bankruptcy. A 51-year-old man in California murdered his own family then killed himself. A billionaire in Germany threw himself under a train after suffering a huge loss. Earlier in my life, I worked with a man who, after suffering an unexpected loss, went out for coffee and never came back.

This is what I felt like doing, just before my wife and I told our two daughters that I was about to declare bankruptcy. They were horrified, devastated and bewildered; any sense of security and safety was completely wiped away. This was heart-wrenching for both my wife and me. The feeling of failure, loss and regret **should** have brought me to tears. I was deeply wounded, filled with pain and shame. But instead of crying, I raged and blamed others. I was a brute, unstable and distraught.

Real Salvation

If it wasn't for my youngest daughter cracking under the enormous shock and loss, God knows where we would all be. She was moody and depressed; at times she threatened to take her own life. She asked repeatedly for help. It was a blessing in disguise. We found a family counsellor and psychotherapist who brought us back from the brink of complete disaster.

This loving and wise man, introduced us to a world of healing resources. All of my family has benefited from his expertise and guidance. I came to realize that I was very immature and out of touch with my feelings. I have gained insight into my life, which had previously eluded me, in spite of my best efforts. Prior to this, I did not cry, being more accustomed (programmed) to suffer stoically or become angry. After all I was a *man*! Suck it up buttercup! Don't be a cry-baby! Don't be a wimp!

Then one day in my counselor's office, as I spoke about my father, I was suddenly moved to tears, racking sobs actually, where I could hardly breathe, a dam bursting, as a childhood memory popped up. I remembered being about 14 or 15, when my father said to me "You know, I don't have to keep you! I can take you to child welfare. Make me want to keep you."

To hide my sudden shock, I argued with him, saying he *did* have to keep me. He just kept repeating himself. I had lost the argument and lost my sense of safety. I was devastated, deeply wounded and traumatized. I didn't know that at the time. I don't think my father knew it either. My sense of being loved and worthwhile went away then. A few years earlier, my father drove into the country and dropped off a stray cat (who had adopted us) at the side of the road. I felt I could very easily be the next thing he dropped off at the roadside. I had been irritating him (as teenagers do) trying to get him to pay some attention to me. He didn't understand; he was annoyed.

Three or four years later he left, divorcing my mother. He left me, by default, as the *man* of the house at 18 years old. At home were my mother and my two younger sisters. This was another huge loss, a shock, and now a huge burden. I felt numb to it all. I "manned up." But I was traumatized, unaware that my new financial blueprint was based on the flight-or-fight survival mode. The dinosaur brain was running my life. I was in a panic and nervous most of the time. I could not sit still.

My alarm was ringing - danger!

Throughout my life, I had huge difficulty accessing and maintaining a clear connection with my creative and intuitive brain. My inner voice encouraged survival-based actions. I made a number of poor financial and life decisions. I did not think of getting help. I hardly knew I was in trouble. I was embarrassed and full of shame. I'm a professional. I should know what to do. I tried everything I could think of doing.

What good is that when you are thinking in a panic? I didn't even know I was in a panic. Then it was too late. It turns out many people are worried about money and may be in a panic. Many are scared. In the United States, according to Helaine Olen in **"Pound Foolish"** countless surveys have been conducted about how people feel about their retirement funds. They all say the same thing: nine out of ten people worry they will not have enough money to retire. In Canada the numbers are similar but slightly lower.

It Isn't Too Late For You

Your life is much, much greater than my or anyone else's laundry list of advice, to-do items and checklists. If it was a matter of whipping through the list and doing it, none of us would have problems. All the self-help books are of little use unless you DECIDE to get real and honestly face the truth of your situation. Not what you tell yourself, not what you hope it is or could be. Now is the time, your time to care about yourself and your family enough to take a good look at your situation. No matter what you see, you can make it better. Don't ignore it unless you don't mind cracking up like I did.

THE BEST TIME FOR DISASTER PLANNING IS *BEFORE* YOU ARE IN THE MIDDLE OF ONE

Decide to take charge of your life now. No one else can do it for you. What will you do if the unthinkable happens? Talk to your partner now. Get professional help now. Prevention is the best cure. Decide to face it, feel it and find the solution. What are you doing to get your financial house in order?

> *"Great Lives Are Made On Making Great Decisions"*
> ~ John Assaraf

Based on what I learned, *if the disaster is happening or has already happened:*

THERE ARE 6 CRITICAL STEPS YOU MUST TAKE IN ORDER TO SURVIVE, RECOVER, AND THRIVE AFTER A MAJOR LOSS OR PERSONAL DISASTER:

1. Get Help Now

First it is vital that you survive this. You will need **COURAGE** and the **grit of an indomitable spirit** to deal with what lies ahead. You will also need **LOVING KINDNESS:**

> *"I am larger and better than I thought.*
> *I did not know I held so much goodness."*
> ~ Walt Whitman

There is no need for you to suffer like I did. ***Decide*** to get help from a financial counsellor in assessing your situation to gain a realistic view of your financial circumstances. Also, be sure to consult with your doctor and family counsellor or psychotherapist.

You are worth it! You are no worse or better than anyone else. Everyone makes mistakes and fails at many things. You just don't hear about it.

Did you know that Walt Disney and Sam Walton went broke and had to declare bankruptcy? Because they had courage, believing they were worthwhile, they decided to give themselves a fresh start. They saw bankruptcy as a tool to eliminate their debts so they could try again.

Disney gave the world fabulous entertainment. Sam Walton forced other companies to sell their products at affordable prices.

Who knows what wonderful things will come from you?

2. Assess Your Current Situation

Notice what is actually going on in your life. If you feel a little queasy as you read this just pause for a few moments. Take three slow, deep breaths to become **present and focussed. Face everything** as it is right now. You can only deal with what you *allow yourself* to see. It is the way it is. Just relax and be honest with yourself. Stay. Don't run away and hide from reality. Tell yourself the truth. Even though it's uncomfortable and painful **you can do this!** You deserve relief from your past mistakes and the freedom to make a fresh start. You deserve good health and joy. You can decide to earn abundantly. For now, you need a clear picture of your situation.

Decide now to accept full responsibility for your life. You are in charge.

3. Talk About It

Talk in a safe non-critical environment with an objective skilled counsellor.

4. Feel Your feelings

Allow yourself to feel the pain, sadness, regret, grief, disappointment, shame and embarrassment. These feelings of futility and loss can lead you to tears. Dr. Jill Bolte-Taylor, a neuroanatomist and author, reported in her book, "My stroke of insight," that the life span of a feeling, without a storyline, is only a maximum of 90 seconds. If a story is created the feeling can persists for days or years. This is awesome if the story is positive but deadly if it is negative. Sustained feelings are like seeds planted in a garden.

> *"Sensation precedes manifestation. Be careful of your moods and feelings, for there is an unbroken connection between your feelings and your visible world."*
> ~ Neville Goddard

You need to express your anger in a safe place so that you will get it out and not traumatize your family, friends or co-workers. You cannot do all this on your own. Feelings that are not felt can morph into monsters that wreck your life, hindering your resiliency or ability to bounce back. Instead, you can easily learn to feel your feelings and turn your life around, building it into the masterpiece it is meant to be.

Once the painful feelings are fully expressed, healing is automatic. Your feelings will be become more and more positive very quickly. You will naturally feel much more gratitude, praise and compassion for yourself and those around you. This will create much more desirable circumstances for you. After all, ***what you focus on grows!***

5. Cry

Allow yourself to give expression about all your feelings of remorse and regret, guilt, anguish of failing, of not being enough, of hopelessness. And of feeling hurt and rejected. In other words everything that feels bad and painful. I have learned that unexpressed sadness or disappointment turns into anger. Anger doesn't make me creative and adaptable. It just turns me into a blunt instrument great at destroying but ***not*** great at building.

With the tears released through crying, stress hormones are released from the body calming the nervous system. The "crying" system is the shut-off valve to the adrenal fight-or-flight response.

Crying can be the gateway to CREATIVITY. This is how we adapt and evolve. Since I am habituated to respond to sadness or disappointment with anger, I choose to stay vigilant and train myself to respond differently.

6. Recover, Maintain and Thrive

You are a new work in progress. Congratulations! This can be very enjoyable and energizing. Just as your car needs regular maintenance so do you.

Here are 6 things that you can do for yourself to make this experience more effective:

6.1 See your counselor/psychotherapist every two weeks.
This way you will keep on track and keep changing. You have decided to be authentic. He or she will help you do this. It takes your courage and willingness. It takes his skill and experience. You will begin to see yourself quite differently than at the beginning. Since you got this far, it means that you decided to grow up and accept full responsibility for everything in your life. You are in charge. Throughout this whole experience, you must be absolutely determined to find out where you went wrong. Dare to look at all of the past to understand it thoroughly, then change each of the elements so you do NOT repeat this program ever again!

6.2 Meditate daily.
This will help clear your nervous system and change your neural programming so that new constructive habits replace old destructive ones.

6.3 Pause several times a day, taking three slow, deep breaths
to become present, relaxed.

6.4 Get plenty of exercise.
Physical exercise is a great way to reduce stress.

6.5 Drink 6 to 8 glasses of water daily.

6.6 Experience your emotions more fully.

Learn to stay with uncomfortable feelings. If you are angry it is quite possible that you feel hurt. Stop, face it and feel what is there. Allow yourself to be vulnerable. This approach may move you to tears; this may be scary but will bring relief.

This will be like magic for you.

I did all these things. I have changed direction, moving into Internet marketing. I am an evolving infopreneur, building an information products business helping people learn how to make money on-line. I have taken my financial and work skills and re-invented my career. I am much more creative, confident and capable. I actually feel my disappointments, sadness and frustrations now. I am lucky to be alive and healthy, lucky that my wife and children have supported me even though I brought them a world of pain. This is true love.

This has made me human again and vulnerable. My intuition-brain is in control, the dinosaur brain at rest. I am making good decisions. I made up my mind to turn myself from being a victim to being a creator. Part of the process in going through bankruptcy is the requirement to set up and live on a budget. This requirement and very limited access to credit helped me change my spending behaviour.

This discipline has huge transformative power that is helping me re-program myself in many ways. I am experiencing renewed financial success.

According to T. Harv Eker, the way to overcome any problem or challenge, obstacle or failure is to grow yourself bigger than the problem. The truth is: you are *already* big enough right now. You just don't know it yet. So you grow yourself bigger through your creative intuition that lies within your subconscious mind. Your access portal is your feelings. If they are clogged up with bitterness and anger, then a mess is created. When the feelings are honoured through recognition and acceptance, your nervous system relaxes and refreshes. It becomes clear and clean. It heals.

When there is deep trauma, as in my case, there is considerable work to be done. Since I now understand how the mess in my life came about,

I am actively working to change my inner pattern of beliefs. Upon taking a closer look at my life I have realized that many of the past shocking experiences have created lasting impressions and beliefs that have re-created similar painful circumstances for me over and over again – stuck in a repeating pattern like a broken record. Now I see why all my efforts and struggle over the years always led to only temporary success.

I realize the *most important thing I can do is change my beliefs and expectations*. I am now learning in a way that builds new neural pathways and new understandings at the subconscious level. The subconscious mind is the true source of everyone`s inexhaustible power to achieve great things. According to Brain science research, the subconscious mind is where 96-98% of one`s feelings, beliefs, behaviors and habits reside.

"As within, so without. There is nothing new about this. The outside mirrors the inside. External action follows internal action"
~ Dr. Joseph Murphy.

I have found an amazing training system that is guiding me in this new deep learning. I am focussed on designing my future including my financial goals. I am building new positive beliefs that will move me to achieve and sustain these goals. This feels natural and joyful, filling me with enthusiasm, confidence and certainty. Obstacles vanish. Life is so much easier and fun! It's as though the Universe comes rushing out to help me with everything, both big and small.

YOU CAN CREATE *YOUR* NEW LIFE AND FORTUNE NOW!

"Our deepest fear is not that we are inadequate, but powerful beyond measure. It is our light not our darkness that frightens us.
We were meant to shine, as children do. We were born to make manifest the glory of God that is within us. It's not just in some of us; it's in everyone."
~ Marianne Williamson

For more details and information, go to: www.davidsmithnow.com

About David

David Smith, of Kelowna, British Columbia, is a new best-selling author and evolving infopreneur. He is focused on helping people successfully reinvent themselves and make money online. David's passion is in helping you achieve your personal, financial and business goals.

His message is that it is never too late to reset your inner blueprint, integrate it with your outer activities in a congruent way and enjoy sustainable success while living your life fully. He speaks from his own ongoing experience.

David has spent many years in management positions with several Canadian financial companies, specializing in client service and sales. His experience includes financial analysis and consulting, both business and personal. He began his lengthy business career at five years of age selling stationery door-to-door.

Throughout his professional life, David has participated in countless self-development and business courses and seminars; his focus is on continuous improvement and profitable results. He approaches life and business with a sense of fun, adventure and humour.

His interests include cycling, skate-skiing, playing piano, meditation and reading.

David is happily married and has two children.

www.davidsmithnow.com

CHAPTER 8

SECURING YOUR FINANCIAL FUTURE IN ANY ECONOMY — Action Steps You Need To Take Today

BY ALAN SCHUH

We are living in different times; obviously it's not the 80's and the 90's anymore. Yesterday's strategies and plans may no longer allow us to achieve our financial goals and objectives. We have lived through two major financial crises in the recent past. The dot-com bubble (also referred to as the dot-com boom, the Internet bubble and the Information Technology Bubble) was a historic speculative bubble covering roughly 1997–2000. The collapse of the bubble took place during 2000-2002 where the average investor lost about 23 percent of their account values (based on the S&P 500 index). Then again in 2008 we suffered one of the worst economic downturns ever, the financial crisis of 2007–2008, also known as the global financial crisis and 2008 financial crisis; this was considered by many economists to be the worst financial crisis since the Great Depression of the 1930s with the average investor losing approximately 38 percent of their account values. It resulted in the threat of total collapse of large financial institutions, the bailout of banks by national governments, and downturns in stock markets around the world. In many areas, the housing market also suffered, resulting in evictions, foreclosures and prolonged unemployment. The crisis played a significant role in the failure of key businesses, declines in consumer wealth estimated in trillions of US dollars, and a downturn in economic activity leading to the 2008–2012 global recession. We are still not fully recovered economically.

Many of us chose not to participate in the economic meltdown as a result of following certain strategies that were able to partially or completely insulate us from financial devastation. We do not make anyone rich; we prevent them from ever being poor. We offer guarantees; guaranteed death benefits, guaranteed income, guaranteed principal and guaranteed returns. In order for our clients to succeed financially, they must commit to new strategies based on these guarantees. Guarantees that can only be provided using specific strategies and products available today. The foundation for successful financial outcomes will be to Never Lose Any Money Again. You cannot defeat taxes, lost benefits, volatility and inflation if you keep losing, getting back to even, losing again and fighting to get back to even. Most people don't realize that a 50% loss requires a 100% gain just to get back to even. Why not try and avoid the losses in the first place?

Many Americans have seen their savings decline or go sideways since 2000. Most realize they don't have enough saved for retirement, and they are looking for a steady income that somewhat mirrors what their parents received from pensions, which they don't have access to. Many Boomers ages 50 to 65 are not adequately prepared financially to retire. In addition, other than government employees, most people will retire without a traditional pension to rely on. All they will have are their 401(k)'s, IRAs and personal savings, and, as we all know, many people have not saved enough money. We now have the ability to help people dramatically improve the income gap they have created due to inadequate savings, without them having to gamble with their retirement assets.

Let's explore some examples of how we were able to help our clients not only survive, but even thrive during some challenging economic times. Specific action steps will be provided later in this chapter.

Most investment brokers base their financial planning on something called Modern Portfolio theory. This theory basically divides up your money and puts it into different investment categories. Another word for this is diversification. The process of diversification is supposed to minimize your losses if the market drops. One thing that is rarely talked about is that it also limits your gains when the market goes up. We have a better idea. What if you could participate in some of the market gains without participating in any market losses? Our emphasis is on preservation of your principal, participation in some of the market gains, and lifetime income that you cannot outlive. We can help you set up a retirement plan you can be sure of. Markets always retest new lows, but when the markets go into the next dive, it won't matter to you once you've escaped the volatility of the markets. You will be smiling, knowing that your hard-earned money is 100 percent safe from any and all market losses. How do we do that? We stay away from stocks, bonds, mutual funds, and variable annuities. All of those are exposed to market losses.

We were always led to believe that if we added money to our 401(k)'s and IRAs on a regular basis over long periods of time, our money would grow and provide a comfortable retirement. What happened to the folks who were scheduled to retire in 2002 or 2008? How well did they fare? If you have most of your money at risk within five years of retiring, you are no longer an investor, but rather a speculator. Many studies have been conducted in recent years regarding the effects of suffering significant losses in retirement accounts during the first few years of retirement. Losing money early in retirement has a devastatingly negative impact on future retirement income. Withdrawing money every year from a declining portfolio will almost certainly lead to you running out of money before you run out of time. Running out of money is a greater fear for today's baby boomers than dying.

EIGHT ACTION STEPS YOU SHOULD IMPLEMENT

1. *Purchase adequate life insurance to make sure your loved ones can remain in their own world should something happen to you prematurely.*

   Our clients have used the ever-popular indexed universal life insurance (IUL) to participate in some of the upside of the stock market, while insulating themselves from market losses. In addition, under current tax law you can withdraw funds for emergencies or to supplement retirement income without taxation if structured properly.

2. *Early retirement.*

When running a retirement calculator, you may want to plan to retire as early as possible. This isn't just because it would be fun to pursue your dream of traveling the world while you're still young enough to do it. Even if you love your job and want to work until you drop, there are benefits to being financially able to retire before you need to. We are utilizing guaranteed lifetime income riders to allow our clients to build private pensions, which will ultimately provide an income stream they can't outlive. Most baby boomers unlike their parents do not have traditional defined benefit pension plans to fall back on as a source of retirement income. It's now all about the 401(k), which becomes a 201(k) every time we have a major financial crisis.

3. *Increase your retirement savings.*

Let's face it. Not all of us diligently saved 15% of our income starting with our first job out of school. Fortunately, you're more likely to be at or near the peak earning years of your career at a time when your children may be out of the house (see the first point) and mortgages may even be paid off. This can provide an opportunity to make up some of those lost savings.

If you haven't been saving 10-15% of your gross income since college, chances are you will face a shortfall in retirement possibly necessitating a reduction in your standard of living. If you can't live on 85-90% of your income while you're working, how can you expect to live on a lot less in retirement? It is a fallacy to assume you need less money in retirement. Don't forget, you now have seven days a week to pursue your hobbies.

4. *Risk Management.*

Risk is one of the most avoided and misunderstood subjects in the financial services industry. This is unfortunate because the primary purpose of a financial professional should be the intelligent management of financial risk. Protecting financial assets against loss while achieving a reasonable rate of return should be the objective of both investor and advisor. This is the critical issue in investing and it is being mishandled by many financial professionals. And it is the evaluation of risk and the way that you deal with investment risk that is critical in planning for a successful retirement lifestyle.

You can insure your risk by transferring any risk of loss to a legal reserve insurance company. The hurdle, which most investors must overcome, is their lack of knowledge that they can insure their investment risk. In the same way you insure your home, your car, your health and your life, you can also insure a retirement which would be protected from any risk of loss, regardless of any market activity and even insure a lifetime income you will never outlive.

5. *Review your investments.*
The composition of your investment portfolio is especially important as you approach retirement, but research shows less than half of Boomers are confident that their investments are allocated properly, and most have not taken a risk tolerance assessment. For one thing, you have more money at stake and less time to recover from a market downturn. In addition, your investment results for the first few years before and after retirement are particularly crucial in determining whether your portfolio will be able to last throughout your lifetime. Invest too aggressively and poor market returns early in retirement combined with income withdrawals can severely deplete your portfolio.

Our client's retirement accounts were largely unaffected by the 2002 financial meltdown and again during the 2008 financial crisis. How were we able to protect their accounts? We repositioned the portion of their savings that they absolutely told us they didn't want to risk into fixed index annuities. FIAs as they are commonly referred to have been in existence since 1995. This strategy utilizes lock in and reset features which provide for reasonable gains when the markets go up but to never ever sustain losses when the markets go down. The more often a fixed indexed annuity resets and the gain locks in, the better for the investor, especially when the market is volatile and has both up and down years. Most of these indexed annuities today have annual reset provisions. This means that any gains are locked in yearly and automatically reset for the next year. With the annual reset feature, the worst case is that the annuity doesn't return anything for a year the markets sustain any losses. Your original deposit plus any gains are always protected from any market losses.

6. *Consider long-term care insurance.*

According to a survey by Sun Life Financial (SLF), there's a major disconnect between people's need for LTCI and the preparation for that need. While just 36 percent of those surveyed believed that they would need such insurance, it's estimated that at least 60 percent of people over age 65 will require some long-term care services at some point in their lives.

The survey also found that 84 percent said they don't feel financially prepared for LTCI. And this is almost surely an understatement for two reasons. First, contrary to what many people believe, Medicare and private health insurance programs don't pay for the majority of long-term care services that most people eventually need, such as help with personal care – like dressing or using the bathroom independently. Less than 20% of Baby Boomers have a long-term care insurance policy in place.

Without insurance, you may have to spend down practically all of your assets to qualify for Medicaid coverage. This is not a remote possibility either. According to the National Clearinghouse for Long-Term Care Information, about 70% of people over age 65 require some type of long-term care in their lifetime, and The 2012 MetLife Market Survey of Nursing Home, Assisted Living, Adult Day Services, and Home Care Costs found the average cost for a private room to be $248 a day, or over $90,000 a year.

7. *Adequate liability insurance.*

Long-term care costs aren't the only threat to the assets you've worked so hard to build up. While less likely, a single lawsuit could cost you everything. Umbrella liability insurance is an inexpensive way to protect you and your property from lawsuits. You don't need it if you have relatively little at stake, but if you've accumulated some assets and have a home, it makes sense to have the policy.

It is recommended that you add an umbrella policy, which starts at $1 million of coverage, to protect against lawsuits even if your net worth is far less than that. The policies protect future income as well as assets and also cover legal fees. To buy the coverage, start with your auto or homeowners-insurance company, which may give you a discount for keeping your business in-house. If your company doesn't offer affordable umbrella coverage, ask an independent insurance agent for quotes.

8. *Estate planning.*

The American Taxpayer Relief Act of 2012 (Act) was enacted on January 2, 2013. The Act makes significant changes that will affect many estate plans. The Act permanently maintains the $5 million estate tax exclusion amount. This amount is adjusted for inflation each year, beginning with 2012. For 2013, the inflation-adjusted estate tax exclusion amount is $5.25 million. This means that a person dying in 2013 can transfer up to $5.25 million ($10.5 million for a married couple) (reduced by lifetime taxable gifts) at death without paying estate tax. Just because the recent fiscal cliff deal solidified the estate tax exemption at $5 million doesn't mean anyone with a net worth under that doesn't need estate planning.

Beneficiary designations and a revocable living trust (RLT) can save your family time and thousands of dollars in probate costs while a will can also designate the guardianship of any minor children you may have. Why are proper beneficiary designations so important? Most retirement plans, annuities and life insurance policies let you decide what should become of your assets in the event of your demise through the designation of beneficiaries. The primary beneficiary or beneficiaries inherit first. If they are dead or they die with you, your assets go to any secondary beneficiaries you have named. You will need to name names. And you will need to determine what percentage of your assets goes to each beneficiary.

Beneficiaries can include those who leap to mind -- spouses, children and other relatives. Or they can include friends, trusts, charities and institutions. Beneficiary designations generally kick in immediately after death and override a will. You need to ensure that your beneficiary designations reflect your most recent wishes because your will cannot override them. Spouses can generally inherit assets from one another without generating estate taxes or, in the case of retirement accounts, being forced into taking mandatory taxable payouts. (Unless the inheriting spouse has turned 70 1/2, in which case normal distribution rules apply.)

Failure to take these actions in time can have catastrophic consequences. But unfortunately, there's no equivalent of a fiscal cliff deadline to spur action. Specifically, you have no idea when you might be forced into early retirement, experience the next stock market crash, need long-term care, be the victim of a lawsuit, or suffer death or incapacitation. That's why the time to take action on these important issues is now.

About Alan

Alan Schuh is a practicing insurance professional in Florida.

Alan has enjoyed helping people safeguard their retirement money. Since 1989, he has helped people protect millions of dollars in retirement assets and not one of those people have ever lost a penny from market downturns. There is something truly wonderful about being able to help people have peace of mind about their finances. Alan is able to sleep at night with the comfort of knowing his client's retirement funds are protected. It is his desire to give you that same piece of mind.

His mission is to teach clients powerful, safe-money strategies. For the past twenty-four years, he has been helping individuals and business owners preserve their assets, increase their income and reduce income taxes. As a safe money advisor, he works independently for your benefit.

His firm focuses on IRA/401(k) rollovers, retirement/income planning and wealth transfer strategies. They provide guaranteed lifetime income that cannot be outlived and inheritances that minimize or eliminate taxes.

They do not make anyone rich; they prevent them from ever being poor! They offer guarantees: guaranteed death benefits, guaranteed income, guaranteed principal and guaranteed returns. In order for their clients to succeed financially, they must commit to new strategies based on these guarantees – guarantees that are only available through insured products.

The foundation for successful financial outcomes will be to never lose any money again! You cannot defeat taxes, lost benefits, volatility and inflation if you keep losing, getting back to even, losing again and fighting to get back to even.

Alan has written articles for industry publications such as Life Insurance Selling Magazine, as well as maintaining a weekly blog.

To learn more about Alan Schuh, visit: www.heritageretirementincomeplanners.com and visit: www.heritageprivatepensioninfo.com or call Toll-Free: 1-855-3-Annuity.

www.HeritageRetirementIncomePlanners.com

CHAPTER 9

HOW TO SOAR DESPITE THE GLOBAL FINANCIAL CRISIS

BY HELENA NYMAN

PART 1:
CREATING HELENA NYMAN'S *SUCCESS TRIANGLE ™ – THE HEART OF THE ORGANIZATION

In 2011, a small a company with 5 million dollar annual revenue called me to do a business diagnostic. This company suffered from the aftermath of the 'Global Financial Crisis' (GFC). The question was whether or not the company should close their doors, or if there was a chance to turn it around. Using my extreme competitive and creative nature and a 'never leave a stone unturned' attitude, as well as seeing the hope and desire of the staff to turn this business around, the owner and I decided to take the direction of growth.

Within 18 months, we turned the business around and increased the revenue from 5 million dollars to almost 20 million. We quadrupled the numbers, while other businesses around us closed their doors.

Coming from Olympic sports, the deciding factor for me getting involved in this challenging project was the commitment of the team. The greatest talent and the best resources can NOT make up for a lack of commitment and fire within!

---

*Helena Nyman's Success Triangle ™: The Shared Vision, the Shared Mission and the Shared Values (Culture) of a company. Helena Nyman calls it also the foundation and the heart of the company.

The Shared Mission:

The next step was to find out the big 'WHY': the 'Shared Mission' – when people have a purpose, they have a stake in it and go 'the extra mile.'

Some questions to ask are:

- Who is affected by our work?

- What is our role and unique contribution to the world around us?

We explored with the team what impact their efforts would have on the community. In a collaborative effort, we created a 'Shared Mission'. While other organizations spent a fortune to create an impersonal mission statement, we created a mission statement that the employees were proud of, and there was a complete buy-in across the organization.

The Shared Vision:

The next step was to take a look at their vision. Their "vision" was the hope not to close the doors. **If I would draw a parallel to a sports team, this team played "not to lose."** I'm wired to win. We spent some time on creating a winning mindset. It takes credibility and trust to penetrate the shell. Having their commitment and a powerful Mission Statement is the foundation **before** you get to the vision. I tried to take short cuts in the past, but I paid dearly for it.

Once the mindset was at a peak, we created BHAGs (Big Hairy Audacious Goals as Jim Collins would say) that were aligned with the mission statement. I always challenge leaders and their teams to come up with extreme goals. Again, sports taught me that either you decide to play at the top, like an Olympian, or you are always going to move around in mediocrity.

I can't stand it when people play it too safe. For me it is a lame excuse under the pretext of being "realistic." Put all your efforts into being solution-oriented and innovative!

Questions to ask:

- What is the ultimate Goal that you or your company would like to achieve?

- What are you most proud of when you think about what your company represents?

To the surprise of the owner, the teams came back with stunning ideas. We synthesized the results, and a 'Shared Vision' aligned with the mission statement, was created. The excitement started to grow, and the teams already started to come up with ideas on how they would get to the peak.

The Shared Values:
The last of the three foundation pieces of Helena Nyman's Success Triangle ™ – the 'Shared Values'- give the tone on how business is conducted and what the company stands for   in other words, its culture.

You can have the best strategy, the best tactics, the best players, but if there is no clear line of conduct, no values and no alignment, then the heart of the company is missing. Bad and unacceptable behavior can take an organization down. Tony Hsieh, the CEO of Zappos, says: "I Fire Those Who Don't Fit Our Company Culture."

Some questions to ask:

- In what ways is our workplace (organization) a great place to work?
- What are our values? How do people treat each other? How are people recognized?

Examples of values:

- Individual responsibility and opportunity
- Honesty and integrity
- Work hard, yet keep it fun
- Continual self improvement
- Overcoming adversity to build character

As a side note:
Small Business Owners/Entrepreneurs: Surround yourself with a group of trusted business owners or entrepreneurs that can serve you as a sounding board and **Mastermind[1]** group. Working in a Mastermind Group can catapult you to extreme and unknown heights, and it can be a great support during transitions.

---

1 Mastermind groups offer a combination of brainstorming, education, peer accountability and support in a group setting to sharpen your business and personal skill. Mastermind group members act as catalysts for growth, devil's advocates and supportive colleagues.

Medium Businesses/Large Businesses: Include all levels of your organization in the process of creating Helena Nyman's Success Triangle™! Have an expert from the outside facilitating these sessions to keep a neutral and efficient process going. This process is very complex with larger organizations, and key people should be properly prepared and trained for this process prior to initiating it. All locations should be visited by the CEO and/or their representatives during this process. Create a campaign to include all employees in the future of the company!

PART 2:
KICK GFC (GLOBAL FINANCIAL CRISIS) TO THE CURB

Frankly, I have ZERO tolerance for people who take the Economic Crisis or GFC as an excuse for their inactivity. I call it pure laziness or a lack of problem-solving skills.

History has shown that many exceptional companies emerged out of a crisis. What did they do? They looked into the eyes of the bull and "attacked" – despite the crisis. When leaders tell me they can't do this or that because of the crisis, I always ask: "What crisis?" Focusing on the problem paralyzes. Again, I like to play to WIN, and a so-called "crisis" calls for extreme actions.

I remember a situation where it was about life or death, and about keeping or losing my business I had built with blood, sweat and tears. My husband was lying in a coma at the hospital after some complications during his emergency heart surgery. There were some additional challenges involved due to an upcoming kidney transplant. Imagine me at ICU (Intensive Care Unit), my husband in a coma connected to life support, me not knowing if he would "make it." I needed to keep my business going. The ICU became my temporary "office," and I conducted my business with the noise of the life support machines in the background. Many times clients commented on the background noise, and I had to tell them that I was in an ICU.

PART 3:
CREATING A WINNING STRATEGY

Having laid a solid foundation with Helena Nyman's Success Triangle™, you now have the buy-in and support of your employees, waiting hungrily to be a part of something big like 'landing on the moon' was for Americans in the '60s. When you have people at that point, they are bursting with mind-blowing ideas.

That's the "tipping point" where you have the opportunity to take your business racing down the highway of success. It's no longer the time to blend in; it's the time to stand out!

Sports prepared me very well for an agile life. I remember at one occasion where we had a New Year's Eve skating show on an outside rink at a castle in Switzerland. It was an hour before midnight, and the audience was ready for our show. Suddenly, all lights went out. After a diagnostic test was run on the lighting system, we were told that the lights were gone. The skaters were ready and the audience was ready. We improvised and saved the night, by jumping into our cars, driving the cars to the edge of the natural, triangular rink and turning on our vehicles' headlights. I think that was the best show ever, and I know we got as much applause for the way we saved the situation as for the show itself.

Now take that experience to your business and apply this concept to your situation.

Creating a strategy can't happen in a vacuum. It involves understanding the external environment, including customers, competitors, new technology, government, and the labor market.

Step 1: Understand the needs and wants of your customers
You have to understand your customers. Who are they today? What will be their needs and wants TOMORROW? Be a step ahead of the trends. Once you go with the trends, its already time for the next trend. Be the pioneer and be ready to live with the possible consequences: It all starts with your grandiose idea. People are not ready yet to hear and understand your message. They may laugh at you and reject you. They may try to take you down and destroy you. Regardless, you must stay persistent and on track. It will take time. But sooner or later, the first followers come on board, and suddenly, everyone wants to be a part of the new trend. You have to be thick-skinned to get through that phase!

I always like to think big and come up with ideas that people sometimes look at me with that look that says "Poor you–keep dreaming." Then I go and do it. It's that simple. People once asked my husband: "How come your wife does all these great things?" and he answered "She's just too naïve to know it can't be done."

Step 2: Assess your competition

Who are your major and most successful competitors? What are they doing? What works? What doesn't? This gives you a good idea where to put your efforts, and what not to waste your time on. If you want to go into details, you can study your competitors and establish a list with all their products and services, and cross-reference the lists. That gives you patterns that can be useful in your decision-making.

Step 3: Assess your Strengths and Weaknesses

After looking outside your organization, take some time to look within.

- What are your or your organization's key strengths and weaknesses?

- What has been working and what has not?

When I assess my clients' strengths and weaknesses, I focus on service, quality and innovation. (For a full version of a strategy, I use the extended assessment).

Service: Is the service 'crème de la crème'? Do you treat your customers like VIPs? Can your customers trust that they are in good hands? Over-deliver on your services and display it with a 'can-do' attitude!

MAKE A DELIBERATE EFFORT!

A friend of mine recently went to the dentist in Philadelphia, PA. At her arrival she received a warm and welcoming smile from the receptionist who asked her if it was her first visit. When my friend answered with a "yes," the receptionist said immediately "Let me be the first one to welcome you!" Then the receptionist gave her an office tour, offered her refreshments, lead her to a comfortable massage recliner, gave her a TV program card and the remote, and asked my friend if she needs to adjust the recliner for her. The receptionist made sure that my friend knew that she was at her avail.

As my friend left the office, she received a personalized coffee cup with a tooth brush and tooth paste. The day after, she received a personalized thank you card from the dental office with a note from the dentist. "It was a pleasure welcoming you to my dental practice!"

Quality: "Good enough" is unacceptable! Quality is non-negotiable!

That applies to your services, your products, your image and your organization's image, and your behavior. You reap what you sow. If your output is not first class, don't expect to earn first class respect.

Innovation: Are you looking to be a cheap copy, or do you want to be a thought leader and/or pioneer? Think where we would be today without Leonardo daVinci, Edison, Einstein, the Wright Brothers and many other brilliant minds. You have to reinvent yourself. Create new footprints.

I also suggest spending some time on the following questions:

- Name up to three major achievements in the past year, and why they were successful.

- Name up to three major failures in the past year, and lessons learned from them.

Everything you do has consequences – either good or bad. Sometimes, you see the impact immediately; sometimes it is apparent later. In order to fine-tune your actions, you need to evaluate your actions and their outcomes. As Einstein said: "Insanity is doing the same thing over and over again and expecting different results." Identify what works, and do more of it. Eliminate what doesn't work. Look for patterns!

CHOOSE INITIATIVES TO BECOME THE BEST

In business, the difference between a winner and second place can mean bankruptcy.

I am so passionate about what I'm doing that mediocrity is not even an option for me. I constantly look for new ways, better solutions, better service, and I love pleasing, no, make that thrilling, my clients.

I go out of my way to offer the ultimate service and experience. Having this fire inside me is contagious. People love being around me, and often they say: "I need a 'Helena fix'."

There is no shortcut to success! My colleagues and I always make fun with the expression: "We worked very hard for the last 10-20 years, so we could become an 'overnight sensation!'"

Are you willing to make the sacrifices? Do you live and breathe your passion?

Identify your company's initiatives that are the best in the industry. Identifying these key initiatives achieves three goals:

1. It enables you or your organization to focus your resources on high priority tactics and initiatives to be the leader in the industry.

2. It eliminates any weaknesses so you can meet – or in my case exceed – your clients' expectations.

3. It points the entire organization in the same direction (shared vision and alignment).

DEVELOP A POWERFUL MESSAGE FOR THE MARKET

A part of the strategy includes choosing messages to differentiate yourself or your organization in the market. A good message communicates the significant and unique value that clients receive from your products and/ or services, and it touches your clients' hearts.

My final word to the reader: If you absolutely love what you are doing, and you 'go the EXTRA mile,' the money will follow. Be persistent! Success doesn't come overnight. It is a process of working hard, constantly adjusting your course, overcoming obstacles, falling and getting back up, over and over, and finally celebrating your and your clients' success!

SUCCESS IS A CHOICE!

About Helena

Born and raised in Switzerland, she immigrated in 1999 to the United States and became Swiss-American in 2007.

Helena Nyman is the President of Nyman Consulting International and the Founder and President of the Executive Center of Excellence. Her background is: Master Certified Success/Executive Coach, Advisor, Consultant, Speaker and Author. She has attracted clients from over 40 countries globally.

In 2009 she received the Global Artemis Award and was inducted into the Women's Hall of Fame.

Having a background in Psychology, her focus is on behavioral change. As a former coach for Olympic Athletes (Figure Skaters), Helena is not only driven, but she's also very meticulous and laser focused on Leadership Development and Peak Performance in Organizations. In the last few years, she helped leaders to turn around their businesses and soar despite the Global Financial Crisis.

She has published several books. Her newest book that will be released in the second Quarter 2013 is: *The Paradigm Shift of the 21st Century Leader: Ignite the Fire WITHIN!*

She has worked in the past with/for: The President of a European Nation, Royalties from Europe and the Middle East, Celebrities, Pro-Athletes, Politicians, Organizational Leaders, Entrepreneurs, and Charities.

"Success is not a matter of chance; it is a matter of choice. It is not a thing to be waited for; it is a thing to be achieved!" ~ Helena Nyman ~

Contact: Helena Nyman
162 Cabin Rd.
Mineral, VA 23117
Phone: (804) 513-3536 * E-mail: Nyman@consultant.com
www.NymanConsulting.com

CHAPTER 10

FROM J.O.B (JOURNEY OF THE BROKE) TO FLOURISHING IN FREEDOM!

BY FELICIA KAYE MAHER

The steps to bravely break away from the J.O.B (Journey Of the Broke) and make a lifestyle change to begin Flourishing in Freedom!

INTRO

Nestled in a secret hideaway, hidden from the world in a home for unwed mothers, was the place where my life began. No one was supposed to know she was there. This couldn't be the way it was supposed to begin and definitely not how it should end. It was becoming difficult to breathe and impossible to see as panic ensued and unstoppable tears streamed down her face. The tension in the air seemed almost unbearable. Imagine the terror of this young girl, pulse racing, heart pounding, torn by the thoughts of the inevitable time rapidly approaching when her only child would be ripped from her arms and surrendered to the unknown! The dreaded day when I would be given up to the courts for adoption had arrived. With thoughts racing, she frantically reached for any resolution. The nuns saw the desperation, love, and fear in her eyes. Reluctantly and compassionately they agreed to do the only right thing; to hide me among the pots and pans in the pantry. When the court social worker came to pick me up, my Mom played out her best role as a unbridled crazy and "showed out"! Shortly and all too briefly afterward, my mother died. I was only four. My beautiful grandmother, Lillie Mae, loving beyond words, stepped in to raise me and my younger sister in a little town called Chickasha, Oklahoma.

Now, unbeknownst to me, even from this early age, I was already beginning to be programmed with a poverty mindset. My grandmother (who from this point will be referred to as "Mama") was on a fixed social security income. She was a seamstress who ironed for extra money. Mama used to pick cotton until arthritis claimed her knees and hands. Later in my high school years, her health would decline to the point of being fully bedridden in constant daily pain as she became blinded as a result of cataracts. Although Mama owned our nice, quaint what I understood to be a middle class home just on the "right side" of the tracks, it was an everyday occurrence for me to hear, "Girl, we don't have that kind of money," "Lisa, now save your money for a rainy day; You never know when you'll need it." And the occasional… "that's them, not us." or her favorite torte, "Now, girl you know, money don't grow on trees!" Then we were showered with the barrage of mediocrity entrainment statements such as, "Now, listen, you"ll have to get a good education in order to make it in this world," or things like… "Now Lisa, a degree is one thing that no one can ever take away from you" which was all affectionate, practical advice. Though it's true that few things can replace the sense of accomplishment and determination it takes to garner a degree, (I earned three), the 85% of students now graduating from college unable to find jobs in their degree fields are not typically finding their diplomas particularly nutritious, or in any way edible even when salted, nor are they a viable way to put food on the table in and of themselves.

Growing up, the only regular male presence in my life had an accepted habit of making moonshine and stumbling down to our house to eat most meals. He also had the customary inclination to mindlessly speak curses into our lives. He would say, under the influence of his homemade concoctions, "Ya'll ain't nothing but orphans and ain't never gonna amount to nothin'!" Thankfully, instead of these sporadic, careless, unintentional words causing irrevocable harm, they only shadowed my thoughts for a brief period of my life. Because of the carefully placed, loving, repetitive, purposeful words of Mama, "Lisa, you can do anything you set your mind to", my subconscious mind chose to cling to her pure, lovely, beautiful, and true words. So, as a result at that early age, I began developing a survivor's instinct that was a little voice inside this shy little girl quietly responding, "Oh, yeah? Just hide and watch!" And thus began the determination for my journey to find a way out of decades of a subtle impoverished mentality.

1. VISION- WHY ARE YOU DOING THIS?

"If you limit your choices only to what seems possible or reasonable, you disconnect yourself from what you truly want, and all that is left is a compromise."
~ Robert Fritz

I can remember as a teenager, driving back and forth to OKC in my little white Fahrvergnügen loudly singing along with Calloway, "I wanna be rich...full of love, peace and happiness!" Though I now realize that money is not everything...just try to pay your mortgage, rent, bills or get around without some! Surely, I'm not the only one who has noticed that poor or broke people have an exponentially more difficult time in life than do wealthy people. James Baldwin wrote, "Anyone who has ever struggled with poverty knows how extremely expensive it is to be poor." The poor pay higher interest rates, are forced to choose options of pricey furnishings at rent to own, throw away excess money at the grocery store for lack of ability to buy in bulk...and let's not even consider the vicious trap of never-ending outrageous payday loans.

As I reached early adulthood I found myself living life as a single mother for 11 years. Ironically, from this difficulty came my real purpose and catalyst for beginning the construction of a multi-generational legacy of wealth. My exceptionally talented daughter had received a scholarship to the premier acting school in New York. The only thing needed was money for housing and living expenses in Manhattan. Oddly enough, the man who had taken no voluntary role in our lives, and who hadn't agreed to even meet her until her high school graduation, I must thank. For, he is doubly the reason for which I chose another path. Firstly, for his role in bringing about the birth of our beautiful daughter, to which I told him then and again echo, would become the most significant person to whom I will ever be connected. Secondly, because by this time he had completed his MBA and had become VPO of a major hospital in the Southwest. When he asked me how long I had been at the company where we had both humbly started, my simultaneously boastful yet embarrassed retort was, "Ten years", to which his reply was, "Wow, you must be running that place by now!" Strangely, I sensed that he meant it and that caused me to think. Are there people in your life who cause you to reflect on where you are as opposed to where you could be? What steps must you take to get there?

Since her father had promised to step up and be responsible for getting our daughter safe and tucked away at New York Conservatory I was relieved. However, a few short weeks later when he "sketched out" on his promise it absolutely broke my heart and caused me to completely re-evaluate my career approach. I realized that I was helpless in making the dream my daughter had worked so hard for come true. After reflecting on all of the years of the stress of working my way through school, obtaining three degrees and working long hours as a top paid professional in my industry for 16 years, why was I not positioned to have all of the things the "American Dream" had promised? I, like many others, was instead living the "American nightmare!" So, I made a decision in that moment that never again would I be in a position where my financial hands were tied. I wanted to be able to say," let me help you." I wanted to leave a blessing, a legacy for my daughters and grandchildren's children. What are your dreams? Have you identified the decision you must make now in order to achieve them?

2. SURROUND YOUSELF WITH HIGHER THINKING

"Show me your five closest friends, and I'll show you your future."
~ Bill Cosby

In business and life there are many ways to elevate your knowledge and mindset. When piecing together an empire fashioned for greatness, being open to teachable moments and maintaining a grateful attitude is the oil that causes the sewing machine of success to execute smoothly. Brian Tracy says, "Develop an attitude of gratitude, and give thanks for everything that happens to you, knowing that every step forward is a step toward achieving something bigger and better than your current situation." Attracting the right people to surround you and work with is paramount. It will ultimately influence the entire outcome of what you're creating.

Investing in yourself is a must, it isn't an option. It baffles me to think about the thousands of dollars over the years I wasted on things that would never bring any return on investment in my life: cable, television in general, and tons of Home Shopping Network and useless infomercial products that I couldn't use or never even opened. I'm still upset about that 'revostyler'! Mind you, a poignant note is that these items found their way into my home as a result of the aforementioned cable! Guard your time and your mind. I'm just sayin'…!

When starting out, the amount of funds available to put toward investing in yourself may be limited. Therefore, books are an excellent resource. Charles William Eliot said, "Books are the quietest and most constant of friends; they are the most accessible and wisest of counselors, and the most patient of teachers." There are numerous conferences available that range from half-day to weeklong seminars throughout the country to attend in person and various online webinars and courses accessible for greater convenience when transitioning out of the rat race. Lily Tomlin said it best, "Even if you're winning in the rat race…you're still a rat!"

Another powerful tool in achieving success and purposing your environment for victory is to seek out and embrace a Master and immerse yourself in their technique. Someone who has conquered the undertaking that you set out to accomplish on a high level and is now reaping the benefits is considered a Master. Success leaves clues; therefore, if a Master has charted the territory and been victorious, it stands to reason that the least painful and most ideal way to learn is from the secondhand trials of others. My favorite book says that "God does not show favoritism"(Acts 10:34). Therefore, if ANY other human has done it, you can do it too! So, if you can emulate the "recipe for success" of a Mentor by embracing the wisdom and steps of someone who has perfected their skill you'll benefit three-fold. You will be able to shorten your learning curve by avoiding some of the common errors made in business, have someone to guide and encourage you along the way when things are difficult, and maintain hope on the journey by physically seeing the outcome of your effort manifested in another person's life.

Wilfred Peterson said, "Walk with the dreamers, the believers, the courageous, the cheerful, the planners, the doers, the successful people with their heads in the clouds and their feet on the ground. Let their spirit ignite a fire within you to leave this world better than when you found it." It's a very common view that when you surround yourself with people who find the blessing in the journey, high achievers, business owners, those who make things happen, you rise to the inspiration around you. On the other hand, when you surround yourself with negative news, people who lack the initiative to challenge themselves, those generally dissatisfied with life, and people who make excuses, they too will bring you down to their vantage point. In other words, your level of success and attitude will acclimate to the ambient temperature of that of your closest peers. With this thought we come to the realization that we have authority to create our existence. How do you want to construct your life? Who do you need to add to or subtract from your reference group?

3. BE UNSTOPPABLE - PRESS INTO YOUR FEAR

"Too many of us are not living our dreams because
we are living our fears."
~ Les Brown

There are countless reasons that we never pursue our dreams. Thankfully, I simply refuse to accept the limitations that most people cleave to. Many simply have never taken the time to stop and evaluate who they are, how they got to this point, and what they want to become. Taking a pause in your life for reflection is noteworthy in purposefully making your life the way you yearn for it to be. Paulo Coelho's character in the Alchemist alludes to the notion that a dream once acknowledged but never pursued becomes a nightmare. Many don't feel that they have the potential within them to achieve what they want. Some take it a step further and don't even believe that they deserve to have the things that they truly desired beginning long ago in childhood when it was considered "safe" for them to dream. They've allowed themselves to listen to the messages of the world, hardships they've experienced, and not so great choices in their lives to cause them to punish or be "practical," and to give up on themselves. One of my mentors once told me that "the average man actually dies in his 30's and just walks around for another fifty years waiting to be buried!" (Matt Morris.)

There will never be a time when all things perfectly align in order for you to decide to have a baby or to start a business. Just begin! Dale Carnegie said, "Inaction breeds doubt and fear. Action breeds confidence and courage. If you want to conquer fear, do not sit home and think about it. Go out and get busy." Had I allowed the things spoken to or about me, to paralyze me from the pursuit of my destiny, or resigned myself to accept the normal route of life that was simply a result of not pausing for station identification, I would have ended up on another frequency destined like 98 % of the world to insidiously continue slowly becoming more broke every day. Chillingly, I cringe to think how different my life would be. I never would have been able to experience the lifestyle that I am now living. Though I in no way intend to make my journey seem complete, without sacrifice, or setbacks, It has afforded me refreshing hope while on the path to building multiple streams of passive income. I own my own businesses, enjoy the freedom of traveling several times a year to many places around the world, and take pleasure in spending time with my family and stellar friends out of preference instead of leftover time. It is my delight to have the privilege of becoming a part of a circle of successful peers whose insight causes me to continually grow and adds value to my life on a daily basis. I am fortunate to live out my passion and educate, coach, empower, and enable many others to achieve their personal goals and dreams, and embrace the reality that we were divinely designed to live in complete abundance in all areas of our lives: physical, emotional, spiritual, and financial.

Mama taught me that going against the grain was for the boldly adventurous and accomplished seamstress. However, every seamstress began as a novice. In the tapestry of life, if you seek to create an audacious existence of doing greater things that will touch more lives, this skill must be relentlessly pursued. If you fail the courage to go against the grain, you'll find yourself under the foot of the machine with the painful needle of mediocrity forever impaling your dreams!

About Felicia

Felicia Kaye Maher, RN, BSN is CEO of Passionate Living by Divine Design, Lifestyle Coach, and Host of The Healthy, Wealthy, & Happy Hour.

After spending years of time and effort dedicated to putting herself through college, achieving an Associate Degree in Nursing, a Bachelor's degree in Applied Arts and Science and a Bachelors degree in Nursing, she had sacrificed years to relentless 12 hours shifts in the middle of the night and found herself still left unable to help her daughter financially in accepting a scholarship to New York Conservatory for Dramatic Arts and Television.

Felicia made the decision to go against the grain, leaving a 16-year career as a top paid Registered Nurse to build businesses that unlock hidden dreams and leverage time so that people can spend more time having fun and embracing their hearts true desires. Felicia is a champion for freedom and healthy living for those who truly desire the "American dream." She mentors and empowers others to become aware that we were divinely designed to live abundantly in all aspects of our lives: spiritually, emotionally, physically and financially.

For more information check out: www.FeliciaKaye.com

www.bydivinedesign.worldventures.biz

Or contact her by email: feewifig1@gmail.com

CHAPTER 11

REMEMBER WHAT YOUR MOMMA TAUGHT YOU!

BY DEBBIE ELDER

Learn from the BASICS for Business Success

Back in 2000, I made a very bold move: I decided to pull my daughters out of public school and enter the world of homeschooling. To say I was terrified by the challenge would be an understatement. Education has always been very important to my family and me, so this was a huge decision! Not too long after making this life change, I came across an article in Reader's Digest. The story was about a man in his early forties who had been asked by his boss to take some clients on a fishing trip. That night as he was sharing this opportunity with his wife, her reaction shocked him. She replied, "Aren't you worried about making a fool of yourself? These are big clients and you don't know how to fish!" It was his reply that had such a profound effect on me. He told his wife he had fished with his uncle one summer when he was nine years old. In his mind, if he could do it at nine, he could surely fish at forty-three!

This article had a significant impact on how I raised my daughters and it gave me new inspiration for my approach to parenting. I was so struck by the incredible truth in this man's words: what we learn to do as a young child remains easy for us as we age. Armed with this new philosophy, I branched out from homeschooling and started a new division for students in my company, **Set Them Up For Success**. Prior to this new venture, I had been training adults in leadership, communication, conflict resolution, behavior management, and other 'soft skills' to improve their relationships both on and off the job. It occurred to me that no one was teaching these very important lessons to kids. I developed an afterschool program that taught students strategies to effectively accomplish their job: being a student. I incorporated all the 'soft skills' that were not being taught, and within months, I had reached full capacity.

The first thing I did was determine the tools needed by a successful person, regardless of their occupation. Once I had my list, I simply incorporated these skills into my afterschool program. My philosophy became the new guide for teaching these students: *once the big decisions are made, the little ones are easy*. In parenting, I had a very clear vision of the kind of women I wanted walking out of my door and into college. This gave me the clarity I needed in making decisions – does it get me to my desired outcome, or not? A little untraditional perhaps, but it worked for my daughters and the thousands of students that followed in their footsteps.

A short two years later, the afterschool program grew into a private school. Again, I watched the market, listened to my customers, and provided them what they wanted. My students' parents wanted more; they wanted their children to be with me all day. Not too long after starting my house school, I set up satellite schools around the city and then around the country. These small private schools were each developed with an intentional culture that encouraged respect for others, cooperative learning, and success strategies.

Finding your niche as an entrepreneur is crucial. Sustaining your passion in a downturn economy requires flexibility, as well as a willingness to think outside of the box and meet the needs of your customer base. Sometimes we need to tweak our products and/or services when faced with a fluctuating economy or a change in lifestyle. I was no longer available to run full-day workshops and travel for work, so I brought the job to me!

In my thirties, I studied successful people and quickly learned that there is a definite recipe to what makes somebody successful. My goal was to instill the habits of success in my daughters, and eventually into my students. This desire was so strong that it defined my "definiteness of purpose," as Napoleon Hill would say. The activities that taught and fostered these skills were non-negotiable tasks; they were practiced daily and became the backbone of our afterschool program. What are your non-negotiables? What principles and values do you hold true regardless of the circumstances? What is the vision driving your business? Once you have identified these key components, create your vision and mission statements. These will provide you with your decision-making guideposts and are invaluable in providing the foundation for a thriving business.

Running a profitable business requires the application of success strategies. When these principles are applied, even in a downturn economy, your business can be prosperous. When you implement the Four Success Strategies, you will find that you are not only fulfilled by this 'definiteness of purpose,' but you will ensure that your business thrives in any economy. Each of the strategies are named with 'momisms': words we all remember hearing as kids growing up…because what you learned to do as a kid, you can easily do as an adult!

My Momma taught me…

1. Your GRATITUDE should always exceed your expectations.

"This is when you say, *Thank You.*"

> *"A grateful mind is constantly fixed upon the best; therefore it tends to become the best, it takes the form or character of the best, and will receive the best."*
> ~ Wallace Wattles

I wanted my daughters to be well-rounded. Not because they had been to McDonald's drive-thru window one too many times, but because they had a true sense of appreciation. With appreciation comes gratitude, with gratitude comes joy, and with joy comes happiness. Life is just too short to not be happy! Plus, I didn't want to spend my day with a bunch of unhappy, entitled middle and high school students! The best way I have found to ensure appreciation is to be grateful on a daily basis. But it is not enough to just want to be grateful; it is important to put strategies in place that ensure gratefulness actually happens. Each school day concluded with a time dedicated to writing in our gratitude journals. Every afternoon, we wrote down five things we were grateful to have in our lives. This forced my students to look for the positive things each day, rather than dwelling on the negatives or simply overlooking the day's blessings.

Pause for a moment and look around the room: try and find everything that is blue. Now I want you to close your eyes recall everything in the room that is red. No peeking! Okay, I know what you're thinking: "Hey! No fair! You tricked me!" But what really happened here? When we concentrate on something, it becomes bolder, bigger, and brighter, and everything else fades into the background. When you looked around the room, everything that was blue stood out, while everything that was not blue faded away.

By actively seeking out the positives each day, we become more positive. The little irritants or annoyances then seem to fade into the horizon. By surrounding ourselves with positive people, we accelerate this process. Take some time tonight to evaluate the people you spend time with on a regular basis. How do you feel when you are with them? Are they upbeat? Or are they 'Negative Nellies?' Toxic people need to go! If you are like me, you value your time – so spend it with people who make you feel good and do great things! I can't think of a time when it is more important to stay positive than in a downturn economy. Stay well-rounded, have joy in your life, and act like the person you want to be!

2. The importance of LEARNING something new every day.

"Bored! How can you be bored? I was never bored at your age."

"Commit yourself to lifelong learning. The most valuable asset you'll ever have is your mind and what you put into it."
~ Brian Tracy

When you stop learning, you stop living. Well, at least living happily! We live in an ever-changing world and in order to be successful in business (or in life, for that matter), you have to continue to learn on a daily basis. At the school, this was our modus operandi: all students were self-taught. They had to learn without the guidance of a teacher, requiring them to have the strategies needed to efficiently dive into information, and then understand and retain it.

It is the same for adults. You are constantly being exposed to new things that are imperative to the success of your business. To be the expert in your field, you must stay current with the trends in your industry, the latest research, and possible pitfalls that need to be avoided. Pursue active learning by scheduling time annually for regular training, continuing to develop your skills, and associating with the other experts in your field. I understand that you are busy. But, only working in your business and not on your business will dramatically limit your growth. So how do you make time for learning in an already overloaded day? Well, the riches are in the niches – that is, the niches of your day! Maybe you are like me and you listen to audiobooks in your car. I find this to be one of the most effective uses of my time. Maybe you subscribe to business journals or perhaps you need to write to learn, so you are an avid online blogger. Decide right now to do something every day to expand your knowledge, stay current, and remain the expert in your field.

3. The ability to OVERCOME adversity.

"I just want what's best for you."

"We are what we repeatedly do.
Excellence, then, is not an act, but a habit."
~ Aristotle

Leaders need self-confidence and we need leaders! A healthy self-esteem does not come from what others say about you. True feelings of self-worth come from what we DO. Being involved in the process of getting the job done and not surrendering to adversity builds our self-confidence. As we experience the valleys in our business, it is the knowledge that we have overcome obstacles in the past which provides the fuel and faith to continue moving forward. But, in order to move forward, you must know where you are going.

By setting clear, specific goals for yourself – both in your personal and professional life – you can stay on track. However, it is not enough to write your goals annually. You need to be rewriting them on a daily basis. Yes, I said daily basis! My students took the first few minutes of their day to write out their goals. Why was this practice something that was non-negotiable? Well, I wanted them to be very focused on the target they were trying to hit. I explained to them that if you can't measure it, you can't manage it. How will you know if you have hit the mark if you can't see or describe it in detail? What exactly is that mark? By rewriting their ten goals on a daily basis, the students were able to stay focused on what was important to them.

Incorporating these two very important tools into your business day will quickly equip you with a successful mindset. According to Napoleon Hill, "If you can conceive it and believe it, you can ACHIEVE it!" But, just like taking a shower, this is a daily activity. If you will commit to the daily practice of goal writing and affirmations, you will be well on your way to attracting the people, opportunities, and end results you desire.

4. The importance of PLAYING NICE with others!

"I don't care who started it, YOU be the one to end it!"

"I want to be clear and here are the values that I stand for. I stand for honesty, equality, kindness, compassion, treating people the way you want to be treated, and helping those in need. To me those are traditional values. That's what I stand for."
~ Ellen DeGeneres

Unfortunately, you don't get it all in life. I encouraged my students to concentrate on their strengths and compensate for their weaknesses. We were able to hone in on this skill in our mastermind meetings. The Mastermind concept was developed by Napoleon Hill, who said, "Two heads are better than one, even if one is a cabbage." Most times, people on the 'outside' of our business will see the trees in our forest differently. Their perspective is fresh and not clouded. I have been a member of numerous mastermind groups over the years and every time, my business jumps to the next level. It is invaluable to have other people who are committed to working on and thinking about innovative solutions to improve your business.

What can you do to help those you serve? How do you give back to your community? Join networking groups and learn about the other business people in your area. How can you help them? Meet with them and listen to what they have to say. Connect them with people you know who need their service or can be of benefit to them. We all know that people do business with people they like, so be likable.

Stephen Covey encouraged readers to "seek first to understand and then to be understood" in his book, *The Seven Habits of Successful People.* Another way to be likeable and understand the people around you is to focus on others as much, if not more, than you focus on yourself. Brush up on your listening skills. Call people by their name. (After all, our name is the most important sound to each of us.) Compliment others with sincere observations. Or send handwritten thank you notes. Better yet, challenge yourself to send a thank you note a day; you will be amazed at how people will respond! Remember, "They don't care what you know until they know you care."

See? Told ya! Momma always knew best! She loved you enough to make sure you learned what you needed to make it in this world. You have the knowledge and the tools for success. If you are lacking in an area or two (which you will, at some point in life), get help! People love to lend a hand, share their expertise, and help out an appreciative 'student.' Take the time to thank those who have given you access to their time and knowledge. Listen carefully to your clients and customers. Learn from them and be willing to make the necessary changes and improvements.

Stay current and up-to-date on what is going on in your industry. Don't get lazy or over-confident. Stay committed to your vision by attacking your goals daily. Plan for success and that is what you will enjoy. Take time each week to work 'on' your business – network, work with your mentor, or join a mastermind group! Stay positive and surround yourself with successful people. Each strategy is important, but when combined, they are very powerful.

You are now equipped with an arsenal of action items that, once executed, will elevate your business to the next level! As Momma says, "Get to work! 'Cause if you don't, just wait 'till' your father gets home!"

About Debbie

Debbie Elder is the nation's leader in motivating students to be peak performers. Her varied background has equipped her to work with any child under any circumstance. While working at the Calgary Young Offender Center early on in her career, she ran the disciplinary unit that housed males between the ages of 12-18 who had committed very serious crimes. Her passion for working with troubled youth continued as a therapeutic foster parent, where she cared for teenage girls who came to her with severe behavior issues. In 1993, Debbie was named the Therapeutic Foster Parent of the Year.

After moving to Houston, Texas, Debbie worked as a substitute teacher at the local elementary school and spent two years teaching Pre-K. In 2003, Debbie joined the Appelbaum Training Institute and traveled the country training in behavior management techniques for the classroom. Debbie enjoyed her speaking engagements, where she was able to interact with 800 – 1,200 teachers each week. Following this venture, she ran a very unique afterschool program for students in grades 3 – 12. This program empowered kids of all ages to take ownership of their schoolwork, develop success strategies, and increase their level of self-awareness. At the request of her clients, Debbie opened a private school that serviced students in grades 6 – 12. The school focused on teaching to the whole child using accelerated learning methods coupled with the same success strategies used by the top producers in corporate America. The concept was so well received that Debbie opened 14 additional schools across the country.

In a continued effort to meet the needs of her students, Debbie worked with families as a college planner. In this role, Debbie utilized a unique process to help parents afford college and ensure their student was ready to be admitted to the university of their choice, including the skills to complete college in a timely fashion. In 2013, a former parent of one of Debbie's students requested that she return to her after-school program. He went on to explain to her the profound effect the program had on his family. He shared with Debbie that prior to her program, he felt like the 'Homework Police' and spent way too much his time badgering his son to finish his daily assignments. But, when his son had the opportunity to attend the Set Them Up For Success After-School Program, all of that changed. He came home feeling successful and satisfied with the progress he had made, and felt relieved that all of his homework was complete. He and his father enjoyed evenings together without any stress or bickering. Family harmony was restored. Debbie is currently offering franchise opportunities to others who are interested in making a difference in the lives of our students. If you would like more information about this incredible opportunity email Debbie at: Debbie@SetThemUpForSuccess.com.

Debbie is a passionate international speaker who "edutains" her audiences. She loves to share her incredible knowledge in simple steps that can be implemented immediately. Her easy-going style is loved and accepted by audiences of all ages. She has experience speaking to students, teachers, corporate America, entrepreneurs, and people who want to be successful in life. She is also the director of the Sugar Land chapter of the Public Speakers Association. To book Debbie for a speaking engagement, call her at 832-419-1455.

CHAPTER 12

THE MAGIC
OF IMAGINATION

BY GERALD ALEXANDER

"The future belongs to those who believe in the beauty of their dreams."
~ Eleanor Roosevelt

Since the beginning of time the world – *as we know it* – is changing. Imagine you're about to embark on an amazing journey. On this journey you can achieve everything you've ever wanted. You can make choices and changes in every area of your life. Discover your true potential and become the person you really want to be. Simply by letting your mind do what it was created to do.

"The potential of the average person is like a huge ocean unsailed,
a new continent unexplored, a world of possibilities waiting to be
released and channeled toward some great good."
~ Brian Tracy

Unlike the other creatures on this planet, we are responsible for our individual thoughts and actions. Human beings in all of our uniqueness are the result of a long evolutionary process. Our expectations and capabilities evolve with every step forward, and each new generation boasts its own set of innovative thinkers.

Everything in our life is a result of what we know, what we experience, and how we interact with our consciousness. These elements make up the ultimate source from which everything evolves.

If we travel back in time, we can see that human technology has dramatically changed the way of life forever. From the moment man first picked up a stone or a branch to use as a tool, he altered irrevocably the balance between him and his environment. From this point on, the way in which the world around him changed was different. It was no longer regular or predictable. New objects appeared that were not recognizable as a mutation of something that had existed before, and as each one emerged it altered the environment not for a season but forever. While the number of these tools remained small, their effect took time to spread and to cause change. But as they increased, so did their effects: the more the tools, the faster the rate of change.

The idea that we could invent tools that change our cognitive abilities might sound outlandish, but it's actually a defining feature of human evolution. When our ancestors developed language, it altered not only how they could communicate, but also how they could think.

> *"A mind that is stretched by a new experience can never*
> *go back to its old dimensions."*
> ~ Oliver Wendell Holmes

My journey of self-discovery began in 1986, when I was introduced to the science of psychology. The idea that my life is the result of how I perceive and respond to my environment - gave a whole new meaning to the word *responsibility* – and I didn't want it. And then to be told that my thinking was a result of my social interactions – well at least this let me blame other people for the mess I was in. Anyway, let's fast-track one year forward to 1987 - when I found the courage to take my head out of the sand and face my fear of this thing called psychology - after all, this is my life we're talking about here.

The idea that someone's perception and behavior can be changed by information received through sight, sound or touch, is rather profound. Even more so is the idea that, through exchanging information and ideas, people can influence and change the course of whole societies. I was fascinated by this belief and wanted to learn more.

> *"The unexamined life is not worth living."*
> ~ Socrates

I had recently arrived in the United States of America, after spending the first 18 years of my life in bonnie Scotland – *I was broadening my horizons*. And yes, I was experiencing something very different about the people around me. Could the reason for this difference have something to do with the culture? Everything seemed possible to the American people. In Scotland I had always been discouraged to think outside of the social norm – just to keep my head down and get on with the job at hand. Could such a little change in one's attitude really create such a BIG difference in one's life?

"The greatest discovery of my generation is that human beings can alter their lives, by altering their attitudes of mind."
~ William James

Consequently, I discovered that a culture is considered to be group-specific behavior that is acquired, at least in part, from our social influences.

Every culture has its own set of symbols associated with different experiences and perceptions. They can be anything that conveys a meaning, such as words on a page, drawings, picture, and gestures. Consumer items such as clothes, cars, and homes, are symbols that imply a certain level of social status.

Perhaps the most powerful of all human symbols is language – a system of verbal and sometimes written representations that are culturally specific and convey meaning about the world.

My fascination quickly became my passion and my passion gave my life its purpose – *to help people realize and achieve their full potential.*

"The human mind is like a fertile ground where seeds are continually being planted. The seeds are opinions, ideas, and concepts.
You plant a seed, a thought grows, and it grows. The word is like a seed and the human mind is so fertile!"
~ Don Miguel Ruiz

All our behavior that is not innate has been learned through social interaction with others to establish an extremely wide variety of values, social norms, and rituals, which together form the basis of humanity. More than any other animal, we are adept at utilizing systems of communication for self-expression, the exchange of ideas, and organization, and as such have created complex social structures composed of many cooperating and competing groups.

Today it's easy for us to understand that technological objects – *such as a computer* – and social structures – *such as democracy* – are human inventions: at one time these things did not exist until a person, or a group of individuals, thought of and developed them.

However, it's very difficult for us to comprehend that – *rational thinking* – at one time did not exist until someone invented it.

> *"What the mind can conceive and believe it can achieve."*
> ~ Napoleon Hill

Our world – *as we know it* – is changing faster than ever before. We live in a digital information age where mobile phones, the internet and satellite technology are considered to be social norms in modern-day life. Our ability to now exchange ideas and share information on a global scale continues to rapidly transform every aspect of human life.

Our creative imagination is now accepted as the innate ability and process of inventing partial or complete personal realms within the mind from elements derived from sense perceptions of the shared world. Both tool-making and language express and provide important evidence for how we have evolved. Technology is at the heart of our understanding of growth. We continue to evolve because someone invents a better and more powerful tool to help us control and adapt to our natural environment.

> *"I'm a great believer that any tool that enhances communication has profound effects in terms of how people can learn from each other, and how they can achieve the kind of freedoms that they're interested in."*
> ~ Bill Gates

Evolution is the change in the inherited characteristics of biological populations over successive generations. The evolution process gives rise to our diversity; with each new day come new strengths and new thoughts. Our affairs are regulated not only by ourselves, but also by the social standards of the collective reason or mind. The question is not will our lives change – the question is what will our lives change *into*?

We can't help the inevitable, change will continue to happen whether we like it or not. Change is one thing that is guaranteed in our lifetime.

Before we created language and became capable of understanding that each individual has different feelings about things, we were stuck in an existence. Life was merely a series of events without long-term significance. Nothing really mattered as we had nothing of value. Evolution is the result of the developing powers of the human mind.

> *"All animals gain a certain wisdom with age and experience, but the experience of one ape does not profit another. Learning among animals below man is individual, not co-operative and cumulative."*
> ~ James Harvey Robinson

Our extraordinary cognitive abilities are what clearly separate us from the other animals on this planet. While other animals live in the present moment, we continually project our thoughts forward to think of *'HOW'* our current behavior will influence our life in the future – *because now we can!*

Let me ask... Why are YOU reading this book?

I believe you have a desire to learn something that can improve your <u>*current*</u> *lifestyle!*

DESIRE is the starting point of all achievement. We continue to develop and learn about the world about us, through the experiences of other people. We can learn from the mistakes others have made. Our connection to others is the key to not only our survival, but also to our happiness and the success of our careers. Building a network of supportive friends, or even one supportive relationship, can be vital to our well-being.

Right now we live in a digital information age. It has never been easier to connect with other people around the world. We stand on the threshold of an enormous leap in evolution. Nearly all technologies are combinations of other technologies and new ideas come from swapping things and thoughts. It's no coincidence that trade-obsessed cities are the places where invention and discovery happened. Think of them as well-endowed collective brains.

The image of a few smart people changing the world with little more than an internet connection and an idea increasingly describes manufacturing of the future.

There are practically no barriers preventing entry to entrepreneurship online: if you've got a laptop and a credit card, you're in business. Manufacturing has traditionally been regarded as something else entirely.

Creativity is our purpose in life – continuous improvement is necessary to enhance productivity and free up the capacity that will provide manufacturers a stable foundation to pursue innovation and growth.

"I do not know anyone who has gotten to the top without hard work. That is the recipe. It will not always get you to the top, but it will get you pretty near."
~ Margaret Thatcher

While we need to envision our future life and career success, our vision is naught if we don't have the will and determination to work hard at making it a reality.

We have to be willing to work hard if we are going to achieve the success we desire. Yes, we need to work smart, not just hard, but hard work is the best way to create the life and career success we want and deserve. Let's face it, nobody enjoys crawling, living in mediocrity. No one likes feeling second-class and feeling forced to go that way. We all want success. Achieving success in all we desire to do is the goal of life.

Success comes in many ways and forms, but what's interesting is that most successful people have very similar qualities.

"Success always leaves footprints."
~ Booker T. Washington

Theory of mind is the capacity we have to understand mental states such as: beliefs, feelings, desires, hope and intentions. It's the way we imagine other people's feelings or thoughts. We can create a mental picture of our own emotions or other people's feelings. This theory of mind enables us to understand that the behavior people display is caused by their inner feelings, beliefs or intentions. We can predict some of those behaviors and anticipate them. Whatever goes on in the mind of other people is not visible, so it will remain a 'theory' we create for ourselves.

The same principle holds good in creative thinking as in creativity in general. Our creative imaginations must have something to work on.

We do not form new ideas out of nothing. The raw materials are all there. The creative mind sees possibilities in them or connections that are invisible to less creative minds.

"Reading is a means of thinking with another person's mind;
it forces you to stretch your own."
~ Charles Scribner, Jr.

What we are intending to do, consciously or subconsciously, is to borrow characteristics from the most successful entrepreneurs we know. There is nothing wrong with that, as we cannot make anything out of nothing.

Once, a distinguished visitor to Henry Ford's auto plant met him after an exhaustive tour of the factory. The visitor was lost in wonder and admiration. "It seems almost impossible, Mr. Ford," he told the industrialist, "that a man, starting 25 years ago with practically nothing, could accomplish all this."

Mr. Ford replied, "But that's hardly correct. Every man starts with all there is. Everything is here – the essence and substance of all there is. The potential materials – the elements, constituents or substances of which something can be made or composed – are all here in our universe."

Our life is an amazing journey of learning and developing the skills that help us to become the best that we can, with all that we have. In order to excel at a job, a sport, or any discipline, a person must acquire and master certain skills. Living life fully and productively is no different.

Where do YOU begin?

Turning information into knowledge and power.

"Do what you can, with what you have, where you are."
~ Theodore Roosevelt

You must realize that you are one of a kind. Your dreams and aspirations make you unique. No two people experience the world around them in exactly the same way. We each filter the sights, sounds and sensations surrounding us through our sensory systems before sending these perceptions on to be processed by and stored in our brains. We are all unique individuals with our own unique imagination.

If you traveled the whole world over, in country after country, among the billions of people here on earth, you would never find another person exactly like you. And to the best of our knowledge, from the beginning of time itself, there has never been anyone exactly like you.

What a marvel and a wonder of creation you are!

Once you truly understand the powers of the human mind, you can program it to obtain anything you want... Evolution is the change we make to survive in our current environment.

> *"Whatever we plant in our subconscious mind and nourish with repetition and emotion will one day become a reality."*
> ~ Earl Nightingale

Success comes in many ways and forms, but what's interesting is that most successful people have very similar qualities. If we look back at the careers of highly successful people, we will find that almost every one of them first imagined who they wanted to be, long before they actually achieved their level of success.

The combination of a sound personal philosophy and a positive attitude about ourselves and the world around us gives us an inner strength and a firm resolve that influences all the other areas of our existence.

B*E*L*I*E*V*E + S*U*C*C*E*E*D
The Key To Happiness Is Having Dreams...
The Key To Success Is Making Dreams Come True.

> *"We become what we think about."*
> ~ Earl Nightingale

About Gerald

Gerald Alexander is a best-selling author and peak performance consultant who is regularly sought out to deliver the life-changing principles and shared characteristics of the most successful entrepreneurs we have ever known. He is renowned for continually asking this enchanting question, "What does success mean to you?"

Gerald is a world-renowned master of the principles, strategies, and characteristics required for the achievement of success. He offers daily inspirations and small actions – exercises – to realize your true potential and coach you to become the person you really want to be. Simply by letting your mind do what it was created to do.

Success comes in many ways and forms but what Gerald finds most interesting is that successful people have very similar qualities. He conducts workshops and seminars for large organizations on a worldwide scale, and is the co-owner and COO of Ibizcon Global Enterprise, a company specializing in the training and development of individuals and organizations.

To learn more about Gerald Alexander visit: www.ibizcon.com

www.ibizcon.com

CHAPTER 13

WHEN THE ERUPTION STARTS, LOCATION IS EVERYTHING

BY GUNNAR ANDRI THORISSON

What follows is a true story on how I began my career in sales at an early age. A lot has changed since then, but the basic principles remain the same in my personal and professional approach. I believe that the values of the story can appeal to everyone that wants to get better results in their life and business ventures.

I have worked as a lecturer, consultant and a specialist in communication and sales in Iceland for over 15 years, helping individuals and companies to achieve their sales objectives and true potential.

It sometimes seems strange, even to myself, why on earth I was so interested in making money as a child. During my youth, I only heard negative things when it came to the subject of money. This fact is one of the first things I think of when I look back at my childhood, along with the unforgettable volcanic eruption in the following story that catapulted my career in sales – at the age of six.

From an early age, I collected wallets and moneyboxes. Most of these were indeed empty, but that didn't matter to me at the time. My philosophy, even at a young age, was that if I had enough wallets and moneyboxes, I would end up getting the money to fill them eventually.

In retrospect, this naive way of thinking seems similar to the law of attraction covered in *The Secret*. And the law of attraction is, of course, a fantastic and powerful principle, but there is one word missing from that particular best-selling book. I would like to add that word into the mix right here: *WORK!*

I also learned early on that if you don't ask, then the answer will always be no. As a young boy, I never asked my parents for money, because there the money simply didn't exist. But when we had visitors that I knew had enough money, I did not hesitate to approach them by asking a very straight-forward, logical and practical question:

"Do you have any money that you aren't using any more?"

This much I had learned: If I wanted money I would just have to make it myself, by asking directly or by shouting out for the attention of buyers – and of course by working hard!

THE KING, THE TROLL, THE GNOME, AND MYSELF

It was 2 am on January 23, 1973 and the earth started trembling. A large rift had appeared in the ground in Westman Islands, an archipelago south-east of Reykjavík. A volcanic eruption had started in Heimaey, the largest of the fourteen islands, and hot magma spewed tens of meters into the air. For the first time, a volcanic eruption was taking place in the middle of an Icelandic village. My family comes from the Westman Islands, but while this was going on, I was safe and sound asleep in my bed in Reykjavík, far away from the melting lava and the ongoing confusion of the Westman Islands.

When the volcanic eruption began, the first reaction of some of the locals was to act on their curiosity and drive right up to the 2 kilometer long rift. There they watched the magnificent natural disaster with amazement, as if they were watching a typical Icelandic New Year's Eve celebration with fireworks and bonfires.

Then it suddenly struck them that what they were watching was not something for their enjoyment or pleasure. They were in fact faced with a life or death situation and the existence and future of their home town was severely threatened. The hot lava ran all over the island, all the way to the sea, and today it's considered a great blessing that no lives were lost during the eruption.

Only two hours after the eruption started, my relatives were safe on board rescuing boats, on their way to the mainland of Iceland. All of a sudden they had absolutely nothing except the few things they had been able to put in their pockets and carry away with them. There had been no time to put anything into bags or suitcases. The situation was a total chaos.

It only took about six hours to evacuate 5,300 inhabitants from Heimaey. What saved the lives of the inhabitants of Westman Island was their response rate and how quickly they realized the gravity of the situation.

My family from Westman Islands was of course in great shock, as everyone had lost most of their possessions and some had literally lost everything. Their homes would also end up being buried by the shower of ash or by the flowing hot lava.

Therefore it became quite strange for me, at the tender age of six, to stroll around downtown Reykjavík the day following these great natural disasters and do my usual rounds of selling newspapers by calling out to the passing pedestrians:

"Breaking news: Volcanic eruption in Westman Islands!"

There I was, the day after my family had lost everything, selling and shouting out, just to get some pocket money...

So it happened that during these fateful events in 1973 my career in sales started for real. The eruption in Westman Islands had caused my relatives to lose almost everything, but I, the best-selling paperboy, rewarded myself with chocolate and candy with the day's earnings.

Every day after school I would sneak to downtown Reykjavík to sell newspapers. I wanted to sell my newspapers outside the national bank, Landsbankinn, because this was considered to be the most profitable location. Incidentally, thirty-five years later that same bank would become one of the largest banks in the world, better known as the bank responsible for the infamous 'IceSave' savings accounts.

IceSave was a giant in the banking sector prior to the economic collapse of 2008, but when I was six years old, Landsbankinn certainly was no giant in my mind. To me the true giant was Óli – 'The Newspaper King'

– an eccentric little man that sold his newspapers across the street from the bank and had done so for many years.

Óli had claimed this busy corner as his own and no other paperboy dared to enter his territory. For a young boy like myself, Óli was indeed a big threat and I felt like a pawn in his presence. He was the opposition. He was my nemesis.

Early on in my career I learned that location is the key, and somehow with my boyish ambition, I saw an opportunity to sell a lot of newspapers because with Óli's location I would be able to reach a larger crowd. I told some of my fellow paperboys about this idea but they told me it was hopeless. *I had no chance going against 'The King,'* they would tell me. Incidentally, I have heard a similar phrasing numerous times over the years when presenting ambitious ideas. And I'm sure you have too.

Anyway, I gathered my courage, went to the corner and began to sell my newspapers. I had only been there for a short while when Óli began to threaten me and tell me he would turn the police on me if I didn't leave at once. *This was his corner!* Listening to Óli's threats made me terrified, but there was a question to be answered:

Was I going to let the fear control me and give up, or was I going to face that fear?

My attitude towards the situation was that I was going to get the corner across from Óli. I was not willing to give up on my dream – there had to be another solution possible. Once you begin giving up, you keep giving up. And that is a terrible habit, because first we create habits and then the habits become us.

I refused to give up against Óli and kept on going downtown to sell newspapers. I started moving closer and closer to the corner next to the Post Office, and by doing so I was able to sell the occasional paper on Óli's territory. My journey towards fortune had started with careful steps in the right direction.

Being able to secure that location, even for a short period of time, did indeed help me to sell papers. I started winning small battles and that made me very proud, even though I had not won the war and the dream had not yet come true.

But this is exactly how you conquer larger milestones – by winning many small victories. And I have learned that the way to commence a large project is by starting taking the smaller steps. Just like Socrates told the traveler that asked him how to get to the top of Mount Olympus:

"Just make sure that every step you take is in that direction."

So, what was my solution to the 'location problem'? The solution had been right in front of me all the time.

There was a grown man that often stood nearby where the rivalry of Óli and I took place. He was a giant of a man, much larger than Óli, and he was collecting money for the poor on behalf of the Salvation Army. Next to this troll, Óli The King looked like a gnome.

"This is a cool guy," I thought to myself. He looked like a combination of a fairy-tale troll and an Icelandic viking. I found myself thinking that I needed to get this guy to join up with me: *"What can a gnome like Óli do against someone like him?"*

I went over and talked to the Troll and asked him how the collection was going. He told me it wasn't going well enough, especially considering the importance of the matter.

I told him that I had an idea that was guaranteed to improve his collection and asked him if he would look into it. He was more than willing to listen. After my explanations, the Troll and I joined forces and he would receive a percentage of my earnings, provided that he would protect me.

The expression on Óli's face, the best-selling newspaper gnome, was certainly not kind when he saw me marching towards him with my new giant friend straight for the corner opposite him, ready to sell my newspapers.

Óli didn't give up without a struggle and of course he tried to bully us away. After all, this was his location. But the Troll was very capable of answering back and rightly pointed out to Óli that he didn't own Reykjavík, let alone the public street corners. The tables had turned and Óli's fear turned out to be uncalled for. We both sold our papers and there was enough business for the both of us.

My confidence grew a lot by this and I was firmly resolved in becoming successful. I realized that the Troll would not stand next to me for percentages if I didn't achieve any sales success. I had to deliver for the plan to work out, and of course I wanted to let the Troll benefit from my success since he helped me achieve that same success.

At that time sales really took off and I was "on fire." I had a burning desire to do well and I felt great. I felt like I possessed more energy than the Westman Island eruption and the Eyjafjallajökull eruption combined.

At the age of six, I was the man!

But the thoughts I had at that time were not only naïve thoughts of a young paperboy. These principles are fully valid in real life, no matter where we are situated in the world or in our personal lives.

I went from selling very well on to selling ridiculously well. In a flash I achieved the highest sales numbers. The pinnacle of my career as a paperboy was when I was informed that I had the highest sales figures of all the other paperboys, including Óli 'The King'. I have felt this exact same feeling later in my career and there is nothing that compares to it.

At this point I was getting all sorts of personal rewards in the form of chocolate, soft drinks and movie tickets. The gnome wasn't a threat anymore. I had proper money in my wallet and I felt like the King of the World.

It wasn't just having beaten Óli, the man I had been so afraid of, but also having won this personal victory by reaching my own goal and being successful on my own terms.

WHAT IS THE MESSAGE?

The reason why I choose to tell this story from my life, out of all the stories I could have told, is that we always have to face our fears, whether they are trolls or gnomes.

In the story, I benefited from the natural disasters, but of course I'm not the first one in history to do so. Recently, numerous travelers became stranded in airports around the world following the eruption of Eyjafjallajökull in 2010. The airlines and travelers lost a fortune, but Icelanders would eventually end up profiting from the eruption. Although many tourists of the world cursed us to hell and back while the eruption took place, following the eruption Iceland would see a huge increase in tourist bookings and arrivals to the country.

I have never met a great sales person, entrepreneur or a business manager that thinks like the average Joe and has achieved greatness. It all boils down to this wonderful feeling of victory and the message is simple:

It doesn't matter if you are a kid selling newspapers or the CEO of a large corporation – you can't achieve great success by mediocre thinking.

Here are my proven principles for Success – going Against The Grain:

1. Knowledge can never be taken from you.

2. WORK is the magic word.

3. If you don't ask a question, the answer will always be no.

4. Location is the key.

5. No one is larger, bigger or higher than you.

6. First we make habits and then the habits become us.

7. Major milestones are achieved with small victories.

8. The solution is often closer than you think.

9. Let others benefit from your success if they have had a part in it.

10. We act outwardly as we feel within.

11. If you want to grow, you must face your fears.

12. One of the dangers of giving up is that it might become a habit.

13. Don't be afraid to ask for reinforcement when you need to strengthen your team.

And last but not least:

14. The giant in your path can turn into a gnome if you have a troll on your side.

About Gunnar Andri

Gunnar Andri Thorisson was born in 1967 in Reykjavík, Iceland.

Gunnar Andri has worked in sales for many years and has sold products, services and ideas. He has been awarded various recognitions and acknowledgements over the years and has appeared on all major radio and television programmes in Iceland.

He has helped individuals and companies in Iceland to achieve maximum sales results and objectives in sales since 1997, the founding year of his company, SGA. Gunnar Andri has provided advice, courses and seminars for companies in all sectors. Among his clients are financial institutions, insurance companies and telecommunication firms.

Gunnar Andri has founded several companies in various sectors, all of which have achieved splendid results, and he has been a guest lecturer at Reykjavík University on numerous occasions.

Gunnar Andri is the founder of **www.happyhour.is** and **www.2fyrir**1.is, the largest online discount club in Iceland. Gunnar Andri also owns **www.leikhus.is**, an information hub on Iceland's theatre life. He released the audiobook *55 Tips On How To Be Effective in Services* and it has gained great popularity in Iceland.

Currently, Gunnar Andri is expanding his ventures from the Icelandic local market into global business, due to the Internet's global reach. More information can be found on: www.gunnarandri.is.

Gunnar Andri's goal is to help as many people as possible, worldwide and throughout all fields and businesses, professional and personal.

Gunnar Andri lives by the following motto: *"Our common goal is that you do well."*

CHAPTER 14

FROM CORPORATE CAPTIVE TO MOTIVATED MAVEN

BY JENN SCALIA

The New Year is a time for celebration and reinvention of oneself. Most people are making resolutions and promises to themselves and I was no different. I was elated and had a feeling of joy thinking of all the things I was going to do this upcoming year. I was especially ecstatic about my new career. I had just taken a job at a high profile casino and resort in Atlantic City in a new position within the marketing department.

I went into work the day after New Year's and was totally motivated. I got in early, started my work and had made serious headway in the 2 hours I was there. I was asked to come into my boss's office, which was usually no big deal. We had a great relationship and I was hoping for some good news. But when the door shut, I knew something wasn't right. I was asked to take a seat. And being the rebel I was, of course I didn't. I knew what was going on and I was instantly devastated. My family was just getting back on their feet financially after I had taken off two years after maternity to stay home with my son. Now, my household income was viciously slashed in half.

I was completely discouraged and destroyed. At 32 years old, I was still trying to figure out what I wanted to do with my life. I spent almost two full months in my sweat pants, feeling sorry for myself. Every day I was told by my parents, my husband and everyone around me that I needed to get out there and look for a "job." But I knew in my heart that there was no way I was ever going back to a JOB. I made a conscious decision to never be a slave to the 9-5 again.

For me, life was too short to continue living someone else's dream. I knew I needed to do something drastic in order to live the life I always wanted and to have complete freedom over my life and finances. With zero income, $50,000 of debt and plain old fear and doubt weighing me down, I made a decision to invest in myself. Within a few short months, I became focused and clear. I found my calling in life and was able to create a profitable business surrounding my passion. I'm telling you this because I want you to know that no matter where you are in your life, you can always move past it and live your dreams. It all starts with YOU.

Whether you are unemployed, in a job you don't necessarily love, or thinking about starting your own business, it's time to focus on your goals and dreams and stop being a slave to Mr. Paycheck. All too often, work and what we really love doing are two very different things. In fact, the vast majority of the world does not enjoy their work. Whether you find yourself out of a job as a result of a layoff, maternity leave or some other unexpected circumstance, this becomes an opportunity for reinvention towards a more fulfilling career path. It may seem like a huge shock at first and will take some getting used to, but it will eventually bring you closer to your true destiny, if that's what you so desire.

Most people have to wait to acquire vacation time or PTO in order to be able to go out there and do what they truly love. We often dream up ideas that get us excited and motivated, but the majority of the time, we fail to act upon them. Fear and/or doubt can hold us back. We emphasize practicality over passion, and we concentrate on being responsible, paying bills and doing what we are supposed to do. Routines are an easy trap to fall into and it can rob years off our lives.

Now, I'm not saying to quit your job if you have one, but if you do find yourself jobless, treat this as a blessing. With the right attitude, you can stop living in fear and open your mind to the possibilities of a new routine and a new life path. My bet is that you've worked really hard all your life, but somehow you barely have enough money at the end of the month to pay your mortgage and do the things you really want to do?

I realize that for most people, quitting their job is out of the question.

Therefore you must devise an exit strategy. Despite ridiculous working schedules and being in a poisonous work environment, most people are discouraged from quitting because of financial repercussions. Even if your stress levels are adversely affecting your health, it's common to feel that weight of your responsibilities, and that ends up keeping you stuck where you are.

If you find yourself in this position, take that chance to turn your hobby or something else you love into a profitable business. Develop your skills and learn to step outside of your comfort zone. You really have nothing to lose by experimenting with your passion. When you are doing what you love, it will be easier to excel at your job and to succeed while you are working. It's a huge misconception that the only way to make money in this world is to work for someone else. By starting your own business you can be sure that you have a wholehearted interest in the bottom line. Find out what motivates you and get started.

Be careful not to think yourself out of ever getting it done. Whatever your objective, it's absolutely necessary to take action. Not just any action, but well-thought-out and inspired action. I will lay out some reflective questions and critical action steps for you at the end of this chapter, so read on.

If you are truly ready to get un-stuck, you must become really introspective and honest with yourself. Your change in direction will be largely guided by your attitude and determination to succeed despite the doom and gloom on the headline news. Each and every one of us has the skills needed to succeed, it's a matter of how you utilize them. Having someone there to guide you and hold you accountable can help you get off on the right foot the first time. Remember, you only get one chance to make a first impression. A coach or mentor can help guide you on the right path.

Sure you can read tons of career books, watch webinars and take online courses, but if you don't have anyone holding you liable, you may be hard pressed to actually apply it to your situation. Creating a new life requires clear direction and it's not easy by any stretch of the imagination. But if you want something, really want it – you can make it happen!

Being stuck and confused are more costly now than at any other time in history. You must think creatively. You must work smarter (not harder). And you must admit that there are some things you just can't do all by yourself. Keep in mind that using a coach or enrolling in courses will cost money, so you must be willing to invest in yourself. I mean really, wholeheartedly invest in yourself. Not your body or your image, but your mind, your brand and your business. Educate yourself and smother yourself in knowledge about your chosen field. Having an abundance of knowledge gives you the confidence and edge to go after what you really want. It gives you leverage in your field and ultimately in your business or career.

This could be one of the most important steps you take in your life or business. You absolutely must invest in yourself. I know what you're thinking, "I don't have the money" or "I don't have the time," but if you really want it, you will find a way. Start looking at it as capital investment, not debt. Bottom line is, whatever you decide to do, you can't 'half-ass' it. You're going to have to invest in your own education and professional endeavors.

Promise yourself to only work with the best and expect only the best, don't ever compromise quality. If you want to really rock it as an aspiring entrepreneur, you're going to have to shell out some dinero – whether it's on certifications, marketing, hiring employees or just keeping things running. And, please, please, please: Do your research! The Internet will put you on information overdrive, and you have to be smart about your decisions. Make sure you are investing in products and services that are accredited and that are in-line with your personal goals. The most successful people say no to the good things, so they can say yes to the best things.

I coach people every day to become self-motivators. I've seen how paralyzing it is not to do what you love in business and in life and, as you know from my story, I'VE BEEN THERE. I believe that everyone is powerful – some of us are just too fearful to go out and get it. It's my job to show you how to become the superstar you were born to be, grow your business and design the life of your dreams.

The goal is to help you identify the good habits which will move your life forward, and the bad habits that are holding you back. Moreover, you need an accountability partner to provide the necessary guidance and support you need to facilitate your goals. You're not stuck where you are unless you want to be. Just know that the right choices can bring you abundant wealth and happiness.

Nine times out of ten, the solution is right at your fingertips, but fear could be blinding you from seeing it. I want you to get really clear on what you most need to do right now to move to the next level in your life and business – quickly and easily. If you are an entrepreneur in particular, you will need to devote time to bettering yourself if you want to be successful in your endeavor.

If you feel like you have a burning desire or untapped potential that you've been unable to grasp or develop, a career coach can help you discover aspects of personal development – including setting realistic and tangible goals, self-motivation, changing habits, improving self-awareness, and identifying your values and beliefs.

Successful people don't make decisions based on money; they make decisions based on their goals. And wouldn't you be happier living the life you truly want, not the one that you are supposed to live? Take a look at the action steps below, and actually do them. Grab a pen and paper and let's discover where your passion lies...

Answer these questions honestly and really dig deep. You will find the right answers.

1. What activities make you feel really alive, powerful and passionate? List things that change how you feel instantly – from pleasure to pain. (It could be music, your family, making jewelry, fishing, etc.) Whatever it is, write it down and do more of those things, starting today.

2. What are you amazing at? (In work or in your life.) That "thing" that seems so easy to you is your talent, your gift. You're certain anyone could do it, but they can't. Write down the top 3-5 things that you are really awesome at.

3. What would you like to stop doing? What activities are you currently doing that's sucking the life out of you? I know it's hard to get out of a routine, but if you are wasting your time and energy on something that doesn't serve you, you are just taking more time away from what you love.

4. What do people say about you? What's that thing that everyone seems to say about you, whether it's family, friends or people you just met. Are you smart, funny, witty, cute? Whatever it is, use that. Use it to your advantage and use it to get what you want.

5. What do you want to be known for? What do you want your legacy to be? Do you want to be known for being an amazing mother, philanthropist, entrepreneur, friend? Really think about this question. Not to be morbid, but when you die, what do you want your life to have looked like?

6. Who do you think is super awesome? Who do you look up to? Who do you learn from? It could be an artist, an author, a musician or even someone tangible that is in your life right now. Who is a true rock star in your eyes. Model yourself after them, but reach further. Maybe even ask them to be your mentor, if you so dare. The worst thing that can happen is they say no. So what are you waiting for?

7. What have you learned from your biggest mistake? I know this is a tough one, because I'm forcing you to dig deep and first recall the biggest mistake you made in your life, and for most people, this is something we've regretted and tried to forget for so long. But if you can't identify your biggest mistake and understand what lesson it taught you, you will continue to make those same mistakes over and over again in your life.

8. What are you most scared of? What obstacles are holding you back from being completely and utterly happy? Where does your fear lie? What is it that makes you disgustingly sick to even think about doing? Whatever it is, maybe you should take the necessary steps to do it. Face your fear and then demolish it. I dare you.

9. What's your childhood dream? What is the thing that you always wanted to do since you were a kid, but somehow you got tricked into not doing it or felt like it was totally out of reach? Now, I don't mean, what your PARENTS wanted you to be. What did YOU want to be? How did you picture your life when you were a child or young teen?

10. What are your dreams? And I want you to dream BIG. Imagine that time and money are not issues and you have the full support of your family and friends. If you knew you could not fail, what would you do? And take it one step further.... WHY?

I hope you got a little bit of clarity by doing this exercise. Now, I strongly encourage you to take action. What steps will you commit to taking within one week to move you toward your dream? I'd love to hear from you and if you need someone to hold you accountable, I'd be more than happy to do so.

About Jenn

Jenn Scalia is a certified life and business coach born and raised in New Jersey. She helps, teaches and inspires aspiring entrepreneurs to gain the confidence and clarity needed to achieve personal reinvention. Jenn started her career as a freelance social media marketer and worked for some of the area's premier lifestyle companies, including a Philadelphia Indie clothing company, a Miami-based fashion magazine and one of Atlantic City's largest casino resorts. She is a published author and social media gal balanced with equal parts of sarcasm and wit. Her no-nonsense approach meshes well with that of the current generation Y-ers. By keeping up with current lifestyle trends, she is able to give her clients a unique coaching experience.

On the verge of financial despair after losing her full time job, she knew she needed to do something drastic in order to live the life she needed and wanted, and to have complete freedom over her finances. With zero income, $50,000 of debt and feelings of fear and doubt weighing her down, she decided to invest in herself by enrolling in an online business school and several coaching courses. Within a few short months, she found her calling in life and was able to create a profitable business surrounding her passion. Now, she helps aspiring entrepreneurs that are in the same position she was in at one time.

Her goal is to help her clients work smarter and make more money than they ever dreamed possible. She believes that every single person has the right to create a fulfilling life while running a profitable business – one that plays on their deepest passions. She empowers her clients on how to consistently attract ideal, high-paying clients, put their marketing on autopilot and create a highly successful and meaningful business.

Jenn uses the law of attraction and a holistic marketing approach to teach her clients to shift their mindset towards abundance and banish the negative emotions about life and business that are consistently holding them back. She offers several online training courses that teach small business owners how to leverage current trends to turn their side jobs into real profits. Through her workshops, courses and coaching programs, she guides entrepreneurs on how to go from zero to 6-figures in their business, all while experiencing more freedom and creating an abundant life.

"I realize, in a logical perspective, that I may not be able to broadly change the world, however, I know I can be an advocate for change. I know I can't save every person from their fears, but little by little, I can help one person at a time..."

To learn more about Jenn Scalia, visit her website: www.BeAwesomeOnPurpose.com

Or just shoot her an email at: inspire@jennscalia.com

CHAPTER 15

SAVE YOUR LIFE & YOUR MONEY – YOUR HEALTH IN A DOWN ECONOMY – MEDICATION REDUCTION

BY KENNETH E. ALBRECHT, M.D.

WHY IS IT that every time I do a presentation nearly every person in the room either raises their hand or nods their head 'yes' when I ask the question, "What is the likelihood that you are taking too much medication?"

WHY IS IT that after meeting with these patients over a rather short interval of time, nearly one-half of them end up on one-half the drugs from which they started?

HOW IS IT that these patients end up saving hundreds to thousands of dollars in a down economy? …which is so important, especially for those on a fixed income or those out of work.

I am Dr. Kenneth E. Albrecht, an internal medicine physician. I did my internship and residency at the University of Michigan after receiving my medical degree from the University of Cincinnati.

As I reflect back on my career, I have always been focused on helping individuals become healthy, wealthy and happy. I have accomplished this through the creation of A.P.P.L.E Medical Network-U.S.A. The

145

acronym A.P.P.L.E. stands for Associated Professionals for Personal Life Enhancement.

A.P.P.L.E. is a creative system of networked health care providers that help patients become both mentally and physically fully functional and fully alive. A.P.P.L.E. is now a benchmark of how healthcare should be delivered in America today. The system is office-based, community-based and is also a home health delivery system.

Throughout my career, I have become highly aware of the "plight of both the patient and the provider." I have created healthcare system designs to address the frustrations of both. As an example, over the years it has been hard for me to ignore one of America's greatest problems; that is, the plight of the OVER-MEDICATED PATIENT.

Therefore, this chapter focuses on medication reduction. Since we are "talking medications", it is important to note that I received my bachelor's degree in biochemistry; I decided to do post graduate PhD work in clinical pharmacology while obtaining my medical degree. Pharmacology is all about advanced studies of medications – for both humans and animals.

In addition, for you to better appreciate my "going against the grain" philosophy regarding the medical industry, I am thinking that you might want to know my take and philosophy on medicine. In that regard, it is important to note that when I finished training in preparation for going out into the real world as a real doctor, I learned two important things that influenced what kind of doctor I wanted to become and did not want to become.

MY FIRST OBSERVATION was the most disturbing. In my attempt to assess how patients felt about the kind of care they were getting from other doctors, I was amazed to see how often patients were dissatisfied with the kind of healthcare they were or were not receiving from their doctor. As a prime example, you yourself may have experienced the long waits in the doctor office and the short time spent with the doctor. Patients often told me, "I felt like I was being treated like a number and was lost within the healthcare system."

MY SECOND OBSERVATION was made throughout my training. I witnessed how disorganized and inefficient the health care system was.

Knowing all too well that this disorganization would have a significant negative impact on my entire career and personal life, I vowed from day one that I would work to be the most efficient and well-organized physician that I could possibly become. In addition, because of my commitment to this principal, I dedicated over a period of some 12 years approximately 5000 hours writing a software system that I felt I needed, and perhaps many other physicians could use, if they too shared the same belief that "there is no way to be as efficient as one could ever be without the right kind of computer software helping you get the job done."

You see, what I knew for sure was that patients wanted one important thing from me, the one thing that could give them everything else they needed from me, and that was quality time and enough of it! Without quality time there really is no way to build a relationship and assess what patients really need - a diagnosis that is well thought out and a treatment plan for which the patient reasonably understands and is in agreement.

About this time, you might say how does this all relate to patients being lost in the healthcare system and overmedicated?

Well, when patients indeed are treated like a number, it is only natural to expect that individualized care goes by the wayside, and generalizations about how to treat the average patient start to prevail. When the lack of individualization or personalized care starts to become the norm, you can expect your unique individual needs will be less met. This is all too often the current state of how most care is being delivered in America today. To make things worse, this level of care somehow becomes the "standard of care" and far too often, it becomes acceptable and tolerated by many patients. This might be your situation?

Perhaps, in a down economy, one might think that the personalization of care could hardly be affordable? Well we have GONE AGAINST THE GRAIN. When one might have thought the personalized approach could not be affordable, we have seen many medical and non-medical economic benefits. As an example, through our commitment to delivering personalized care, my team of healthcare professionals discovered the problem of the over-medicated patient. As a result, in a down economy, we have saved a lot of patients hundreds to thousands of dollars on medication costs.

In looking back at our discovery, it was one thing to notice the reduction in medication for many of our patients, but even more surprising was seeing how our patients' quality of life improved. Fewer drugs lead to less side effects and general improvement in well-being. This was seen in both mental and physical function.

In looking back on our experience, we have discovered a clear understanding on how the overmedicated patient came about. These are the main reasons:

1. Too often, physicians are under pressure to see more patients in less time, and patients (particularly those more senior), are not seeing physicians as often as they should.

2. Too often, when one finds themselves lost in the system, the phrase "leave well enough alone" often prevails.

3. Too often, another phrase prevails..."once hypertensive, always hypertensive" and "once diabetic, always diabetic." For some patients that is true, but for many it's just not the case.

And how do I know that is true? I frequently say, "Having seen what seems like a million patients in my entire career," my team has been witness to all the above and more.

We actually have gotten many patients off meds and they are no longer diabetic, and those hypertensive are no longer hypertensive. Here is the added bonus. They are happy to no longer pay for medications they no longer need, and many no longer have the side effects those meds may have caused.

You might at this point be asking how can you tell if you're on too many meds? How can you tell if you are one of those people who may, at one time, might have been diagnosed with a medical problem that you no longer have? At one time you might have been told you have high blood pressure, or were hypertensive, or diabetic, or have high cholesterol or hyperlipidemia, but is that still the case?

Well here are a couple of scenarios to consider. There's nothing like talking to your doctor and getting his or her opinion. However, from my experience having listened to the stories from thousands and thousands of patients, that does not seem to be working too well. I say this because

I have encountered way too many patients on too many drugs for far too long. So here is some help if you want to get proactive in working with your doctor or choosing another doctor. It is important to understand that there is everything to gain in your quest if you are trying to find out if you are one of those who can benefit from medication reduction. It's one of those "everything to gain and nothing to lose" scenarios. If your approach to this "going-against-the-grain-of-not-leaving-well-enough-alone" is done correctly, you will know for certain what diagnosis you do or don't have. You will know what drugs you do or don't need. Most importantly, if you do need medication, you will discover the lowest effective dose, with the least cost and least side effects and greatest benefit. That is what I mean by the "everything to gain and nothing to lose" by this "going against the grain approach."

If you are going to go on this journey, the first thing you need to know, right now, is whether your medical problem is well controlled or is not well controlled on your current medications at their current dose. You might think this is rather straight forward, but too often the labeling of a patient "well controlled" is not often that obvious, and more often a matter of individual physician opinion as it should be. Literature opinion can vary as well. So for you to not be confused, having a "meaningful discussion" with your doctor is so important. The reason why I emphasize the word "meaningful" is because by the time that meeting with your doctor is done, both your doctor and "you" should have a good understanding of whether or not your specific problem is well controlled. This should not be a one-sided understanding. Your physician owes you a reasonable amount of education for you to feel reasonably comfortable as to where you stand with your diagnosis, treatment and current level of control.

All that being said, with current labs, vitals and measurements having been done, if it has been determined that you are well controlled... unless your are choosing to "leave well enough alone," your next step is reducing your meds or titrating your meds down while doing the appropriate monitoring for each diagnosis you may have. The steps for each diagnosis vary and can be made available to you in another publication on request.

In either case, here are some common next-best steps to medication reduction. Some medications, depending upon their type and dose, can simply be stopped. Others need to be tapered down over time, and if proven unnecessary, eventually stopped as well. I am often asked the question as to whether you can stop or taper more than one medication at the same time. The answer in general is yes, but it is not often done with medications for the same diagnosis.

During the taper, the appropriate measurement, labs and vitals need to be monitored along the way. The steps for this can be made available to you in the other publication listed above.

All in all, I can assure you of this. Taking a good look at where you stand regarding what diagnosis or what medical condition you have, and seeing whether you are a candidate for medication reduction, can provide you valuable information that will have a significant impact on your life, if not even save your life. You will discover at least three things regarding your medications. You will know if are over-medicated, under- medicated or just right. In addition, you will learn to what extent you do or don't have an ongoing drug side effect of which you may or may not be aware. As an added benefit, medication reduction provides you an opportunity to be as fully functional and fully alive as possible both mentally and physically. Why expect or accept less?

To be fine-tuned both mentally and physically at anytime in your life makes the most of living your best life, the only one you will ever have. Know this as well, and consistent with the theme of this book in a down economy, mental and physical performance is important for good health, job performance and continued employment.

Finally, in wishing you a healthy economic wellbeing, let's not forget about the significant amount of money you can save if one "goes against the grain by not leaving well enough alone," by challenging your diagnosis and the amount of medication you need or don't need.

About Dr. Ken

Kenneth E. Albrecht, M.D. is an internal medicine physician. He received his training from the University of Michigan, Ann Arbor.

He is the founder of **A.P.P.L.E Medical Network U.S.A. (A**ssociated **P**rofessionals for **P**ersonal **L**ife **E**nhancement). Dr. Albrecht has dedicated his entire medical career to the development of personalized cost effective systems of health care delivery.

His focus has always been on helping individuals become healthy, wealthy and happy. This has been accomplished through creative personalized systems of networked health care delivery that helps patients become both mentally and physically fully functional and fully alive.

A.P.P.L.E Medical Network has been established as a benchmark of how healthcare should be delivered in America today. This system is office-based, community-based and also a system of home health delivery.

Dr. Albrecht, as an innovator in medicine, is one who wrote the software that drives this system of effective healthcare delivery. Through out his career, he has been highly aware of what he refers to as the "plight of both the provider and the patient." He has created system designs to address the frustrations of both patients and providers.

He is an avid lecturer on topics that address the above issues. Three of his outstanding presentations include:
1) How to Talk to Your Doctor - So Your Doctor Will Talk To You
2) How to Live Your Best Life on the Least Amount of Medicine
3) The Challenges of Healthcare Delivery

Dr. Albrecht is married to Lizbeth, has four children and lives in the Chicago land area. His personal interests include music and the entertainment industry. Since the age of 5 he has had a strong interest in music and has become an accomplished front drummer. He created a new form of musical entertainment for musicians and singers alike through the development of The CD's Come Alive Band. The band is a fusion of both live and CD sound.

He is entrepreneurial in both the medical and entertainment industry. He is inventive with four inventions. He has written five screen plays for production and is a consultant to the movie industry. He is a licensed pyrotechician, author of two books and a software developer. Outdoor interests include fishing, skiing and astronomy. He also is a safe rider of Harley Davidson motorcycles.

www.AppleMedicalNetworkUSA.com
email: DrKen@AppleMedicalNetworkUSA.com, Tel: 630-204-0164

CHAPTER 16

HOW TO RELEASE YOUR SELF-SABOTAGING LABELS AND HAVE A HIGH PERFORMANCE LIFE

BY KATE UPCHURCH

I was born in a small Texas town, population 350. Being the only person in town my age didn't help a shy and introverted child learn how to interact with other kids. This was especially true when I started school, which was in another town. Children in my class immediately began making fun of me and mimicking me, because I was different. I had buck teeth and a crossed right eye – a prime target for bullies.

To make matters worse, my doctor categorized my particular situation as a physical handicap, now called physical challenge. It was an extremely long childhood with a lot of self-sabotaging labels.

After college, I became immersed in self-improvement. I read book after book, but I soon discovered most were all theory. There was no *how to* in them. I felt like a loser because I couldn't figure it out.

At the age of twenty-four, I got married. Seven months later my husband died of a massive heart attack, he was thirty-six. His best friend was a hypnotherapist in Los Angeles who agreed to help me with my grief. I was soon on a journey that would change my life forever.

IT TOOK JUST ONE WORD

After experiencing how rapidly hypnosis changed my life, I also became a hypnotherapist. One of my first clients was a teenage girl who came to me for test phobia. At least, that's what I was told.

Her mother said she wouldn't graduate from the eighth grade without summer school and maybe not then. She had been diagnosed with ADHD and was on medication. Due to her ADHD she was in the special education program at her school. She was an introvert without any friends and didn't have much contact with her father. Her parents were divorced.

For the first three hypnosis sessions, I didn't believe we made much progress. Then we had our fourth session…

I offer the option to my clients to either verbalize what they are feeling or silently experience it. She had chosen the latter. So I was actually working from instinct, and any unintended verbal utterance or facial expression she gave.

About twenty minutes into this session I had a strong urge to tell her she was loved. I told her how much her mother loved her and was proud of her. Next I told her that even though she didn't see her father often he also loved her deeply.

When I said this I saw complete peace come over her face…actually over her whole body. It was fantastic to watch! When she was back to her full consciousness, I asked if she would share what she experienced, she did. She had never known her family loved her. *She had always told herself she was unlovable*. The word *LOVE* had just changed this teenager's life.

After this session, I didn't hear from her again.

Fast forward three months…her mother called glowing and wanted to give me an update. Her daughter passed the eighth grade at the end of the term; she didn't need summer school. Even better, in the fall she would be in regular classes. Her medication was in the past. She was making friends and having sleepovers. She had joined her church choir and the ROTC.

All of this in three months by simply releasing a self-sabotaging label and having a different belief about herself, *she was loveable.* A whole world of options and possibilities had just opened. She had gone from being totally withdrawn to a high performer at lightning speed.

(I'm not saying, or implying I cured her ADHD. I'm not a doctor. I'm only reporting what her mother told me before and after I worked with her.)

WHY SHOULD YOU CARE?

You may say, "That's a terrific story Kate, but why should I care? How does this relate to me... this story has nothing to do with business." Those are legitimate questions; ones I'd like to answer through continuing this journey of discovery.

After the mother's call, it was like a lightning bolt in my head. – What if other people could increase their level of performance not just a little, but by leaps and bounds with a change in their internal labels?

First, I had to explain what a **self-sabotaging label** is compared to negative self-talk and negative thoughts. I also needed to explain what I mean by **high performance**, so we have a benchmark to monitor change by.

My definition of a **self-sabotaging label**: what you believe to be true about yourself whether there is a basis for that belief or not. A label you repeat to yourself so often that it becomes part of your identity. *(For example – I'm fat, I'm ugly, I'm a failure, etc.) When it becomes part of your identity, it works against you by becoming a self-fulfilling prophecy.*

Negative thoughts *are thoughts you have about any topic where you only see the negative viewpoint.*

Negative self-talk *is similar to self-sabotaging labels, but to me they have one difference. Self-sabotaging labels are so ingrained they have become part of your identity, whereas negative self-talk creates doubt for you by what you are saying to yourself. However, when repeated* *enough and believed, it can become a self-sabotaging label.*

How I see **High Performance**: *High Performance is feeling fully engaged in your life with joy and excitement. It is to outperform your history deliberately and consistently to the point that you grow into your ultimate self.*

With this clarity, I researched, tested and refined this theory. I was shocked at how quickly and successfully it worked for most people. Did it work for everyone? – No!

The distinctions I discovered that made it work or not work were:

- *Was the person ready to change?*

- *Were they willing to take responsibility for their life or did they need to be a victim?*

- *Would they push the limits of their current comfort zone and grow?*

Some of the changes I've seen: one client had always dreamed of writing a book, she became a bestselling author. Another woman moved out of the projects and off welfare into her own apartment and full time job. Then other people were happy to have money left over after paying their bills. Each story is unique and different.

What I do know from working on myself and hundreds of others, we all have or have had self-sabotaging labels to some degree. Also, these labels can be fatal to achieving high performance and your ultimate self.

I've also discovered that *where you go, so go your self-sabotaging labels.* Whether that's the boardroom, the executive office, small business owner, factory worker, stay-at-home mom, professional athlete, etc.

Here's the good news, once you release your self-sabotaging labels you will experience freedom. You can then create new positive labels and move to a higher level of performance and happier life.

HOW DID YOU GET THERE IN THE FIRST PLACE?

If a person, I'll call her Sue, says to two people, "You'll always be a failure." One of the recipients may reply, "You're wrong! I'm successful and always will be." The label is rejected. The other person may respond, "If Sue said that to me it must be true," and a negative self-sabotaging label is born. – "I'll always be a failure." It can also come from something you read, hear or see and strongly identify with.

If you hold on to that self-sabotaging label, even if you're not consciously aware of it, you will somehow sabotage successful change in the area of the label. Why? It's part of your identity, and you must fulfill that identity to feel whole. This can hold true even if you have a certain level of success, but you bought in to what Sue said. If the level of success isn't to the extent you'd like, it may still be the same self-sabotaging label, but you believe it less.

PROGRAMMED FOR NEGATIVITY...

According to a UCLA survey, the average one-year-old child hears the word *NO* more than 400 times a day. When you consider they're usually told "no, no, no" instead of just "no," it's easy to see how it adds up.

Another study estimates the average child hears "no" or "don't" over 148,000 times while growing up compared to a few thousand "yes" replies.

I'm sure you can see how this can set someone up with a tendency toward self-sabotaging labels.

HOW TO GET RID OF SELF-SABOTAGING LABELS...
NO HYPNOSIS REQUIRED

I've worked with hundreds of people, to help eliminate their self-sabotaging labels. Some used hypnosis and others did not. Hypnosis isn't for everyone, I know that. I'm not here to judge but to help.

Therefore, I've created a system that allows someone to work alone to achieve outstanding results. My goal and hope for you are that you clear all of your labels and achieve an exceptional level of high performance – a level you've never dreamt of, one where you reach your ultimate self.

Please read through the following steps and instructions several times before you begin the exercise. In other words, know the steps before you start.

Important: This exercise isn't meant to be used if you suffer from severe emotional or physical trauma. Also, if during this exercise you have emotions well up that you feel are too intense to handle on your own (terror, rage, suicidal thoughts, disturbing images, etc.) please seek the assistance of a professional therapist.

1. Sit in a comfortable place, where you won't be interrupted for at least 20 to 30 minutes. (Don't do this exercise while driving a car, operating machinery or doing anything that requires your full attention and eyes open.)

2. Now read through the list of common self-sabotaging labels below. Note: if you know you have a self-sabotaging label(s) that isn't listed here or yours is worded differently, *write yours down*.

3. When you read through the list of self-sabotaging labels notice any body sensations. Do you feel a twinge, a knot in your stomach, sadness, or any other feeling or sensation? Do you have a reaction such as "this doesn't apply to me" or something similar? (This is an indication that it does indeed apply to you.) Write down any word or phrase you have a feeling or reaction to.

   It's critical to read through the words and phrases at a normal speed. Do not dwell on any particular word or phrase. If you do, you may get a false reaction.

   Again, *write down anything you feel applies to you.*

4. Now shut your eyes, take several deep breaths and picture yourself in a remarkably peaceful environment where you feel totally safe. Hear all the sounds as though you were actually there... imagine the setting. (For example, my peaceful setting overlooks a waterfall with deer, squirrels, and other animals moving around. I hear the waterfall and the animals.) Having this tranquil image simply helps you relax.

5. Recall one word or phrase from your list. (Do not try to work on multiple words or phrases at one time, this creates confusion.)

6. After you have your word or phrase in mind, ask yourself for the *POSITIVE* learning this self-sabotaging label is trying to give

you. *Yes, positive learning!* The first few things that surface may be negative. Just let them float by. Again ask for the positive learning.

For example:

Self-Sabotaging Label – *"I'm a failure."*

Positive Learning – *"I can choose not to believe what is said about or to me."*

(Your self-sabotaging label and positive learning will probably be different from mine. Yours will be unique to you.)

I promise there is a positive learning; you just have to keep asking until it surfaces. If after a dozen times of asking it still doesn't come forward, end your session. It may not be ready to release. If that's the case, don't get discouraged. Try it again tomorrow or a few days later.

7. Once you've completed step 6, ask yourself what a positive replacement label would be. Say it to yourself. Then declare to choose this new label. An example:

New Label – *"I'm successful!"*

Declarative Statement – *"I now choose to believe I'm successful in everything I do."*

8. Open your eyes when you're ready and write down your new label and declarative statement. Also write down all the new options/possibilities that have opened to you with your new label.

9. Read the list you created in Step 8 everyday, preferably several times a day until you begin to see these options/possibilities occurring.

HERE'S A LIST OF COMMON SELF-SABOTAGING LABELS:

a coward	fat	not worth loving
a failure	have no value	not worth respecting
a loser	heartless	screwed up
a nobody	helpless	self-centered

a nothing	I can't	selfish
bad	I'm not capable	something is wrong with you
black sheep of the family	incompetent	stupid
can't cut it	inconsiderate	ugly
can't do anything right	inferior	undesirable
defective	insignificant	unimportant
dishonest	insufficient	unlovable
disposable	irresponsible	unreliable
don't measure up	just like your parents, sister, etc.	unsuccessful
don't count	lazy	unworthy
don't have what it takes	less than	useless
don't matter	no good	worthless
dumb	not good enough	wrong

NOTE: If you don't believe the label has cleared and you're not ready to try it again, go on to another label and clear it. Sometimes when one won't clear and feels *stuck* it's because it's connected to another. When you discover the *core* label, the other *stuck* label will release.

How do you know when the label is gone? Simple – you don't experience a sensation in your body when you read that word or phrase.

Stay the course! In most instances, you've had this/these self-sabotaging label(s) for a long time so be patient. It may take a little while to get it/ them cleared. You may even have to repeat the process several times on a specific word or phrase. – That's OK, nothing is wrong.

IS IT YOUR TURN?

It doesn't matter how old you are, what your career path is or what happened in your past. Now it's your turn to make the decision to release your past or stay the same. I know change isn't easy and I honor you for choosing it. Once you've released your self-sabotaging label(s), you'll enjoy new freedom. You'll discover that moving into your future without the baggage of your past, opens up so many options/possibilities.

The remarkable thing is now you have a tool that can help you remove any self-sabotaging label that comes up. Thank you so much for allowing me to be a part of your change, I am humbled.

In closing, may your life be filled with positive self-labels and on a scale of 1 to 10, may your high performance go to level 12 and beyond.

About Kate

Kate Upchurch is a Certified High Performance Coach (CHPC), Certified Health Coach (CHC) and Certified Hypnotherapist with an emphasis in Conversational Hypnosis (C.HT). Her mission is to work with Women Entrepreneurs, so they have a high performance lifestyle. This includes having a more profitable business and more time for themselves and their families.

Kate has been an entrepreneur for over 33 years. She fully understands the struggles and daily challenges women go through in the workplace and in their personal lives.

As a coach, she assists her clients to discover why they don't have clarity, energy, productivity and influence in everything they do. She helps them learn to work more efficiently and to see what's getting in their way and holding them back from having their ideal career and personal lives. She views this as the foundation for a high performance lifestyle.

Then she works diligently with each client on how to, quickly and easily, turn any challenges around. They understand what they need to do to achieve their high performance lifestyle – a life where they feel fully engaged with joy and excitement in everything they do. Where they out-perform their history deliberately and consistently to the point where they grow into their ultimate self.

Kate has worked with Entrepreneurial Women with all types of businesses and backgrounds. Her client list includes individuals from 23 countries and 38 US states.

She is President of Wahu Topa, Inc. the parent company of Kate Upchurch Coaching (kateupchurch.com) and Music by Marcey™ (www.musicbymarcey.com). Music by Marcey is an independent music label that has 1000s of healing testimonials. Composer Marcey Hamm's music has been credited with dramatically changing people's lives.

Kate would love to hear your success stories and testimonials from the Self-Sabotaging Label Exercise.

To learn more about Kate Upchurch go to: www.kateupchurch.com.

www.KateUpchurch.com

CHAPTER 17

THE TOOLS TO BUILD A SUCCESSFUL COACHING BUSINESS...FAST!

BY JOHNNY TARCICA

During my life as an advertiser working for Foote Cone & Belding, I had many memorable events that happened while managing the accounts of my clients. One of the particular events happened in Miami during a Latin American account review with Pizza Hut around 1990. After the two-day meeting, we were invited to go bowling, both their staff and us – the agency guys.

During the game, I noticed a group of three that were not playing but observing, and somehow all my client´s staff was paying attention to them. I suddenly remembered having seen the same group in the meetings, sitting in the back, taking notes, but not participating.

I could not hold my curiosity and asked to my fellow players: "Who are these guys?" The reply was, "They are from Human Resources and are assessing us to select who will be promoted."

I was impacted by this answer. At that moment, I immediately realized the power of Human Resources in organizations. *They could select the new marketing team.*

So, suddenly I started reading all the HR material that I could get. These were pre-Internet days, so it was very difficult to select appropriate material, as there were no online reviews to rely on. Living in Costa Rica, I had another difficulty, which was the limited amount of material I could get in English, as many books in Spanish at that time were lacking the latest trends.

Anyhow, I slowly began to learn the different components of Human Resources, and still, while being a full-time advertiser, I started getting involved helping the HR department in the company I was working in.

The task they assigned me seemed an easy one at the beginning, I was in charge of recruiting Creative Directors for the different offices we had in Latin America. A Creative Director is the most valuable asset an advertising agency can have, as those are the guys that produce the big campaigns that in the end result in attracting and retaining big client accounts.

So I started my journey contacting creative directors in almost all important cities in Latin America, thinking I would only need to interview them, see the creative work they did for their current agency, and if appropriate, make them a good salary offer and hire them. Easy task I thought. During the first interview I was doing in Santiago, Chile, I suddenly realized I was missing a very important point. Creative Directors do not work alone. They have assistants and copywriters who produce the material they use in their campaigns.

So, how could I determine if a great campaign I was shown was the result of the Creative Director's great idea, or just the result of having a great team that produced it. I immediately realized I had to develop a quick and easy way to test their skills.

THE WATER GLASS TEST

So I figured out a very simple test that consisted in giving them a glass full of water and ask them to write a campaign to advertise it. Very soon I was able to find who were great, and who were only the result of managing a great group of copywriters.

MY LIFE AS A RECRUITER

I started my own recruiting company with my wife in the early 90´s and used my valuable contacts from my advertiser days to get assignments.

My practice grew fast and suddenly I was searching for top talent for big clients around Latin America. I started receiving invitations to speak at events, in conferences and to grad students. I felt great.

Then I was invited to conduct consulting, in some cases, being hired by the same managers I had recruited. I thought life was great.

HOW I DISCOVERED THE DISC MODEL

I was sitting in the office of one of my clients, a big pharmaceutical company, and the manager shared with me a DISC Profile of his marketing director. I started reading the report and was impressed by the extensive information it provided and the accuracy of the results.

I started researching the DISC model, and found out it was published by a Harvard University professor named William Moulton Marston in his book "Emotions of Normal People" in 1928. I thought how important this model should be, to be still current sixty years after its first appearance.

I managed to get a copy of the book (which was a very difficult task at that time) and was intrigued when I started reading the first paragraph that says "Are you normal?"

LEARNING THE DISC MODEL

The DISC model represents four different behavioral styles:

1. Dominant

Action oriented. Quick at solving problems, makes decisions and takes on risks.

Dominant personalities like making decisions for themselves and for others.

2. Influential

People oriented. Interacts well with others and is skilled in the art of persuasion.

Influential personalities like socializing and leading others through persuasion.

3. Stable

Procedure oriented. Stays centered and balanced. Seeks harmony and does not like surprises.

Stable personalities enjoy working alongside others as part of the team.

4. Cautious

Explanation oriented. Requires accurate information, researches in depth, analyzes carefully.

Cautious personalities pay a great deal of attention to detail and stick with a plan until it is completed.

DEVELOPMENT OF THE DIAV MODEL

During my years as an advertiser, I had the good fortune of being exposed to the growing trends in research toward consumer insight and behavior.

Successful advertising campaigns, the ones that really produce millions in sales, are the result of combining brilliant creative strategies with top-notch production and effective media mix.

At that time, psychologists that had mastered the intriguing world of consumer insight and behavior were conducting focus groups all over the world, trying to figure out what were the desires, interests, attitudes and values of the consumers of a particular brand or product.

When I moved to human resources, I always had the feeling that the same techniques and fundaments could be used to communicate better with employees.

If the boss has a way to better understand what the motivating factors of the employees are, wise management can be achieved and better results will follow almost always. So, one weekend I got inspired and created the DIAV Model.

LEARNING THE DIAV MODEL

DIAV means four motivating concepts: Desires, Interests, Attitudes and Values.

The objective of this model is to help to understand why each individual reacts in a unique way and produces different outcomes when exposed to the same situations.

According to the DIAV Model, there are six types of persons:

(i). Social

Desires: sharing and belonging

Interests: connecting with everyone

Attitudes: sympathy and communication

Values: popularity and prestige.

(ii). Artistic

Desires: harmony and depth

Interests: an environment that is pleasing to the senses

Attitudes: feeling and pleasure

Values: beauty and meaning

(iii). Enterprising

Desires: new challenges

Interests: progress and well-being

Attitudes: confidence and energy

Values: success and rewards

(iv). Conservative

Desires: a peaceful life

Interests: to keep things "status quo"

Attitudes: to listen and mediate

Values: tradition and family

(v). Analytical

Desires: understanding everything

Interests: careful investigation

Attitudes: trust but verifies

Values: accurate information

(vi). Balanced

Desires: effective coordination

Interests: combining a bit of everything

Attitudes: is eager to contribute

Values: open to variety

MORE COACHES AND CONSULTANTS EVERY DAY

Being so close to the corporate world, I started noticing that many mid-age corporate refuges were facing difficulties getting new jobs, and were starting consultancy and coaching services.

Consultants are usually behind the scene with limited exposure to the final outcome of their advice.

Coaches by the other hand are permanently visible through the progress of their clients. Like a personal trainer in a gym, results are visible to everybody – just by observing the shapes of the bodies of their clients.

Many of my corporate former clients started calling to offer these types of services. Many were rising to the stars and others folded in a couple of months.

I was intrigued by what made the difference between their success and failure, so I started some simple statistics, and suddenly discovered some common patterns:

SUCCESSFUL CONSULTANTS AND COACHES:

1. Had established a very particular niche where to provide their services. Failures were among who tried to bid every single opportunity, regardless of the field and their expertise.

2. Were using very precise and standardized frameworks to conduct their practice.

3. Incorporated top-notch technological tools in their practice.

4. Had an ongoing new client prospecting program, even when they were full of existing clients.

5. Produced outstanding results and got word-of-mouth referrals that resulted in additional business.

6. Participated as speakers and wrote articles. Got recognized in the community as experts in their field.

BECOMING A COACH

I made a transition from consultant to coach in a seamless way. It simply happened. I started to become very concerned about the results my clients were achieving from my consulting services, and realized that in almost all cases, unsuccessful projects were the result of lousy implementation. In most of the cases the client did not implement the recommendations or executed them in a less than desirable manner. It was frustrating to see brilliant ideas sitting in the file cabinets of my clients, or being killed by lousy execution.

So I decided I always wanted to be involved and accountable for the end results of my projects, so I become a coach. Or at least I thought so.

DEVELOPING THE TOOLS

I tried to get the best tools that were available in order to provide a sound professional service. I found many and started using them, but very soon I realized I was lacking the most important of all.

I needed a tool to engage and establish immediate rapport with my coaching clients. The tool would need to produce standardized results but in a very personalized manner, to avoid a "one-size-fits-all" situation.

BECOMING A SUCCESSFUL COACH

My first intention was to become a world class coach. I had traveled around the world. I had many valuable contacts in three continents, and my hair was starting to get gray. At least, I felt I had the required pedigree to start a coaching career.

But during the development of the new tools, I suddenly realized that I could be much more valuable to the coaching community by developing tools and systems to help both existing and 'aspiring-to-be' coaches around the world to start and conduct successful professional practices.

This approach to coaching would also be more rewarding for me, and provide the motivation to build new and innovative tools. With online distribution through the Internet, my audience would be huge.

So, FuturaDISC, FuturaDIAV and FuturaDDI were born.

I had created a framework that could help coaches to produce long-lasting engagement with their clients. Now all I needed was to spread the word, translate into different languages and start validating the tools. I developed a built-in validation scheme that uses the client´s input and rewards them for their participation.

HOW TO START A SUCCESSFUL COACHING CAREER

Successful coaching techniques always start by asking questions. Not any question. You need to ask the right questions. And you need to make your best effort to get the right answers.

So, you should start asking yourself this very important question and produce a very realistic answer:

Do I really want to become a coach?

A successful coach is somebody that has decided to conduct a coaching practice as an ultimate career goal in life. It is not somebody looking for a temporary source of income until the next job opportunity arises.

If the answer is a definitive YES, then you should move your mindset to become not only a coach, but also a highly successful coach, which in many cases are not equal.

BLUEPRINT: 10 STEPS TO BECOME A SUCCESSFUL COACH

1. Define a precise niche where you will offer your services. It is wise to explore within your area of expertise in order to streamline the process and not lose valuable time learning new industries. If you have spent the last twenty years in logistics, it makes more sense to become specialized in coaching distribution chain organizations than starting a health care coaching career.

2. Define the target of your coaching practice. Usually you can mix some of them, but you will get best results if you stick to a specific target audience. Following are some examples:

   • Personal Development for Individuals

   • Organizational Development

• Sales Coaching

3. Get the right tools. As in the old Wild West, you cannot enter the saloon unarmed, if you really want to produce an impressive first appearance. You need to use the latest technology to impress your prospective clients. Nobody will trust a coach that uses outdated systems.

4. Create a standardized framework for your services. If you start tailoring everything to the minimal requests of your clients, you will end up with a lot of work and very little money in the bank. You need to develop a flexible framework, and you need to use it in every project, so you will benefit from economies of scale, and you will be able to work smarter, not harder.

5. Develop a USP (unique selling proposition) to be used in all your marketing materials, explaining what is unique in the service you are offering. It is more important to be unique than to be the best, so people will remember you more easily.

6. Use a top-notch CRM (Client Relationship Management) system and start filling it with all the contacts you have from your former life. Whenever you contact a prospect, do not be shy to ask to be referred to additional prospects they may know who could be interested in your services.

7. Establish an ongoing marketing campaign to get new clients even when you are full. You can easily outsource this task, but never stop. You cannot be successful if you run out of clients.

8. Start to be recognized as an expert in your field. Volunteer to speak at conferences, participate in workshops, write articles, be an active blogger in your area. Get testimonials from satisfied clients. Show your success stories to your target community.

9. Provide outstanding service. If possible, always over-deliver. Impress your clients. Run the extra mile. Do not charge for minor incremental assignments. Let word-of-mouth spread.

10. Do not look back ever. Even if you have a bad day. You are not running for a specific date. Accumulated results are what count and will put money in your bank account.

ONE FINAL WORD

Coaching is one of the most rewarding careers available. You can help so many people to achieve their goals. Be your first client. Coach yourself to success. Go for it. Never look back.

You can learn more about my Coaching Framework visiting: www.futuracoaching.com

About Johnny

Johnny Tarcica is the Founder and CEO of Empleos.Net, a leading Job Portal in the Internet for Latin America. He is also the creator of the FuturaDISC and FuturaDIAV assessments, which include personality, behavioral, desires, interests, attitudes and values tests, used by Human Resources departments, recruiters, trainers, consultants and coaches all over the world.

Johnny is a well-known entrepreneur, marketer, advertiser, talent acquisition expert, headhunter, international consultant and coach. Wearing so many hats; he has developed multiple relationships in different industries around the globe, with a variety of clients, partners, business associates and friends.

A self-taught software developer, Johnny wrote the first code for: www.empleos.net. He launched the company as a one man shop (himself), and worked his path to become one of the best-known and most popular recruiting platforms in Latin America.

An avid traveler, he divides his time between creating new software tools and attending conferences and workshops, to make sure he is always current with the new trends.

Always creating and developing new projects, he is also the founder of: latinojobs.com, an Internet job portal for the Latino community in the US that was launched in 2013.

Johnny is also an enthusiastic golf player. He plays just for fun, to enjoy life. Many people seek to play with him just as an opportunity to spend four valuable hours talking and receiving his normally sound advice. He also founded the Happiness Bank for Latin America, where People can open accounts to keep track of their good actions, and include them in their resumes...

In business he usually over delivers, besides being extremely flexible and targeted; so there is no wonder why his clients love him and love doing business with him. A famous tale recounts a prospective client he met on a plane who asked for a service that was not provided at that time, and Johnny created and quoted it. Business was closed before the plane landed.

With so many projects and business ventures, when somebody asks Johnny to define which of them he thinks provide more value to the world, his answer is always FuturaDISC. It consists of an online testing platform that can be easily used for employee training and development, career planning, individual performance coaching and many more uses. This platform has been constructed following worldwide best practices using a multicultural team that provided input through different countries and continents.

If you are interested in starting or expanding a consulting or coaching practice, there is no better tool than FuturaDISC for establishing and engaging in a long-lasting relationship with your clients and also with your prospects.

You may contact Johnny at: jtarcica@futuracoaching.com,
Or visit: www.futuracoaching.com

CHAPTER 18

SUCCESS-FILLED FACTORS
From Knowledge to Action

BY MYLES MILLER

SUCCESS is something that many aspire to achieve and some do, but many are challenged by how to get to the level of success that they desire for themselves. Having spoken to tens of thousands about SUCCESS and what they can do to acquire it in their life, I often pose the question, "So how many of you want to be 'SUCCESSful'?" Amazingly or not, every hand in the room will go up. Then I follow-up with the question that gets to the heart of what this chapter is all about…"How many of you know how to become 'SUCCESSful'?"

During my career as trainer and speaker, having created one company which has grown into seven in just four years, many would look at what I have accomplished and say that I must be successful, but I am still honestly growing and striving to reach new heights and achieve more success.

So, how does one go from wanting to be SUCCESSful to what I call "SUCCESS-filled?" It begins with an understanding of who you are now and who you truly want to be. Do you work for someone else, but want to work for yourself? Are you staying in one place, but see your potential growing, if you focused on another area? Have you seen what others have done and imagine that you could do the same, if you only knew how?

There is no magic pill or silver bullet that will work for everyone because, no surprise, your circumstances are uniquely different from everyone else. But the good news is that what makes you different will also help you in your efforts to become SUCCESS-filled. This is counter-intuitive to what you may have heard on late-night television or from other proponents that say you can become successful overnight. While we may want that quick fix similar to going down the drive-thru lane and being handed a bag with everything in it we need, the truth is that most, if not all, successful people have become that way due to the actions that they have taken, and steps and plans that they have made, to achieve the success they want.

Before I share the **ACT**ions that you can do starting today to achieve the SUCCESS-filled life that you want, understand that no matter your current circumstances, you can achieve the success you want. But don't define success based solely on what others say. Your success may not be measured by wealth, power or other means that define success for some. Maybe success for you will be more time with your family and friends. It could be getting a promotion with your employer that will help you achieve more. Perhaps you want to start your own company, but have no idea what that takes or where to begin.

That is my story, having worked for many corporations for almost three decades. As part of a severance package at my last employer, I was provided with a career-transition counselor. Honestly, I had never heard of this role and didn't even know they existed, but let me assure you they do, and what a difference this person made in my life's direction. His name is Joe and from day one, Joe challenged me do something that I always wanted to do and thought it was a great idea ("Yes, I want to be SUCCESSful"), but I just didn't know how. I had tried becoming successful over the years by selling insurance, vacuum cleaners, hearing aids, vending machines and many items and products that I thought would make me successful, but ultimately they made others money and did not produce much money or success for me. I have learned that the main reason for me not being successful with these efforts was that I truly had no passion or drive or ambition connected with what I was doing. What did I really want to do? I wanted to own my own company, but honestly I was scared of what that meant and really did not know where to begin.

Now back to Joe and his challenge to me. As part of his service, he provided a variety of personality tests that came back with the same results I had received previously. No surprise there. Who I am has been the same for many years. So what was Joe's challenge to me? …"You will only be happy if you start your own company."

Talk about a challenge. Hitting on the one thing I have always wanted to do. Well, I jumped at his suggestion. Not really, I actually was stymied at the suggestion and verbally shared numerous reasons why that was not a good idea for me. Ever make excuses for why you can't do something. Well, realize if you want to be successful that has to change. It did for me.

Every two weeks for many months Joe would keep his challenge in front of me and I would say, but Joe, I have a daughter in college to pay for, a wife that is working but needs my income as well so we can pay our monthly bills, and on and on. Excuses, excuses, excuses.

Joe never gave up in his persistence and I am so glad he didn't stop. So in January 2009, with literally very little money, I started my first company.

So, what did I do that will help you in your efforts to achieve your own SUCCESS-filled life? I took **ACT**ion steps to begin filling my life with success.

What are these **ACT**ion steps?

Think of the word **ACT**. Remember how in my story I had to **ACT** to get from where I was to where I wanted to be. This is what Joe helped me to realize and the **ACT**ions I pursued helped move me forward to my SUCCESS-filled life.

To **ACT** you must have these three elements working daily to achieve your SUCCESS-filled life.

- **A = Attitude of SUCCESS**

- **C = Connections to SUCCESS**

- **T = Tenacity for SUCCESS**

Let's look at each area in more detail and begin today to understand more fully how you can go from thinking about and wanting to have success, to actually achieving it.

1. ATTITUDE OF SUCCESS

"Your attitude, not your aptitude, will determine your altitude."
~ Zig Ziglar

It is a vital first step that you adopt and maintain an attitude that is one of positive focus and thinking each and every day. It will be next to impossible to achieve success in your life without this all-important first step that will be the foundation that all other steps will be built upon.

Now, what does it take to maintain an attitude of SUCCESS daily? Well, immediately purge your mind of all those ideas and thoughts that have been implanted by you and others, that you are not good enough, or capable enough, or pretty enough, or smart enough, or on and on enough. Enough already!!! You are what you believe yourself to be. No matter what you have been told by "well-wishers," parents, friends and others who have your "best interests" in mind. Remember in many cases they are telling you what they believe to be true about themselves, and conveying that to you so you will adopt the same thought process. Thank them for their concern and then do otherwise.

We must create a mindset and thought processes that ensure that we always have positive ideas and responses flowing throughout each day. It is much simpler to believe in negative talk, which we are flooded with all day, everyday…in the media, …in the workplace, …in our homes, …and in our neighborhoods. Fight back against this constant stream of negativity and stem the flow of its influence on your life and direction. As the title of this book alludes to, you must go "against the grain" to achieve more and succeed more than others you might know.

We are naturally wired to be negative in our thoughts, word and deeds. This is part of our humanity, because of our early need in less lawful communities to protect what was ours at all costs. In the distant past, we had to protect our families from harm and our property and possessions from theft. Many still are doing this same thing in parts of the world today. But when laws were created and enforcement of those laws was mandated, others took on the responsibility of protection for us. Still, we harbor those negative foundational ideas after all these generations, and therefore we believe the worst sometimes about others and ourselves. This is then perpetuated by our surrounding social systems and by those in our circle of influence.

Thus the battle against the flow of negativity persists, but you can combat it daily by flooding your mind with positive quotes and messages. Read books, yes, books or articles which focus on positive ideas that you can leverage and use to combat this negative flood trying to invade your mind. Surround yourself with positive thinkers and motivators, like my good friend, Joe, who will encourage you to do and be more than you are right now and never let you settle, if you want to be truly SUCCESS-filled.

Now that you have the right and positive attitude for SUCCESS running through your mind each day, let's move on to the next step to build upon to achieve the SUCCESS-filled life you want.

I alluded to this idea earlier while we were focusing on maintaining positive thoughts, and it is to surround yourself with "connections" that will help you in your efforts to become more SUCCESS-filled.

So here is the second step in taking **ACT**ion…

2. CONNECTIONS TO SUCCESS

"Only through our connectedness to others can we really know and enhance the self. And only through working on the self can we begin to enhance our connectedness to others."
~ Harriet Goldhor Lerner

One key aspect that helped me when I started my first company and has continued to be beneficial to me throughout our growth, are the "connections" I have made.

For you to reach and achieve beyond your current level to NEW levels of SUCCESS, you must be willing to leave the comfort zone that you have created for yourself. You need to be willing to meet and talk to perfect strangers that will be able to help you learn and grow on the path to the SUCCESS-filled life that you want.

Let me ask you this, if you could talk to anyone about what makes them successful or how they achieved their success, who would be on your list? Maybe Oprah Winfrey, Donald Trump, Sir Richard Branson, Melinda Gates, Jill Abramson, Angela Merkel, Steven Spielberg, Jerry Seinfeld and many more you may or may not know.

Would you be willing to take the steps to try and contact them and ask for advice? Maybe that might not be a first step, so let's consider trying locally or regionally for a start. Are their people in your communities that you view as successful? Could you pick up the phone and contact them and ask this simple question, "Would you be willing to meet me for 15 minutes over a cup of coffee to talk about your success and how you achieved it?" Now I know what you are thinking, "I could never call and ask someone that." Guess what, that is what the majority, over 90% of people believe, and that is why they never realize success in their life and are stuck doing what they are doing and still just thinking about being successful.

One key aspect that changes you from thinking about SUCCESS to becoming SUCCESS-filled, is doing what most would not do.

So, if you have been filling your mind with positive thoughts (remember the "Attitude of SUCCESS"), then your confidence should be growing each day. The next step is to make "connections" that help you along the path to SUCCESS.

Where do you begin? If you want to move into a new career path or move up in your workplace, talk to and meet with the people that are in these roles and ask them over that "cup of coffee" what they did to get there. Here is a little secret you may not know, most people are wired to help others when asked, but guess what, most people never ask. This is how connections are made, you start asking and believe me, people will naturally want to help. As you approach these people, be humble and state your intentions clearly up front. Let them know you value their time and expertise, and want just 15 minutes of their time to learn from them what has made them successful.

As you build these relationships, keep expanding your sphere of SUCCESS and these "advisors" will be instrumental in your growth to your SUCCESS-filled life.

Finally the third step, one that will carry you through the challenges as you are reaching and achieving the success you want, is to be tenacious.

3. TENACITY FOR SUCCESS

"Let me tell you the secret that has led me to my goal.
My strength lies solely in my tenacity."
~ Louis Pasteur

At this point, you have filled you mind daily with positive thoughts (Attitude of SUCCESS), you are surrounding yourself with people who can advise and help you with your growth (Connections of SUCCESS) and now you are ready to face head-on the challenges that pursuing your SUCCESS will bring.

To maintain your efforts and keep you moving forward to your goals, you must constantly maintain a drive to be tenacious. In this regard, don't settle when an obstacle or barrier stands in your way. Always find ways to resolve any problem or issue you face. Remember every situation you face has a solution; you just need to work at finding it.

One approach that has worked for me for many years is to always have a 'Plan B' in any situation I approach. This simply means, always think through alternatives prior to the steps you take, and be prepared to move in a new direction if your first steps don't work out as originally planned. This will help you to always be moving forward and being the "tenacious" person that you need to be, to achieve the SUCCESS-filled life you want for yourself.

Now you have the knowledge, and I believe you have the will within you to succeed. The next step is truly up to you. No one can do it for you. You must decide to do it for yourself.

Starting today, to have the SUCCESS-filled life you want, you must ACT.

About Myles

Myles Miller is the CEO and Founder of LeadUP (www.leadup.biz)
LearningBreaks (www.learningbreaks.com)
SUCCESSHQ (www.successhq.net)

In January 2009, Myles started his first company, LeadUP, focused on providing customized training solutions to companies and individuals that will take them to new levels of success.

Other companies followed and his efforts, along with those he has partnered with, continued to expand their market impact beyond local and regional companies to becoming an internationally competitive training and professional development company.

Each of his training companies was created with the foundational ideal to offer a variety of customized training, educational and speaking opportunities to professionals and their companies that need to gain new and greater expertise in Project and Program Management, Business Analysis, Leadership Development and Team Building, Decision-Making, Critical Thinking, Problem-solving and much more.

During his career, Myles has influenced and impacted tens of thousands of people through his speaking and training efforts. His leadership and guidance has led corporations and non-profit organizations to new heights and enhanced abilities.

One life philosophy that Myles has tried each day to live out is to impact one life in a way that will last a lifetime. He puts this at the top of his To-Do list for each day, and through a variety of methods he takes steps to cross this item off this same list daily.

Myles has 30 years of experience in the project management field, across multiple industries including retail, defense, hospitality and the state and federal government. During his varied career, he has led projects ranging in budgetary size from $100K to $500B. His team leadership has impacted national and international companies, as well as governments and non-profit organizations of all sizes from 100 to over 10,000 team members.

CHAPTER 19

STAND OUT AND BREAK OUT!
HOW TO GO AGAINST THE GRAIN WITH STORYSELLING

BY NICK NANTON & JW DICKS

Samuel Joseph Wurzelbacher, recently divorced, found himself at a crossroads. He had decided to leave his telecommunications job to return to his roots as a plumber, a trade he had learned during his years in the Air Force. He thought the career move would help him spend more time with his son. But there was a bigger potential career move looming down his street that he never saw coming.

He was playing football with his boy in his front yard on October 12, 2008, when he saw then-Senator Barack Obama, three days before the final presidential debate with John McCain, campaigning down the block. So Wurzelbacher, a conservative, strolled down to where the event was taking place. There, he directed a question at Obama about his tax plan – and commented that he thought it might threaten "the American dream." After a brief discussion, Obama wrapped up his response by saying, "…I think when you spread the wealth around, it's good for everybody."

Suddenly, other prominent conservatives were using Obama's answer to attack him for advocating wealth distribution and what they considered to be socialism – and they lionized Wurzelbacher for putting Obama on the spot.

Just as suddenly, Wurzelbacher was given a new media-driven name – "Joe the Plumber." Not only that, but three days later, Joe the Plumber became a prime subject of the third presidential debate, with McCain mentioning him repeatedly throughout the night and Obama responding by talking directly at the camera as if he was speaking directly to Wurzelbacher. Yes, within 72 hours, the guy who had been just playing football with his kid was now being addressed by name by the President of the United States.

Wurzelbacher couldn't believe his newfound fame. He appeared on *Good Morning, America, the CBS Evening News with Katie Couric* and *Fox News*. Retelling his story became one of John McCain's main campaign strategies in the closing weeks; an ad was created by the Republican Party featuring other different small business people looking into the camera and saying, "I'm Joe the Plumber."

McCain might have lost the election, but Wurzelbacher suddenly became a winner. He wrote a book, he became a motivational speaker, and he was hired to appear in commercials. And, in 2012, he came full circle, as Joe the Plumber went from campaign prop to candidate and won the Republican primary for Ohio's 9th District Congressional seat and went on to challenge the Democratic candidate, Marcy Kaptur.

HOW STORYSELLING CHANGES LIVES

That October day just down the road from his house, Wurzelbacher literally stumbled into one of the most incredible StorySelling situations ever; he instantly became the perfect "working class guy" symbol for the Republican Party and was used to create a new narrative for McCain. Because he went "against the grain" to create a StorySelling scenario that caught fire with a certain section of the public, he became a star.

In this chapter, we're going to set the stage for the StorySelling that could make you a star in your field in equally powerful ways. We're going to talk about the four key factors you need to have in place to StorySell effectively – and also about what you need to consider before you implement your StorySelling methods.

In StorySelling, as in many things in life, the first steps are often the most critical ones – and we want to make sure you get off on the right foot.

As we just mentioned, there are four key factors that, when combined, create the perfect climate for StorySelling success. They are:

1. Simplicity

How many stories do we hear in a day? How much information do we end up taking in? The answer to both of those questions is the same: a scary crazy amount. That means if your story isn't simple and easy to grasp, most of us, unless we're already intensely interested in the story, aren't going to hang on to it. Our lives are too busy and our minds too cluttered to take in something that's not directly relevant to what we're dealing with at the moment.

2. Authenticity

We are also bombarded with marketing campaigns night and day – and most of us can smell a sales pitch a mile off. If your story only seems like an effort to get your audience to buy – or, even worse, if it doesn't have the ring of truth – no one is going to take it seriously. The only exception is if that audience has already heavily bought into your StorySelling and feels the need to defend it, even in the face of obvious falsehoods.

3. Visibility

Obviously, the public, or, at the very least, your target audience, has to have access to the story you want to tell. There are a lot of channels you can utilize to deliver your narrative. The point is, you can't expect your potential leads to come to you, you have to find a viable way to bring your story to them.

4. Relevancy

It also has to be a story that people want to hear. Again, we have so many people out there trying to sell us their stories that we block out as many as we can, just to keep our sanity. That means your narrative must be one that your audience is predisposed to hear for one reason or another – and that reason should be a powerful one.

Let's return to the story of Joe the Plumber – and review how these factors came into play for Wurzelbacher.

We'll start with *Simplicity* – because this scenario had it in spades. The situation was easy to grasp and instantly arresting: some guy goes up and directly engages one of the two candidates for President of the United States. Not only that, but he gets that candidate to say something that the opposition can immediately leverage against him. The moment was brief, easily replayable across all media channels, and it captured everyone's attention as a real "David and Goliath" moment, in spite of one's political leanings.

The only thing threatening that Simplicity? Well, "Wurzelbacher" is not the simplest name in the world – but that small problem got solved when he was quickly renamed Joe the Plumber, a very memorable moniker, by everyone in the media. What could be simpler – or easier to remember? What better captured his "Average Joe" status?

Authenticity was also present and accounted for. Wurzelbacher wasn't a political plant – he was a dad playing football with his son who took a minute to confront a candidate. He came across as a "real guy" because he was – and he was obviously saying what he personally believed. There wasn't anything phony about the situation or the participants.

Visibility? A no-brainer. The media already had all their cameras on Obama that afternoon and that's how the entire encounter got captured. After the fact, the video of the confrontation between Joe the Plumber and Barack Obama was endlessly shown on cable and network news channels as well as online; anyone following the presidential race couldn't help but see it.

Finally, there's the matter of Relevancy – or, in other words, exactly who wanted to hear the story of Joe the Plumber? If you answered, "The American voting public did," well, that's close, but not quite the right answer – the group that actually wanted a story like this, even desperate for a story like this, was the *Republican Party*. The McCain campaign's poll numbers were bad. They needed some kind of outside boost, and suddenly, they were given the gift of an everyday American articulating their talking points right to Obama's face. McCain's people made sure Joe the Plumber became a media sensation – and both the Right and the Left seized on his story for their own political reasons.

In short, Wurzelbacher fulfilled a *huge and immediate relevant need* – and, because he was authentic, because his story was so simple, and because his story was so visible, the StorySelling of Joe the Plumber took flight.

AVOIDING STORYSELLING PITFALLS

Now, the overwhelming majority of StorySelling cases do not happen this quickly and this powerfully; with Joe the Plumber, there was a perfect convergence of the four key factors we just discussed. It usually takes some time to StorySell a Celebrity Brand. But the four factors we're discussing here still *must* come into play, no matter who the person in question is or at what speed the StorySelling process happens.

But here's an important qualifier – just because those four factors are in place, and just because a StorySelling opportunity does present itself, *doesn't mean you should follow through on it.*

Wurzelbacher's story initially made people feel good about supporting John McCain – he was a "real guy" and voters could identify with him. Because Joe the Plumber became famous so quickly, however, nobody really knew that much about him – including the McCain campaign. And, as we've seen over and over, when the media spotlight shines intensely on someone who's not prepared for scrutiny, every possible imperfection gets magnified.

For example, someone examined the records and found out that Joe the Plumber wasn't legally licensed to be a plumber in Ohio. They also found out he had a lien placed against his house in 2007 because he owed about $1200 in back state taxes.

More damaging for McCain was the fact that Wurzelbacher was far from a seasoned politician – he was still very rough around the edges. For example, he started weighing in on foreign policy and said that "a vote for Obama is a vote for the death of Israel" in an interview with Shepherd Smith on Fox News. When the interview was done, Smith looked directly at the camera and said "Man, it just gets frightening sometimes."

Suddenly, it was clear that Joe the Plumber wasn't going to help McCain expand his base – not if he was going to alienate anchormen even on Fox News. Joe the Plumber, it turned out, was no Average Joe – instead, he had opinions that could possibly alienate more people than they attracted.

Again - *just because you can take advantage of a StorySelling opportunity doesn't mean you should.* When you set into motion a StorySelling narrative that can't sustain itself, you set yourself up for disaster.

The fact is when you do launch StorySelling that the public is ready and willing to buy into, you risk more damage than benefit if that narrative ultimately will defeat itself. Stories that connect with people hit them in a very deep subconscious place - and that subconscious place gets very angry if the story it bought into isn't for real.

StorySelling is a two-edged sword. It's truly the most powerful weapon in anyone's personal branding arsenal – *but you must be careful which narratives you choose*. Not only that, but once you've picked one that will work long term, you must be committed to remaining *consistent* with that narrative.

Consider the following infamous incidents:

- Tom Cruise jumping up and down on Oprah's couch like a lunatic and, a few days later, lecturing Matt Lauer about psychiatry
- Mel Gibson spitting out a drunken anti-Semitic screed at a policeman
- Peewee Herman getting busted in a porn theatre

All of those moments substantially damaged these stars' careers, because they publicly and severely contradicted their StorySelling narratives. Suddenly, without much warning, Cruise wasn't the cool in-control guy, Gibson wasn't the happy-go-lucky action star, and Peewee was no longer suitable for children. And since their fans had invested so much into those narratives, they felt doubly betrayed when these unpleasant occurrences were publicized by the media.

WHEN NEGATIVES DON'T MATTER

Of course, StorySelling contradictions don't have to be fatal – it really depends on how much credit you have in the StorySelling bank, so to speak.

For example, here are three historical figures whose StorySelling continues to this day, even though they're no longer with us:

- **Mother Teresa** – the nun who traveled all over the globe to help the neediest people in the most poverty-stricken areas of the world.

- **Abraham Lincoln** – the American President who saved the Union, freed the slaves, and paid the ultimate price.

- **Gandhi** – the Indian leader who led his people to independence through non-violent means.

The above names conjure up strong, straightforward narratives that are simple, authentic, and still relevant, because these three people went beyond the call of duty to deal with issues that still haunt us today. They also remain highly visible through movies, books, television documentaries and school courses. They not only represent the four key factors of StorySelling in very powerful ways, they also represent the best of humanity. They make the overwhelming majority of us feel good about being human beings; we want to believe in their stories.

Of course, if you examined their actual lives a little more closely, you would find the usual human contradictions and complexities that all of us share. For example, did you know…

- Mother Teresa's orphanages were investigated for abuse and neglect?[1]

- Lincoln's attitudes towards race were so confused (as anyone's in the 1800's would be) that one prominent 1960's historian called him a "white supremacist?"[2]

- Gandhi in his later years slept naked with his grandniece to test his willpower (a test we hoped he passed!)?[3]

Now, all of the above facts are true – but these peoples' legends and good deeds are so powerful that a few potentially scandalous pieces of trivia can't do them much harm.

But…you don't have to be Abraham Lincoln to keep your image a positive one.

---

1 "Sins of the Missions," The Guardian, October 14th, 1996
2 Bennett Jr., Leronne, Forced Into Glory: Abraham Lincoln's White Dream, pp.35 -42, (2000) Johnson Publishing Company
3 Parekh, Bhikhu C., Colonialism, Tradition and Reform: An Analysis of Gandhi's Political Discourse, (1999) Sage Publishers

For instance, you probably know the story of Jared, the guy who lost a ton of weight just eating Subway sandwiches. It was the chain's most popular campaign – as well as an excellent example of StorySelling success. Well, ten years into his run as a Subway spokesman, he ended up gaining some of that weight back. There were even a few ads where Jared's waistline was disguised by big bulky coats.

Subway actually turned this into a positive – as they had him train for the New York Marathon, which gave them an entirely new narrative to StorySell with their sandwich star and also guaranteed that he would again be svelte and commercial-ready.

Subway could get away with all that just because it had been a decade since Jared had signed on – that was more than enough time to prove his weight loss story had been for real. People are willing to deal with a lapse or contradiction in a StorySelling narrative as long as it's not too severe and it's addressed in a positive way.

Just like with any other powerful force, StorySelling is awesome to use – as long as you can maintain some control over it. When you implement it correctly, it goes "against the grain" of conventional marketing – and can suddenly transform you into a breakout star in your area of expertise!

About Nick

An Emmy-Award-Winning Director and Producer, Nick Nanton, Esq. is known as the Top Agent to Celebrity Experts around the world for his role in developing and marketing business and professional experts through personal branding, media, marketing and PR. Nick is recognized as the nation's leading expert on personal branding as Fast Company Magazine's Expert Blogger on the subject and lectures regularly on the topic at major universities around the world. His book *Celebrity Branding You®*, while an easy and informative read, has also been used as a text book at the University level.

The CEO and Chief StoryTeller at The Dicks + Nanton Celebrity Branding Agency, an international agency with more than 1800 clients in 33 countries, Nick is an award-winning director, producer and songwriter who has worked on everything from large scale events to television shows – with the likes of Steve Forbes, Brian Tracy, Jack Canfield (*The Secret*, Creator of the *Chicken Soup for the Soul* Series), Michael E. Gerber, Tom Hopkins, Dan Kennedy and many more.

Nick is recognized as one of the top thought-leaders in the business world and has co-authored 26 best-selling books alongside Brian Tracy, Jack Canfield, Dan Kennedy, Dr. Ivan Misner (Founder of BNI), Jay Conrad Levinson (Author of the Guerilla Marketing Series), Super Agent Leigh Steinberg and many others, including the breakthrough hit *Celebrity Branding You!®*.

Nick has led the marketing and PR campaigns that have driven more than 1000 authors to Best-Seller status. Nick has been seen in *USA Today, The Wall St. Journal, Newsweek, BusinessWeek, Inc. Magazine, The New York Times, Entrepreneur® Magazine, Forbes*, FastCompany.com. and has appeared on ABC, NBC, CBS, and FOX television affiliates around the country, as well as CNN, FOX News, CNBC, and MSNBC from coast to coast.

Nick is a member of the Florida Bar, holds a JD from the University Of Florida Levin College Of Law, as well as a BSBA in Finance from the University of Florida's Warrington College of Business. Nick is a voting member of The National Academy of Recording Arts & Sciences (NARAS, Home to The GRAMMYs), a member of The National Academy of Television Arts & Sciences (Home to the Emmy Awards), co-founder of the National Academy of Best-Selling Authors, a 16-time Telly Award winner, and spends his spare time working with Young Life, Downtown Credo Orlando, Entrepreneurs International and rooting for the Florida Gators with his wife Kristina, and their three children, Brock, Bowen and Addison.

About JW

JW Dicks, Esq., is America's foremost authority on using personal branding for business development. He has created some of the most successful brand and marketing campaigns for business and professional clients to make them the credible celebrity experts in their field and build multi-million dollar businesses using their recognized status.

JW Dicks has started, bought, built, and sold a large number of businesses over his 39-year career and developed a loyal international following as a business attorney, author, speaker, consultant, and business experts' coach. He not only practices what he preaches by using his strategies to build his own businesses, he also applies those same concepts to help clients grow their business or professional practice the ways he does.

JW has been extensively quoted in such national media as *USA Today,* the *Wall Street Journal, Newsweek, Inc.,* Forbes.com, CNBC.com, and *Fortune Small Business.* His television appearances include ABC, NBC, CBS and FOX affiliate stations around the country. He is the resident branding expert for *Fast Company's* internationally syndicated blog and is the publisher of *Celebrity Expert Insider,* a monthly newsletter targeting business and brand building strategies.

JW has written over 22 books, including numerous best-sellers, and has been inducted into the National Academy of Best-Selling Authors. JW is married to Linda, his wife of 39 years, and they have two daughters, two granddaughters and two Yorkies. JW is a 6th generation Floridian and splits his time between his home in Orlando and beach house on the Florida west coast.

CHAPTER 20

SUCCESS STARTS EARLY WITH MINDSET

BY RICK APPELT

Do you remember your high school days when a counselor in the school office tried to help you find a possible career path? How about graduation day when all your relatives showed up and each one asked you what you were going to do with your life?

Do you remember when you were in college and a counselor tried to help you complete all your coursework and then pushed you to apply for a position at specific companies? At least by that time you had chosen a specific major in which you were interested. Then you woke up to find you still had two main fears at that point: would you get a good job, and the sudden realization that from now, life on your own really just began.

So where did all these people with advice go once you entered the workforce? Did you ever wonder where that workforce counselor was when you were in the early stages of your career? Would you even have listened at that point in your life? One of the greatest gifts we receive from seeking knowledge is learning from experience. But how do you learn when you have no experience? You learn from others that have been there, done that, and are willing to share their experiences with you. You have to be willing to listen, take advice, and endure constructive criticism along the way. How many times in your life have you heard the phrase, "If I only knew then what I know now." It is a simple yet powerful sentence. I believe most people would take their knowledge of life at 40 and go relive their twenties. I know I would.

Having that experience and being able to share it with others is a rewarding feeling. During my professional career I had the opportunity to visit college campuses to recruit college seniors for potential employment. I did more than simply recruit for my company when I went to speak to these seniors that were soon to enter the workforce. I took knowledge that I received from the workforce and from life experiences and shared it with these young minds that were overflowing with book smarts. I gave them something that I wish someone had given me when I first entered the workforce – direction…direction that included a pathway to success that starts when you first enter the workforce.

This path involves not just young college students, but anyone entering or re-entering the workforce at any age. The earlier one begins this approach, however, the sooner in life one can reach career goals and financial success. It is the initial mindset of people entering the workforce that creates this success. It is this success that allows one to achieve not only a level of self-fulfillment within the workforce, but also financial freedom. This financial freedom allows one to: retire early, retire wealthy, start a new business, overcome hardships, or prepare for lean economic times. This chapter outlines five fundamental steps to follow when entering the workforce to help one achieve these goals.

1. RESIST DEBT

One of the most popular phrases I hear ringing from the voices of college seniors in interviews is, "I can't wait to finally graduate so I can buy ----." You can fill in the blanks with most anything people feel they deserve as a reward: a new car, boat, etc. This is the single most tempting mistake people can make when entering the workforce. Do not reward yourself for one accomplishment by burying yourself in debt before you start working on your next accomplishment. When you take a new job and then immediately sink yourself into debt, you risk becoming controlled by your job.

One of the greatest feelings you will ever welcome in your career is the ability to walk away at any point. You cannot do that if you are worried about paying your bills on a daily basis. Step number one on your path to success is to resist debt. Never get yourself into a situation of debt where you cannot walk away from your job if you completely disagree with your boss, the corporate culture or a violation of your personal principles, morals, or values. If this happens to you and you cannot walk away because you will be unable to pay your bills, you are stuck. When you can go to work and not fear for your job, it is a liberating experience that allows you a sense of self-fulfillment in your career and decision-making.

Before you started your new career, especially if you were in high school or college, you probably learned to live a simple life and make sacrifices. If you are starting your career over, you might have lost your job at some point or you went back to school to learn a new career, but you also learned to make sacrifices and live more modestly. Keep that mindset and continue to live simply and modestly. If you cannot pay cash for something and have to charge it, maybe you really do not need it. Do not get trapped by a lavish lifestyle, or become overtaken by material possessions and the desire to outspend your neighbors. Keep life simple and resist debt.

2. KNOW YOUR BUSINESS

Entering or re-entering the workforce, relying on your education, and showing up to work to put in your time is not enough to excel in your career. At this point in your working career you lack the one thing that others in your field already have – experience. From a manager's viewpoint it is hard to place a value on experience. One may overcome the lack of experience with a combination of education, determination and natural talent. The easiest way to overcome the lack of experience is to *know your business*.

Do not be intimidated by others in your field. Remember that everyone had a first day of work just like you. They too had to learn the business and gain their experience over time. Research your field, know how others succeeded, learn all the new technologies and advancements in your field and always keep learning. Remember that what you learned in 1993 may not apply in 2013 and the only way to continue moving forward is to continue learning.

Let me share a real example of fundamental step number two – knowing your business. As president of a large commercial construction company, I had to hire young project managers out of school to manage new construction projects. These young people were educated but had no field experience. To know the business they had to know their project and their project bible consisted of the contract, the blueprints, and the project specifications. Studying all three of those, taking direction from the main office, along with guidance from the field crew, the young project managers succeeded at these projects. They were usually intimidated in the beginning by elders with more experience, but as long as they knew everything in those documents, they could not be easily manipulated.

So learn your business and learn how your role impacts your company. Also learn how your position relates to other departments, what your next level of promotion involves, and how you plan to get there. Develop a roadmap to success within your particular business. If it involves more education, see if work will pay for your training, your continuing education, or even your master's degree or doctorate. Remember, that in the workforce, if you are not learning, you are falling behind.

3. KNOW WHEN TO SAY NO

The third fundamental step on the path to success is knowing when to say no and when not to say no. Earlier we discussed the ability to say no when it comes to burdening one's self with debt. This decision then affects the ability to say no when one is confronted with a moral or political dilemma within the workplace. Never compromise your personal principles within the workplace. You will always maintain a level of self-fulfillment and also gain respect from peers for standing up for the ideals in which you believe.

Never say no to a difficult project. In fact, ask for the hardest project at work; the project that nobody else wants. Ask for the high-profile project; the project that has others scared for fear of failing in front of their peers. Do this, work hard and take all the required measures for your success on this project. When you succeed then you become the go-to person. You become the person in the office that superiors look to for success. You have to remember that when you succeed, your superiors also succeed and the business succeeds. When the business succeeds there is more of an opportunity for superiors to share the wealth. Be successful and be the first in line to deserve a bonus. Your successful completion on the difficult project usually places you at the front of the list for the next project or even promotion. You also benefit from placing your name at the bottom of the list if the company is faced with the unfortunate task of cutting costs, including job reductions and lay-offs.

Do not sit and wait for opportunities to happen. Be proactive and make your opportunities happen. If you sit and wait on others, it could take an entire career for something spectacular to happen. Strive to be the best at what you do and everyday always do your best. You cannot ask anymore from yourself. When you give 100%, you will not have any regrets.

4. TRAVEL

If you take heed to step one above and resist debt and continue to live a simple life when entering the workforce, then you will be in a better position to accept the challenge of step four to your success – travel. This is another time in your early career when you should eliminate the word no. Similar to the earlier example above of taking on the hardest project, stay flexible enough to travel when the company need arises. Be the person that can leave town to make a sale, close a deal, or go work on a project. You will once again put yourself in a position of trust and accountability for your superiors. You will end up being the person they call on first again the next time. That is a position of success and of leverage.

Let work pay for you to see the world. Travel usually means extra pay for the burden and inconvenience to your personal life. Your expenses are covered when travelling and typically you are not dipping into your own pockets for meals and other items that you would normally pay for while at home. You will probably be able to save more of your normal pay than usual.

Experience other cities, other countries and other cultures, if possible. See the world before your journey to success makes your life busier and a little more complicated. I can say personally that I have seen more countries, cities, and cultures through my professional career at this point than through my personal travels and vacations. The trips have typically been for longer durations and have allowed me to experience all a city has to offer during that time. I enjoyed meeting a diversity of people, experiencing different cultures, experimenting with different foods, visiting all the local landmarks, and all while being paid to do so. If I was to never go back to these same cities again for work, I would choose another destination for vacation to see and experience even more of the world.

5. MONEY MINDSET

One of the hardest topics to discuss with family, friends, spouses, children and especially with new people entering the workforce at any level is money. It is the tool with which we pay our rent or mortgage, buy our food and gas, and everything else in life from basic needs to our personal desires. Money is the driving force behind our job, our profession, our career and eventually our retirement. It is time to introduce the most controversial step on the path to success – your money mindset.

From high school to college most people have an approximate figure in mind when they discuss annual salaries regarding a particular profession. Disregarding bonuses, commissions, and sweat equity in business, most professions have a definitive range of a salary from the low end to the high end. Unless you are a professional ball player, movie star or something else totally out of the ordinary, your annual salary is not going to set you apart from most other people.

The hardest mindset to recondition in people in the workforce is that of pay and salaries. Let me tell you now that it is not your salary that is going to make you financially more successful than others. It goes well beyond the annual base salary. I am personally a firm believer in getting paid for performance. Over-achievers and under-achievers should be justly compensated for their personal success in relationship to the success of the business. Financial success that sets us apart from others occurs in performance bonuses, commissions, and incentives such as stock options and equity shares in the business. The financial freedom that sets us apart from others is how we save and invest those monies and ultimately watch our money work for us. So do not place a major emphasis on an annual salary and raises and instead look at companies that reward individuals based on performance. Look for these reward incentives mentioned above in an employer and question the availability of a 401k plan also and fund it with maximum amounts allowed. When you narrow the field of potential employers, do not hesitate to research their incentive programs and negotiate terms up front.

CONCLUSION

The direct path to success in your career starts with the initial mindset when entering the workforce. Resist the temptation to incur debt and keep life simple. Learn and know your business, develop a roadmap and always continue learning while working. Know when to say no to debt, unethical practices and issues that confront your personal and moral principles. Seek the most difficult and high-profile projects and opportunities within the organization. Give 100% to the success of these challenges and continue to succeed at every level. Never pass up an opportunity to travel and to become the person the company goes to when they need a leader. Check your money mindset and know that salary is simply a monetary base and that rewards and incentives based on excellent performance will increase your ability to save and invest.

After difficult economic times over the past few years in this country, one can only learn a valuable lesson to save more and spend less. In a nutshell: save early, perform higher, produce more, and invest wisely. This path will bring self-fulfillment in one's career and financial success that will allow one to retire at an earlier age, retire with more money than the average person, and have a resource to tap into during lean economic times or in the event of an unforeseen tragedy.

About Rick

Rick L. Appelt is currently an author, professional consultant, speaker and mentor. Holding masters degrees in both Construction Management & Technology and Project Management, he has been a leader in the large construction industry ranging in scope from semiconductor, industrial, manufacturing, commercial, government, hospitality, airport, civil and transportation industries. During his career he was known as a clean room guru building semiconductor and biotech clean room facilities around the world for such high-tech companies as Motorola, Intel, Texas Instruments, Samsung and many others.

During his career, Rick spent rewarding time as a university speaker and a college recruiter. He continues to mentor young college graduates entering the workforce.

Opportunities in private business through operations as president and business owner have afforded Rick the opportunity to give back. His successful journey now allows him to do speaking engagements, mentoring and training, construction consulting, professional contracting, and also writing. He trains managers and also mentors entrepreneurs for improved operations in small business.

To learn more about Rick Appelt and opportunities for consulting, speaking, contracting, training, mentoring, and other writing, please visit his website at: www. RickAppelt.com.

www.RickAppelt.com

CHAPTER 21

SUCCESS LEAVES CLUES: WHERE AND HOW TO FIND IT

BY BRENDA LEE

I have only been on one job interview in my life. Every position that I have held I got because someone knew that I needed a job and offered me a position. Ever since I was very young, growing up in a less than desirable environment in the Washington, D.C. area, I have always worked at least two jobs. As the eldest of nine children in a home without a dad around, I have worked two jobs most of my life to help my mother out. I learned in my close-knit family, where we all helped each other out, that a person has to play the hand they are dealt and that where you grow up, or live, or your circumstances does not determine who or what you can be. I also learned a work ethic that has been a double-edged sword getting me jobs when I needed them, but alternately, perhaps keeping me from exploring some opportunities along the way.

Sometimes push has to come to shove before we leave a comfort zone to follow a dream. In 2011 on the eve of my two-week vacation from my "good job," I received a call that my mother had a massive stroke and the next day she had another that further ravaged her body, this one disabling her left side. What followed was quadruple by-pass surgery to relieve the blockages that were the root cause of her strokes and a four-month long recovery at two different facilities. As the eldest sibling and the one with the fewest family conflicts to keep me from the hospital, I was delegated to spend the bulk of those four months at the hospital with my mother. So much for my planned vacation, and quickly, so much for the hours of paid leave that I had accummulated through hard work and rarely being sick myself, as I used those hours to take care of my mother.

If necessity is the mother of invention, my mother's necessity in having someone to attend her needs caused me to invent a new vision for my own life. Navigating through hurdles and negotiating with management to secure a schedule conducive to consistently managing my mother's care left me certain that there must be a better way and determined that I would find it. While four months of juggling my work schedule with my employer illuminated my need for a schedule that I controlled, it also led me to some quiet, reflective and creative time away from my daily job – where I could really consider my goals for my future. A new vision emerged, a lighthouse to a new life, my new life. At every step along my new path, this lighthouse guided me and kept me from venturing toward the rocks—which is exactly what I wish to do for the reader. Whether necessity, or sheer boredom, propels you to seek a new path, you must change your course or you shall never arrive.

CHANGE YOUR COURSE

The moment when the realization dawned that I needed greater control over my time and my income, a co-worker of mine approached me with a network marketing opportunity. I asked him to give me a month to consider the option. When faced with any new business proposition, due diligence is required to thoroughly vet the business, its principles and the people involved in that organization. During that month, I selected a business partner to mentor me in the company and embark on a new course to financial freedom. I attended a meeting where a 24-year-old man with no college degree spoke about his success and the freedom of never having to work another day in his life, should he choose to do so. Another couple spoke, he as a former metro driver and she a former government worker, who had become millionaires via the business opportunity I was considering. I looked around the room and figured, "why not me?"

SUCCESS LEAVES CLUES

If blessed with an opportunity, do not miss out because of fear. Look at the success rate of the people doing what you are considering doing. Success leaves clues. You can find much of the information you need from the comfort of your own home via the internet. We are naturally skeptical about business opportunities that seem too good to be true; however, sometimes opportunity only knocks once. Do your due diligence. Look for a company where the successful people are accessible to you. When presented with a marketing plan, sales figures or income levels, investigate them. Verify everything you can.

When you are ready to dive into your new opportunity, don't hold back. Allow the new experience to change you. If you hold onto your old mindset, you might as well hold onto your old job, old life and old level of success as well. Additionally, you might miss the clues to your success if you look at a potential opportunity with the same set of eyes and thought processes you used before. By expanding my thinking within this new network marketing company, I have become a better leader as I mentor other new business people.

FIND YOURSELF A MENTOR (OR TWO)

Even a leader who is mentoring others needs his own mentor. Your mentor will do more for you than cheer you on. Seek a mentor who has done what you want to do. If you want to write a book, find someone who has written a book—or several—to mentor you. The person who has walked a similar path can assist you in recognizing the stones or boulders in the road you are traveling.

Mentors are available all over. When I began my new career, I knew that I needed a mentor, but I was still working my day job as I built my business. I despaired of having time to consult with a mentor in the few free hours I had after work and caring for my mother. Fortunately, mentors are available through books, videos and on the internet via everything from webinars to online chats to daily motivational advice on Facebook. If you seek a mentor, you can find one to meet your needs and your schedule. Choose your mentors wisely. The perfect mentors are the people who are hugely successful themselves and whose stories inspire you—think Warren Buffet, Bill Gates or John C. Maxwell. If you are unsure about finding a mentor or about your new opportunity in general, it may be time to consider how badly you really want a new life.

HOW BADLY DO YOU WANT IT?

Whether or not you achieve something correlates directly to how badly you want it. When the Verizon Center was preparing to open, a friend and I heard there were some good jobs available there. We decided to attend an employment event for the venue. We went on our lunch break, which was only an hour, and arrived to a line of thousands seeking the same jobs with only a half-hour left before we needed to return to the office for our day jobs. Seeing the line, my friend quickly passed on the opportunity. I maneuvered my way to the front of the line—flashing my government badge all the way--as though I had the authority to clear the line. When I reached the front, the interviewers asked me why they should interview me ahead of all the people waiting in line. I replied that they were going to give the job to me anyway. I got the job.

If we are not fighting for something, we don't want it badly enough. The "why" isn't strong enough. The "why" is the reason a person builds a business, and the "why" is not money. For most people, money is not a strong enough motivator to push us toward a goal because money is not emotional. Get to the heart of "why" you want to succeed in a new opportunity; is it the freedom of a flexible schedule, or the vision of the luxury lifestyle your additional earnings will bring? Truthfully, most of us don't fight for what we want until we are backed into a corner or beaten down so much that the only option is to fight. Do not wait for fate to back you into a corner. Find your "why" and be proactive instead of reactive. Act like your child's life depends upon your success and light a fire under yourself. Then allow your mentors to be the bellows to fan the flames.

BE IN THE RIGHT PLACE, WITH THE RIGHT MINDSET

Be careful of trying to gain too much knowledge before stepping out to do something. Sometimes we use the excuse that we need to investigate something even when our gut tells us that the decision is right. We don't get what we want because we fail to put ourselves in the right arena. Positioning yourself mentally to succeed, in other words believing that you will not fail ensures that small setbacks are not mistaken for the need to move mountains. When you change your mindset, you change your life. What we think on a continuous basis, we will achieve. We limit ourselves only by our mindset. Wealth is one area in which our mindset tends to be self-limiting.

WEALTH MINDSET

It goes against the grain to be wealthy. Most of us never learned that we could be wealthy or have money in abundance. I was raised in a community in which having a solid job with a guaranteed paycheck was the best life for which one could hope. Media portrays the weathly as different from the rest of us and places them on a pedestal revered for their creativity and drive. There is nothing to stop any one of us from acquiring the same creativity and drive, and thus earning the same wealth.

Bear in mind that the laws of attraction apply: we attract what we produce. Negativity repels people, especially the right ones. Our thoughts manifest themselves in our whole being, therefore, others can "see" your positive success or negative failure in the manner you carry yourself. Watch your thoughts; they become your actions.

ORGANIZATION

While keeping your negative thoughts in check, organize your thoughts as well. A person cannot expect to build an inspiring, new empire on the rubble of yesterday's disorganization. Clean up and organize your world. If you are not by nature an organized individual, get there. Organize your thoughts by writing them down. I have learned that to achieve rapid power and wealth, you need to have control over everything that moves or changes in your life. Organization is imperative when beginning a new venture, as it will help you to keep on track. Properly managing your family, health, spiritual life, financial life and business life allows the clarity needed to succeed.

Organization leaves room for your new vision. You cannot win the race when you are swimming against a current of chaos.

A NEW JOURNEY REQUIRES A NEW VISION

If you are with any company and you do not know what your next step to advancement is, you are with the wrong company. Determine your needs. Do you want to: Change careers? Write a book? Run your own company? How much income do you require? Do you want or need more flexible work hours? Do you desire to work in an office or work from home? Take the time to map out your ideal situation. Your needs and your family's needs guide your vision. Determine what you want to do and put it on paper. Create a plan for yourself. When you have your plan, seek a support system to help you stay on task as you implement your plan. Friends and supporters are the walking stick to lean on during your journey; they will help you stay the course.

While friends and family offer support, only your inner strength can move one foot in front of the other for you. Creativity comes strongest when you are self-sufficient and in charge of your own journey. Marcel Proust said "We don't receive wisdom; we must discover it for ourselves after a journey that no one can take for us or spare us." Invest in yourself. Learn something new for yourself or about yourself everyday. You have the strength inside you right now to create the life you want for the very reasons you want it. Success leaves clues; follow the trail to your own success, wealth and happiness.

About Brenda

Brenda Lee is one of nine children raised in Washington, D.C. where she still resides. The type who is rarely idle, Brenda has always worked at least two jobs. Her varied and successful career includes many leadership roles, but the one of which she is proudest is her latest adventure as entrepreneur. Through the tutelage of such powerhouses as John C. Maxwell and Brian Tracy, Brenda found a passion for leading others to success.

Brenda takes her mission seriously, perfecting the necessary steps to assess one's goals and take control of one's life. She happily mentors others toward higher aspirations and achievement of goals greater than they have ever imagined for themselves. Brenda believes that "success leaves clues" and teaches others to follow the trail to personal success.

When Brenda is not building her business, she enjoys spending time with her large extended family and caring for her mother.

To learn more about Brenda Lee, email her at: leej.lee74@gmail.com

CHAPTER 22

STOP AND FOCUS

BY ANDREA REAKA, PhD

Confucius say, *"The man who chases two rabbits catches neither."*

Now imagine trying to catch five at the same time. Chaos, right? But that's what most people do, all the time. If you want to change that, read on. Now don't get me wrong. Multi-tasking is not all bad. In fact, I spend part of my work day purposefully multi-tasking, but I also spend part of the day really focusing on important projects.

I have very limited time, which has helped me form the habit of being able to focus. But, this wasn't easy to learn how to do. When I was in graduate school, I was dreading my qualifying exam. I knew what I needed to study, and it was somewhat overwhelming due to the volume of information that I needed to know. I knew the first thing I needed to figure out was how long I thought it would take me. I had examined how people used their time and I realized that for the really important things, people clear their schedule. I had never done that before, but I decided that since this test may determine the course of the rest of my life, it probably qualified as something that I could clear my schedule for. People would have to understand that I just wouldn't be available.

People have a hard time hearing "No" and I have a hard time telling them. But I kept thinking about what my mother always told me, "You can be anything you want to be, as long as you want it bad enough." I had never really understood this. But, when I was planning out how to study for my exam, I realized that this is what she was talking about. This was important enough to me that I would actually turn people's requests for my time away. In some ways, it was about figuring out my priorities, and this was number one. Once I really figured that out, it was easy to schedule my time.

One month before the exam, I spent a week organizing my files of information, notes, textbooks, and library access. I moved appointments, rescheduled meetings, and cleared my calendar. I actually told some people that I was going out of town. Then, I spent the next three weeks doing nothing but studying and focusing on the information for that exam.

The first day I had a lot of trouble sitting all day, so I paced around my apartment reading through my books and notes. I put my cell phone out of reach and on silent mode. I knew that this was the most important thing in my life right now. I had to focus on it. I would check my phone every two hours or so as I finished a section, using it as a reward for finishing another step. I put on some music, but found that I couldn't listen to music with words in it, because I would start to sing along and not understand what I was reading. But, having no music put me to sleep. By day two, I found that classical music with a quick beat kept me energized and able to focus.

My next hurdle to overcome was those pesky little tasks that popped into my head: shelves needed dusting, floors needed cleaning, laundry needed to be done. Thus, my To Do list was born. I kept a notepad close to me so that I could jot down those tasks that kept calling me. I found that once I wrote them down, they would exit my mind and I no longer thought about them. In the evenings, once I had accomplished my goals for that day, I would allow myself to do one or two mindless tasks on my To Do list. (Vacuuming and dusting became a reward for me!) As I continued to do this day after day, I got better at it. My body and my brain got used to being able to set aside daily distractions and focus for hours at a time.

At the end of the three weeks, I had taken in a lot of information and solidly exercised my ability to focus. When I went in to sit for the four-hour exam, I wondered if I would be able to sit for that long, but remembered that I had been doing that for 3 weeks. The exam was tough, but when I got the letter two weeks later saying I had passed my qualifying exam and was now a candidate for the doctoral program, I could not have been more relieved and happy. My sacrifice was worth it.

After 20 years, I don't remember a lot of the information that I learned for my exam, but the lesson I learned on how to focus will stay with me for the rest of my life.

Now, I run a business and my day gets split up. Like most jobs, I need to answer the phone when it rings and send email messages promptly to prospective clients. I can't imagine my day without multi-tasking. It's a necessary skill that I have learned over the years to help manage not only my work, but also my family's day-to-day activities. I cook supper while helping my kids with homework and returning texts about sharing rides to practices, all while having the television on in the background. I am aware that each of these tasks are not getting my full attention and certainly are more prone to mishaps. On the other hand, I am also aware that there are some tasks that require my full attention. For example, writing this is something that requires my full attention and I know I cannot do another task simultaneously.

When I go in to work in the morning, I spend a little time checking email and checking my phone messages, but only to see if there are urgent problems. The non-urgent messages get written down on my To-Do list to address later. I keep a pad of paper next to my work area so that I write down tasks to do that pop into my mind. The list also includes things that I need to do that didn't get done the day before. Once they are written on my list, I can put them out of my mind. Then, I get to work. My philosophy follows Brian Tracy's "Eat That Frog" method. I look at my To-Do list and find the thing that I am dreading doing the most. I also consider what will have the greatest impact on my business. For example, should I do marketing or should I do my financial report and pay taxes. All of these tasks are things that I hate doing, so they are equally big, ugly frogs that I need to eat. But getting rid of the frog that will help my business the most can clear up the order that I 'eat the frogs' (or do the tasks).

In the afternoon, when my students start coming in, I can no longer focus on just one task. Parents want to meet with me, appointments need to be rescheduled, my instructors come to me with concerns about students, I need to talk to potential new clients, evaluate students in the classroom, and answer teacher questions. I need to be *available*. I used to try to get "real work" done during this time. But, I realized that is just not possible because then I am not doing something that is very important to my position as owner and Center Director, which is being available to my clients and staff. Being available is the most important thing I need to be doing at that time. I keep my To-Do list close to me to jot down the things that people have asked me to do (and I have promised them that I would). And, I make myself available. I definitely multi-task during this time. But it is deliberate. And when I do have time...I can STOP and Focus.

Amit Sood, M.D. wrote in an article about learning how to focus – (http://www.mayoclinic.com/health/how-to-focus/AN2168): "Many people find it hard to focus, but it is a skill you can develop...Any skill worth having requires practice. Learning to focus is not different." I couldn't agree more. The more time you spend focusing, the easier it will be to do; and, the easier it will be to quickly re-focus when necessary. When I find myself with a little time on my hands (unexpectedly or not), I quickly remember my mantra to STOP and Focus. That is, I need to eliminate distractions that include Screens, Tasks and Obligations, and work on my highest Priorities: STOP and focus. You can too. Here's how:

Step 1 is eliminating all Screens. First of all, put your cell phone on silence and put it in a drawer where you won't even hear it if you get a text message or the vibrations from a phone call. If you are at home, turn off the TV. Don't even leave it on in the background, it still uses up part of your brain to block it out. Instead, play music in the background, but be careful to select something without words. If you are doing work on your computer, leave that screen on, but close all other programs, especially your email so that you are not temped to check them during your STOP and Focus time. Other programs you should close include: the Internet (Facebook), iChat, your calendar, and even your address book. Set an alarm so that you do not even need to look at the clock. Then, you can just put your head down and work until the timer goes off, thinking about nothing else.

Step 2 is to eliminate Tasks. When you sit down to work, inevitably tasks will pop into your mind. So, keep a small notepad close by to jot down those tasks. I have found that if I do not write them down, they do not go away, they only get louder. But, once you do a brain dump, you can let them go to worry about later.

Step 3 is to eliminate Obligations. This can be tough at first, but once you get used to it, you will be surprised how easy it is. Have you ever forgotten your cell phone when you went into a store and then missed a phone call? Did the world end? No, you simply returned the phone call once you got the message. This may have been an inconvenience to the person trying to get ahold of you, but if it was important they will get over it and the job will get done. If you set clear boundaries by letting everyone know what you are doing and when you will be available to get back to them (and do it consistently) people get used to it very quickly. If you have not done this before, it will be hard for people to understand, but hold your ground. Eventually they will understand, especially as they see your productivity increasing.

Step 4 is to evaluate your Priorities. Once you have eliminated distractions, the final step is to focus on the project in front of you. If you have clear priorities, it is easier to see value in the task and focus clearly on it. To really mentally buy into this, you have to believe that it is the most important thing you can be working on right now and worth the time you are spending on it; you have to believe that this project will change your life. Before you begin, think about your goals and evaluate if this project will move you toward them or away from them.

Many people procrastinate so much that they already know how to do this. That is, they have gotten behind and now have had to eliminate all distractions and work solely on a project to get it done, because it now has a deadline looming with major implications if the project does not get done. I always think to myself, "Imagine what you could accomplish if you could harness that power of working at the last minute to beat that deadline." You can harness that power.

Imagine this: You call your spouse on Monday to say that you will be working late to be sure that you get the project done that is due on Friday so you can make it to your son's baseball game on Thursday evening. Then, imagine showing your boss your work on Tuesday so that tweaks can be made to it and it can be finalized by Wednesday. Then they have two days to work on it before they present the project to their client. When you tell your boss you need to leave early on Thursday to go to your son's baseball game, what kind of response do you think you will get?

Try it. It's fun!

In this day and age, time is precious and needs to be protected. You have to carve out time to focus. When you sit down to work, it will help you eliminate distractions and focus to know that this is the most important thing you can be doing with your time right at this moment. You can return those phone calls and e-mails later when you are multi-tasking and generally being available. So, STOP and Focus.

"Concentration can be cultivated. One can learn to exercise will power, discipline one's body and train one's mind."
~ Anil Ambani (Billionaire Businessman)

About Andrea

Andrea Reaka received her Ph.D. in Biomedical Engineering from the University of Illinois at Chicago in 2002. She did a post-doctoral fellowship at Washington University in St. Louis, MO and started a tenure-track position at the newly-founded School of Pharmacy at Southern Illinois University, Edwardsville in 2005. After two years, she quit her position at SIUE and started a Tutoring Center in Edwardsville – where she has impacted the lives of hundreds of kids in Edwardsville and the surrounding areas.

Her goal is to help parents teach their kids focus, motivation, and goal setting so that they can follow their dreams and make the most out of their own lives.

You can follow her blog: EducatingParents.info.

CHAPTER 23

AGAINST THE ODDS

BY CHARLES SIMONS, DDS

Leadership inspires, such leadership can coach one to become a "catalytic converter" by aiding an individual or group to attain their goals of success through a well-defined process or plan based upon their principles and values and driven by their people and processes. The right people, the right strategy, the right exccution, and the life blood of a sound financial base can prioritize, measure, and create a momentum that will propel the business, organization, or cven individual to a level of success and dreams desired. Whether it is a tool-and-die product business, an affordable housing agency, or an orthodontic practice, success is built upon the regimen just described.

I remember my beginning student years that were filled with hesitation, fear, and trepidation. We were told that we would be lucky to start 32-40 cases our first year: i.e. about one/week; that the general practitioners would resent us as specialists; that the public would not afford our services; that we would have to go to our banker to beg; that we should be careful not to invest too much in ourselves and our situation (physical plant, staff, supplies, etc.); that we must be extremely careful of being too confident, and that we should not expect much for the first 3 to 5 years. Rather, that we should go to that glamorous place we wanted to live, "open shop" and have fun! While the last sentence sounded wonderful, it didn't make much 'dollars and cents' sense to me knowing the overpopulation of orthodontists in these areas. The previous advice was not what I had envisioned, nor was it what I had calculated. Yet, "did I dare go against the grain?"

I had studied and worked so hard; what did all this mean? If I were to make $500/case, my wife and I could not survive on $20,000 per year—even in 1970! Did it really mean that my referrers would dislike me; why would they refer; would they refer? If the public could not afford me, would I be doing charity? This was not the way I wanted to do charity! I liked quality, the best of the best, luxury, beauty, ease and happiness. We'd have to not only pinch, but actually squeeze the penny, and not invest much in myself? I wanted to embrace the next phase after the academic process. I was being told I had to be this or to do that. I loved people, and I wanted to straighten teeth and smiles in the most perfect way and in the nicest setting that I could. I didn't have the money for the mansions and the exotic playgrounds. What was I to do? I was not going to make the commitment to live on someone else's (bankers) money by BORROWING! That was a naughty word. Luckily I had not purchased a new car; rather, I had paid for my schooling and saved the extra dollars from my wife's teaching during my schooling.

What was I to do! Wouldn't it be too risky to go "against the grain?" Yet, this was a story of defeat—before I even got started! I didn't like what my mind was perceiving. What kind of an attitude was I going to have? I didn't like this picture. Maybe I preferred my old job of life guarding—but by now after all these years of sitting at a desk studying, I needed to cover up the gut; well, it wasn't that bad, maybe; but it was no longer worthy of exposure, either. Days went by, weeks went by, disappointment and self-doubt were brewing, and depression was setting in.

Suddenly, I realized I had to get straightened out. I had to become a little more strategic, even if it meant "going against the grain." I had to develop a mind-set that would carry me to "the success I was born to be!" Why think any other way? Say it like you want it to be repeated; like you want to believe it! After all, I just might achieve it!

As I began to think about this, I realized that I wanted be surrounded by happy (the right) people; I didn't want to blunder along and not plan on too much—I wanted a plan of action that headed toward what I thought of as success: happy people with growing revenues. I wanted a plan that would profit everyone, be efficient and effective—without needless and useless struggle resulting in exhaustion. But I would need cash—the life- blood of any business or professional practice or service. Would my meager savings be enough?

I would need to prioritize, quantify, and qualify where I was going and what I was doing. Once started I would have to keep the momentum going. The process, and the patterns along with the people (my staff, customers, and everyone with whom I would come into contact as well as myself) would be what would make this happen. I couldn't/wouldn't control others; I could only control myself. I could only "coach" and inspire. I could be a catalyst, "a catalytic converter." Others would have to be conscientious, engaged and step up and take ownership. They would have to be motivated by inspiring leadership to step up and to take ownership for the success of the practice and their/our situation.

I shared my vision with my wife of the possibilities, as well as what my/our mission and action based upon our values would need to be— as I perceived them. We took a deep breath! We took Brian Tracy's "The Phoenix Course" to become inspired in ourselves and our innate capabilities—to believe in ourselves!

I wondered: "Who am I; who are we to think that we can "go against the grain?" Just two small-time people with a little different idea from what we had been taught or from what we had heard and been lead to believe – was the answer. We decided maybe we had better turn to some others for confirmation, affirmation, or even redirection before we would get out there on that limb all by ourselves. So, we turned to consultants for standards and systems, to attorneys for the incorporation and to accountants for correct addition, subtraction, government paper work, and to coaches who would listen – to learn and ask to empower; not to namby-pamby coaches that were there for the big pay check, and to orchestrate the next quarterly meeting for another big pay check; but to a coach that would care and smile with reassurance or raise an eyebrow and say: "Are you sure about that? Would you like to check with your accountant or your attorney?"

Our advisers had the experience, knowledge and expertise to tell us about the numbers and dollars, the articles of incorporation, the systems of wires to straighten the teeth. Our consultants told us about the required number of starts to accomplish our goals and to sustain our venture, (and the new baby on her way). Our coach held us accountable to our plan, and for our actions by asking us those hard questions that we would otherwise have dodged to remain in the comfort zone of naivety.

WOW! Did it work? Well, we arrived in town two months early, set out to meet every general dentist, attended our church functions, searched for an office (wasn't too hard to find as only one became available, and was it small!), bridged a business phone number to our residential phone number (next to which we kept an appointment book in our apartment), and found a teaching job for my wife which permitted her enrollment in the university to finish her master's degree. The small office was just fine for my one dental chair, a bright and happy yellow color. The office had a small reception room, a small lab, a small back office for my paper work and a restroom. I papered the treatment room with a large bright yellow smiling sunflower wall paper and purchased relaxing wicker furniture and green carpet for the reception room where there would be coffee, children's and adult's reading materials, and goodies for our guests. We were ready to entertain and to arrange (…teeth, that is!).

You wouldn't believe the attractive, talented, smiling three ladies I interviewed and hired (receptionist, lab assistant, and chair-side assistant). My wife did the bookkeeping at our residence during the evening after her school day and evening classes while I did the evening meal (snack!) and made my "care calls." We were on our way to 40 starts! But not in the first year, not in the first month; but rather, the day I unlocked the office's front door to say: "Welcome, please come in; we are so glad you are here!" The rhythm and patterns seemed to continue. But were they really sustainable? Big question! So "my" ladies and I met consistently, measured results, prioritized, kept to our simple plan based on our values, vision, and mission statement and worked very continuously with joy and celebration in our hearts. We'd gather at the end of the day and celebrate the little child that came in with a tear in the eye and left with a smile on the face; as well as the adult who would come in with his/her hand over the smile and leave walking a little taller. We'd go home energized by what we had done and how we had done it., knowing that there was more cash in the drawer than when we had started the day (actually, I took the cash to the bank each night, myself!). The next morning we would return to the office for our morning huddle, and renew and review our commitment of ownership by each of us, our values, hopes and dreams for that day's patients and for each other. We had a partnership based upon trust in, and respect for, each other and ultimately, in our patients. It was one grand family. We would come in in the morning enthused and leave in the evening energized and with more cash in the box.

The practice grew, and grew! So did we! Within four years we had patients standing in the hallways and a telephone that couldn't handle all the calls. Then our landlord informed us that he had sold the building and that we would have to vacate within 6 months. Remember, there were no other offices in town.

What were we to do? I didn't want to lose my office location identity of being next to the hospital and just off the two major highways. Across the street was a car dealership, now closed. The property was way over-priced. But it might work. But I didn't have that kind of money! How could I ever make the payments that would be required by borrowing money. Then in a quiet moment I thought: "Tenants! I can do for them what I do for myself, and we, all of us, can make the payments together! Yeah! Celebration! And so we did. Fourteen suites and two buildings, on the most expensive per square foot land ever sold in the city/county. Again, we were "off to the races." Now, I was in the commercial-professional office space rental business, with tenants paying rent and referring patients. Again, I had become a "catalytic converter," but only because of "here's what, so what, now what" attitude and mindset. The people, the plan, the process, and the discipline with the catalyst to inspire a CEO mindset, was the beginning to success. All concerned were conscientious and engaged with an attitude of ownership in the business, to make it happen for the sake of all concerned.

Forty-two years later, retirement is inspiring me to continue the "catalytic converter process" of making whatever it is to happen: energized by the process, with minimal stress (no dis-stress) and more cash at the end of the day, not only for ourselves to thrive, but also to help feed the hungry, quench the thirst of many, heal the sick and hurting, clothe the naked, remove the cataracts from the blind, entertain the sullen or despairing, and to just be your friend.—all by "going against the grain from tine to time."

"Can we, shall we have a conversation?"
Dr. Charles M. Simons

About Dr Charles

Charles M. Simons, D.D.S., M.S.D. – Specialist in Orthodontics

Dr. Simons is a specialist in orthodontics. His primary focus is tooth-straightening and jaw alignment for children and adults. Attention is given not only to the teeth and the most current technologies of invisible, removable, and traditional dental braces, but also to the individual patient's needs and desires in order to enhance their quality of life, individual accomplishments, and achievement of their goals.

Dr. Simons established the primary location of the practice in Kokomo, IN, in 1970. There are also satellite practices in Frankfort, IN, as well as in Peru, IN.

Dr. Simons is a graduate of DePauw University as a Rector Scholar, Indiana University School of Dentistry, and Indiana University School of Dentistry's Department of Orthodontics earning an M.S.D. He is a Board Certified orthodontist and holds status as a Diplomat of the American Board of Orthodontists. His practice as a specialist in orthodontics is limited to the practice of orthodontics for adults and children.

Dr. Simons has been president of the Indiana Dental Association, Wabash Valley Dental Society, Howard County Dental Society, Indiana Orthodontic Association, and the Great Lakes Association of Orthodontists. He co-chaired the American Association of Orthodontists Annual Meeting in Anaheim, CA, in 1989. Nearly 20 years has been spent in the House of Delegates for the American Dental Association as well as many years in the House of Delegates of the American Association of Orthodontists with assignments to various committees and councils.

Dr. Simons is an active member of dental honoraries. He is a Fellow of the American College of Dentists as well as the International College of Dentists of which he is a Past President of the USA Section (over 7,000 members), secretary of the USA Section Foundation, and Councilman of the College at large (over 8,000 members worldwide). He holds the Distinguished Service Alumni Award from the Indiana University School of Dentistry. He is only the second person ever to have been presented an honorary membership in the European Section of the International College of Dentists.

Dr. Simons has served his community on many boards as an active participant and officer. He served two Indiana Governors as an Indiana Arts Commissioner for a total of ten years. He is a past president of the Kokomo Symphonic Society, and is currently serving on the board for the Kokomo Children's Choir. He was awarded the highest gubernatorial award by two different Indiana governors and was named a Kentucky Colonel.

Dr. Simons married his wife, Alice Grace, in 1968. They have a son (a patent attorney in Denver, CO) and a daughter (a retired financial planner in Minneapolis, MN and now a realtor in Edina, MN), both of whom are married and with children for a total of six grandchildren.

He is currently a retired orthodontist after 42 years, and is serving as business coach to business executives and professionals who want to grow their business and become energized by the process, enjoying less stress and more cash at the end of the day. He likes to engage an audience with stories, humor, a message and inspiration.

CHAPTER 24

FIT FOR THE PROFESSION

BY DREW SCHULTZ

To be an outstanding personal trainer, it is not enough to just get certified. In order to be successful in any industry, you must be fully committed to mastering your trade. Despite the down economy, I've doubled my business in five years - in an industry where the customers are spending discretionary income.

In the pursuit of mastering my trade, I have studied the habits that lead to success. Here are ten principles that I codified as a standard to which I hold myself. These principles are transferrable across any industry.

1. PASSION

If you don't have true passion for what it is you're doing, you can forget the rest. If you have true passion, then you earnestly believe in the service you are providing. Rather than seeing it as merely a monetary exchange that is a means to an end, you are truly providing for a need – providing a solution to a problem. Both you and your clients benefit, and society is better for it.

Ultimately, people buy you as your passion shines through in the way you do your job, conduct yourself as a professional, and service your clients. As Simon Sinek says, people buy your "why".

2. EXCELLENCE

You have to resolve to be absolutely excellent at what it is you do. This includes being excellent at the next eight principles, which are all necessary to excel in your profession. There is no substitute for this if you wish to be successful.

3. YOU MUST BE AN AUTHORITY IN YOUR FIELD

If the prospect/client knows more than you do about the service, then why are they hiring you? You must demonstrate that you are more than capable of addressing their goals and needs. Uncover any hidden needs by being observant and by asking pertinent questions. Get them to answer more than "yes" or "no" to your questions. Show why the information you learned from them and your ideas for them are relevant to what they wish to accomplish. You will gain their confidence.

For example, you are meeting with a prospect. She states that she wants to lose weight and tone up. You notice that she has postural imbalances such as slouched shoulders. You ask her about her occupation to confirm that she is seated during most of the day. During the fitness assessment, you see that her knees cave in when performing a squat. "Mrs. Prospect, we're going to need to correct these postural imbalances to safely and effectively perform the exercises necessary to help you reach the goals that you outlined." You are making her aware of the deeper extent of her situation, and are demonstrating that you will deliver more than she expected.

4. EFFECTIVE COMMUNICATION

Fully 85 percent of outcomes in life will result from communication. Effective communication occurs when a message is sent and received. The prospect may or may not have already formulated an idea in his head that he is open to purchasing your service, but you will make or break the deal based on your communication— whether it is during his first impression, your presentation, or your closing. You must be in tune with them throughout the entire process without distraction or deviation. This demonstrates you are exclusively focused on them – you already value them before they have even bought.

This process includes more subtle, finer points such as body language, tone of voice, and grooming. One rule of thumb – listen 70 percent, speak 30 percent. Silence is golden. Pause while they think, so they can fully absorb what you said. It also shows respect because you're not trying to talk over them. You will gain their trust.

5. ALWAYS BE MINDFUL OF YOUR OBJECTIVE

This is applied to all key development areas. Complacency is the death of progress. We must always be restless, because we have no guarantees. Customers move, change jobs, have personal challenges, lose interest, etc. Even the most loyal customers will have things occur that are unforeseen. In order to build customer loyalty, a great personal trainer must take the initiative to still deliver – particularly from continuing education.

You must add new customers. Always be alert to new opportunities. To find new customers, a great personal trainer must take the initiative to prospect – floor prospecting, asking for referrals, etc.

6. CONTINUING EDUCATION

Whether formal or self-initiated, it is absolutely necessary. Knowledge doubles in each industry every two to five years. This means in two to five years, if you have not kept up with the latest developments in your industry, you will only be 50 percent as competitive as you are today. You will be obsolete. This means you have to double your knowledge of your industry every two to five years just to stay current. Remember, you must absolutely demonstrate that you are an authority in your field. If you don't, the competition will eat you for lunch and take your customers, too.

The best part about continuing education is you will be building increased value for your customers. I often tell clients that they're not just paying for the hour or half hour during the appointment, but included are all of those unpaid hours of my own time behind the scenes – coming up with new exercises, planning new strategies, staying current with new information and continually upgrading my knowledge and skills to be the best I possibly can – resulting in continued progress for them. It is a great return on the law of utility for both parties. Ultimately, to earn more you have to learn more.

7. BUILDING THE BUSINESS

It is not just enough to maintain, but to continually find ways to build on your success. We can always take one more customer. As previously discussed, it is not enough to be content with our current workload and customer volume. There will always be a revolving door, and one goal as a businessperson is to keep that exit as small as possible. Because some clients will take a break or leave for often unforeseen reasons, we must be diligent in pursuing new business. We love referrals, and it validates the value of what we do for the customer. They trust us enough to stand behind us with their good name when referring someone.

However, going back to initiative, we must take action ourselves. This is what I call "saturating every pathway." You exponentially increase your chances of success if you can pursue every path possible. You can also ask for referrals. I believe in reciprocity, and giving at least a free session for every referral. Often the client does not even expect it, but that's ok. It again validates our good standing with them by showing appreciation and building upon the relationship.

The best way to get new business is to go out and get it! At least 50 percent of my clients, maybe more, come from this approach. Many people are uncomfortable with prospecting, because they may feel strange about engaging with a perfect stranger, or they fear rejection. Both problems can be overcome. When engaging with a prospect, simply ask questions while being genuinely friendly. "Are you new to the club?" "What type of workout are you doing today?" "I noticed you are using the foam roller. May I can show you another way to do it to get the best results?" "I noticed you were working on xyz. Did you recently have an injury?" The list goes on. This is where you again demonstrate that you are an authority in your field and uncover hidden needs. You show a personal and genuine interest. You first built rapport, now you are building trust.

The prospect is much more likely to purchase a service from someone whom he trusts and respects vs. someone who just wants money. You can invite members to try a complimentary workout. "I noticed you were doing cardio. Are you including any resistance training? I could take maybe thirty minutes or so and show you some exercises that would be very beneficial." "I heard you say you hate cardio but really prefer resistance training. Why don't you try a kinesis workout sometime? You get a cardio workout built in with resistance training, because it's a continuous pace and you're using a lot of muscle groups at one time. You also get balance and flexibility training that will directly carry over and improve your weights workouts. How does that sound?"

Overcoming the fear of rejection comes through repetition. Anything we find difficult becomes easier over time with repetition. It becomes second nature. If they say no, it is the same as if you said no and never tried. Therefore, you have at least a chance. Remember, if you really believe in your service, you're simply offering something that may be of benefit or value to a prospect. They are free to accept or reject it. You are free to offer it.

8. TAKE ACTION, NOW!

You must decide right here, right now, to take action. Do not delay. Do not procrastinate. Procrastination is the enemy of progress. Resolve this moment to take action on all of these key development areas. It goes back to: "Always be mindful of your objective." When an opportunity arises, seize it. When an obstacle or problem presents itself, deal with it without delay. It is always necessary to take a first step to pursue your goal. It is the small victories that add up to get you to your larger goals and objectives.

If you have a break between sessions, engage in floor prospecting. Catch up on information relevant to the industry – continuing education. Rather than being tempted to go out for coffee or surf the internet, make the best use of your time possible. Take action when there is a hole in your schedule.

9. YOU ARE PRESIDENT AND CEO

You must realize that you are President and CEO of your own success corporation. The average person changes jobs every two years, and can experience fourteen different full time jobs in their adult career. Rather than shift with the winds, decide you are responsible for yourself and accept no excuses. Many a personal trainer expects the club to hand them new business. We are very thankful when something like that happens, but it is the exception, not the rule. Even when we are provided with new member assessments, all of these key principles are just as relevant. When you get new business, review what went right. This is a better approach than focusing on what went wrong with prospects who did not purchase your service. Decide that you fully own your successes and failures – no excuses. Brian Tracy says, "As the president of your own professional sales corporation, your current employer is your best client!"

10. ACCOUNTABILITY

You are being held to account, whether you wish to be or not. You are always on display. Hold yourself to account because everyone else is already holding you to account. To paraphrase Warren Buffett, it takes decades to build a reputation and five minutes to destroy it. Do what you say you are going to do, then deliver more. Always exceed expectations. People are watching. Even if 95 percent of the other members in the club are not your personal clients, you must make sure your conduct would in no way cause them to think or say anything but something positive. Human nature is such that people often take for granted what they expect or are pleased with, and will be more vocal about what displeases them. If someone has a negative experience, on average they will tell nine other people, who will then tell five others a piece – that's forty-five people's minds who have been tainted.

Remember that the client is paying a premium. Stay absolutely focused on them. Tune out distractions. Hold yourself to account and to attending behavior – don't slouch or stand with one arm leaning on a machine, and no hands in your pockets. Have pride in your appearance, grooming and dress. Your clothes cover roughly 95 percent of what the customer sees. Have respect for yourself and you show respect for them. Excellent posture, grooming, and attentiveness will actually make you feel more professional and productive, and if you think and feel more professional and productive, then you will act that way.

You may see that each of these skills overlap one another. You can't get new business from prospecting without excellent communication and you can't be an authority in your field if you're not continually learning. Even improving just one key area can make a dramatic difference in your business and will automatically upgrade your effectiveness of the other skills. Resolve today to hold yourself to account, to upgrade yourself and to be the absolute best professional you can be.

Always be mindful that these principles raise the standard of your professionalism. People will notice—your clients will notice, your prospects will notice, and so will your co-workers. When you decide to raise the bar for yourself, you will be seen as the "go to" person in your field.

About Drew

Meet Drew Schultz, President of Live Well Longer, LLC (www.lwlcoaching.com), a company specializing in wellness consulting for employees. Drew's goal is to help lower health insurance costs by giving employees the tools to make confident decisions regarding their health and fitness. Drew works with employees of Fortune 500 companies and small businesses alike.

Drew is a top personal trainer at O2 Fitness, the Raleigh-Durham Triangle area's premier fitness club. He has been recognized for top personal training sales in the company for several years. For over a decade, Drew has worked with professionals, executives, and business owners.

What started as a lifestyle passion grew into a career. Drew's dedication to wellness started at the age of thirteen, when he realized it was a lifestyle commitment. While pursuing several fields of study at North Carolina State University, Drew was just as involved in his commitment to his personal training clients as he was his to studies. Majoring in History, he attained a Minor in Fitness as well as a Design Minor. Drew is certified through NCCPT/Smartfitness and IFTA. He is also a certified instructor in Kinesis and TRX.

Drew believes that committing to fitness and nutrition goals go far beyond the cosmetic benefits we see, resulting in positively concrete changes in other areas of our life – for the rest of our life.

CHAPTER 25

TWO FOUNDATIONAL PRINCIPLES LEADERS REQUIRE TO DO THINGS DIFFERENT IN TOMORROW'S WORLD

BY JASON C. PLATT

"A ninety!" "Ninety!" I screamed. My golf game by no means is superb. I try and play once or twice a week with my uncle, Mark. For me, golf is a time to enjoy being outdoors, get a little exercise, and recoup. As we approached the eighteenth green on this Friday afternoon in August, I knew my scorecard was in bad shape. I had a six-foot putt for par. If I made it, I break ninety. If I miss it, I shoot ninety. As I stepped over the ball, my hands gripped the putter and a couple of sweat bullets dropped from my forehead to the green. I stroked the ball smooth and right in line with the hole. It took a peek in the hole and bounced around it, landing less than an inch from the hole. I tapped in for bogey and belted out a loud scream, "Ninety!" "I haven't played this bad in years! The more I practice and play this game, the worse I get! I am not coming back!" For you golfers, you always go back!

Mark, who was beating me by multiple strokes, said something that stuck with me. He said, "Jas, you have been putting *against the grain* all day! The "grain," in golf course terminology, is the way in which the individual blades of grass are growing on the golf course. The term is a characteristic of the green, where the grain can significantly affect putts. If you putt against the grain, it will be slower; if you putt with the grain, it will be faster. While to most people it is a simple golf term, for me this little saying was life-changing. I have thought about it and used this term as an analogy in my life. To me, "putting against the grain" is doing things different, not conforming to the norm, being creative. This has made all the difference for me in my life, and to be a successful leader in tomorrow's world, you must do things different than you do today. *My job is to share with you two foundational principles that leaders require in order to do things differently, and thus, be successful in the new age we are in.*

TOMORROW'S WORLD

When I was in high school and studying the Civil Rights movement, I can recall reading John F. Kennedy's Address to the Nation in June 1963. One of the lines of this speech is: "a great change is at hand." My parents are big classic rock fans, I can still hear the Bob Dylan song lyrics in my head, *'these times they are a changin.'* Even the great philosopher Heraclitus' words pop into my head, "the only thing constant is change." I find it interesting that philosophers thousands of years ago, Presidents and songwriters all know and understand that how things are today, will not be how they are tomorrow. The "great change" John F. Kennedy was speaking of those many years ago, is indeed, upon us right now. The most successful leaders of today's world understand that we are going through the most signifanct changes in all of human history. I have studied, interviewed and even been personally coached by some of the best leaders and I have found that there are two principles that stand out – that they all have in common. It is my hopes that you will use the following two principles in your own life to navigate the tides of change. Those principles are: Purpose and Creativity.

THE FIRST FOUNDATIONAL PRINCIPLE IS PURPOSE.

One of the most overused and misunderstood word in business today is "passion." "Find someone who is passionate." "John is sure passionate about this customer." "Jane's passion was clear in her presentation." "Find what you are passionate about and do it." The common misperception is the meaning on what passion is. Passion is a result, it is always the result. Passion is derived from purpose. If you know your purpose, you get passion.

According to a study by Gallup, seventy-one percent of American workers are not engaged with their work. That is, they are uninspired and not reaching their full potential. If people know and understand what you or your company stands for, you will therefore attract the kind of people who share your same belief system. I call these people the principled employees. It is your job as a leader to elicit the potential in people around a deeper purpose. That is why purpose is one of the foundational qualities.

I must admit, one of my favorite movies is *The Family Man*, starring Nicolas Cage. If you have not seen the movie, the plot is about a wealthy and talented businessman, Jack Campbell. Jack lives the bachelor life of luxury, living in a Manhattan penthouse, driving a Ferrari and making tons of money. When fate intervenes, he is given a glimpse of the life he could have been living had he made different choices. He wakes up one morning to find himself living in suburban New Jersey with a wife and two kids, driving a minivan that doesn't start and making a meager living selling tires.

One of the most memorable scenes in the movie is when Jack is having dinner with his wife, Kate, in a NYC restaurant. He is describing his love and passion for his work in his old life:

"I remember I used to walk to work, and I had a warm bialy in my hand, and a hot cup of coffee from Dean & Deluca, the crisp feeling of the Wall Street Journal, the smell of leather from my briefcase, I used to be so sure about everything, confident. You know, I knew exactly who I was and what I wanted...I was the guy who had it all figured out."

As I watched this scene, I thought to myself, isn't that what we all want and strive for in a job, work projects and a career? Even life? ...That intangible feeling of what Simon Sinek calls "your Why." The feeling Nicolas Cage's character has in the movie is what gets him out of bed in the morning, it's a deeper sense of purpose and direction. I remember a time in my own career where I would almost be bummed it was Friday, and I couldn't wait until Monday morning to get back in the game! I loved the smell of fresh coffee on my counter in the morning, the pre-dawn commute into work listening to a good audio book, and the Monday morning staff meetings. Following the meetings was the quick hustle and bustle of a late afternoon flight to either coast. Now, that feeling certainly goes *against the grain* of 71% of the American workforce, and why? I have a purpose, a deep sense of direction, and a core set of beliefs.

How Jack describes his old job in the movie is exactly what engagement is! So, how do we raise engagement? Easy, find your purpose. Once you do, you will attract the principled people you seek because of what you and your organization stand for.

Principled VS Paycheck Employees

I have noticed that there are two types of employees in this world. Those that will work for your paycheck and those that will work with their blood, sweat and tears because of the principles you embody around a purpose. What I call the P/P employees. Let's take a deeper look into the two types.

First, let's look at the Paycheck employee. We all know and have these employees in our organizations. These people show up at 8:00am, put in their 8 hours, and go home. They contribute; only to the level they are paid. They will attend meetings, run reports, and do exactly what it is you say. They are great foot soldiers. They cash the check every other Friday, and are happy with the status quo.

Now let's look at the principled employee. We all have these types of individuals in our organization as well. The people show up in the morning early, work with all their heart and soul. They go home only to reflect on the day's events, and ask themselves how can I do better tomorrow. They contribute and add much more value than they are paid. In fact, money is not why they work hard. It's not title, parking spot, corner office, bonus, or perks. Their work has intrinsic value. Their work comes from their purpose and is inspired by the leader's or company's vision and mission. They also cash the check every other Friday, but they are not happy with the status quo.

Let's look at the number one metric that businesses use today, for both types of employees. Numbers. How much revenue did we generate? How much did we keep? What is our A/R percentage? Vacancy Rate? Or whatever numerical measurement you want to pick.

Paycheck people don't feel bad when they let the number down. John's goal is to secure 10 new prospects a week. I call John on Friday afternoon and ask him how many new prospects did you secure this week John? Answer – 7. John doesn't feel bad because he let a number down. Number is only a measurement for progress.

Now let's look at JoAnn. Joann has the same goal as John, only JoAnn is a principled employee. I call Joann on a Friday afternoon and ask her how many new prospects did you secure this week JoAnn? Answer – 7. JoAnn feels bad because she let me down, not a number. It's now personal. She works extra hard the next week for what I, or the organization, stands for. The number doesn't know or care about the purpose. I am disappointed that she did not hit her goal for the week. The number is not.

So, I challenge all of you to answer the question...can you describe your job as Jack Campbell did in the movie scene? Your life? If not, find your purpose, and you can be enjoying the smell of leather from your briefcase as well. It will not only fill your life and business with meaning, but also inspire your employees to do the same.

THE SECOND FOUNDATIONAL QUALITY IS CREATIVITY

Creativity is the root of all innovation.

"Jason, get your call volume up or the next conversation will be that of termination." I was shocked. How can my team lead be telling me this? I am doing a good job, so I thought.

I am a recruiter by trade. I started my career many years ago "working a desk" as we in recruiting call it. Actually, I was literally working on the desk. I was working for a private equity funded start-up company, and the only furniture we had was old card tables. My tools consisted of a phone to make calls to potential candidates, a computer to capture the leads, and a flathead screwdriver to support those tools! All I had to do was source, recruit, and hire. I thought I was doing a good job. Why was I being threatened for termination?

Part of "desk management" was what my bosses called "primetime" – and we were measured on it. That is, from the hours of 9:00 am – 11:00am and 1:00-3:00 pm we were to be on the phones, calling potential candidates and selling them on our jobs. We were measured on how many calls we made, how long the phone calls were, and what the conversation rate to hires was, among other measurements. The other four hours of work, we were to be sourcing candidates to build our pipeline, doing reports, attending meetings, and other administrative tasks. The basic philosophy of the leadership was, *if you're not on the phones during "primetime", then you're not making hires.*

I subscribed to this philosophy for a while. I was making phone call after phone call after phone call. All I got in return was the lovely sound of Bertha. Bertha being the nickname of whom I talked to the most – voicemail! "I'm sorry, but the subscriber you are trying to reach is not available. Please leave your message after the tone." Occasionally, I would get ecstatic when I would hear the person's own personal greeting on the voicemail. A real live human, even if he or she was a recording!

Finally, after a lot of thought and determination, I decided to do the exact opposite. I went *against the grain* and started to get fantastic results, almost immediately. I had record hires for engineers, a very tough recruit. During the "primetime" hours of 9:00 am-11:00 am and 1:00pm – 3:00pm I would only source for candidates to call only while everyone else was on the phones. I would do research on job boards, even schedule meetings, and complete my required reports. I had a slate of people to call; I just wasn't going to call them during "primetime" any longer. The other hours of the day, 7:00 am-9:00 am and 4:00-7:00 I would make my phone calls. How did I come to this conclusion? It was so simple! Most people who we were targeting were passive candidates, they were already working and most were not actively looking for a job. So, when do these candidates take recruiters phone calls? Before and after work! I would drink my coffee in the mornings from home, or in the office and call people. I would crack a beer in the evenings by the pool and call people whom I had sourced for during the normal "primetime." Bertha was no longer a gatekeeper.

According to *USA Today*, one of the most important skills hiring managers look for in a potential employee is the ability to think creatively, second to only the ability to communicate. Here is some good news – any business skill is learnable, including the ability to think creatively! You want to learn to read financial statements, no problem. You want to learn how to calculate your return on investment capital (ROIC), no problem. You want to learn to think creatively, to tap what Brian Tracy calls your *"Superconscience Mind"* to solve a problem, no problem.

I challenge you to take any aspect of your life – a business problem, a community problem, a relationship problem, even the most complex political problem – and do something different. Do not accept the results you are getting if you are not pleased with them. Start small or big, but challenge yourself to go against the grain and you, too, will be able to have your own "primetime."

My golf game has changed rather considerably. My swing (or score!) has not improved, but I know when I am putting *against the grain*. I also know when I am going against the grain in business too. Against the Grain is creating change, fighting to bring my vision into reality, inspiring around a purpose and doing things different to get the desired results. When I stand over and read putts on every green, I am reminded of why I make the conscious decision to do things differently, because it makes all the difference.

About Jason

Jason C. Platt was born in Garland, Texas, a suburb of Dallas. He and his family moved to Houston when he was four years old and he has called Houston home ever since. Jason grew up in a wonderful, loving home, playing all kinds of sports, and, of course, picking on his younger brother Trey.

Scientists have studied and some believe that you figure out what you will do with your life between the ages of 7-14. At age 15, Jason started working by walking ditches in a nearby developing community picking up trash for minimum wage. He jokes about the scientists' study and says *"I don't have any proof that their hypothesis is correct, but at the age of 15, I know what I didn't want to do - and that was pick up trash, in ditches, in August, in Houston!"*

At that point, he knew he needed to become a different person. But, without realizing then, he had a problem. He thought he wasn't as smart or couldn't learn as fast as the other students. *"I always believed I wasn't as smart as everyone else,"* he laments.

It wasn't until his senior year in high school that he decided to enroll in the "advanced" government class. After the first half of the year, and seeing his poor grades, his teacher called him to the front of the class. Publicly, and humiliatingly, his government teacher said he should seriously consider dropping the advanced class and enrolling in the academic course if he wanted to graduate.

"I was completely embarrassed. It was almost like it was validation for me that I was dumb," Jason says. However, it was the turning point for him. *"Right then and there I decided to prove to him, and more importantly my assumptions about myself, wrong."*

He became a quick study, going in early, seeking tutoring from smarter people, going home later. He locked himself in his room and re-wrote all of his notes several times. *"I started to 'get it.' It clicked. Learning, comprehending, getting along with other people, discipline. It was like I figured out how to open a safe that has been locked forever. It just opened."*

After high school, he went on to attend Texas State University – San Marcos where he led multiple collegiate organizations. *"I learned more lessons on leadership and management in college than any of the previous years combined, and the majority of those lessons came from outside the classroom."* After college, he went to work for a leading transportation company in Houston, TX where he says he grew as a leader exponentially. *"Those were truly magical years. The people made me better."*

Jason earned his undergraduate degree in Organizational Communication, became a certified Human Capital Strategist, and has since helped lead organizations to success through developing and managing their human capital departments. He has written, spoken and been coached on leadership and human capital principles and his passion is combining the two to develop great organizations through leadership and human capital development.

To learn more about Jason, and to subscribe to his leadership and human capital blog, visit: www.jasoncplatt.com

CHAPTER 26

AVOIDING COMMODIFICATION

BY DR. JOHN FORNETTI

My father was a dentist in a remote, small town in the Upper Peninsula of Michigan called Iron Mountain. When I became a dentist, I joined the ranks of a successful family of dentists. In fact, the conferrment of my son's D.D.S. degree marked the ninth Fornetti dentist, most of whom practice in the same area.

When I returned to Iron Mountain in 1983, the unemployment rate was over 20% and the interest rate was almost 20% in the area. My wife and I bought a house with a mortgage payment of just over $300, but I worried many sleepless nights over how to make even that small payment. I owned my own business however I shared office space with my two brothers who are also dentists. After a year, I still had not collected a paycheck and the cleaner and dental assistant were making more than I was. I was paying bills, but that was about it. On Sunday nights, I went to my office to review the schedule for the week ahead. One particular Sunday I remember with crystal clarity because when I opened my calendar the only thing I had scheduled for the week was one measly appointment on Thursday. That was an epiphany for me. I knew I had to do things differently; I did not know what or how. Coming from a family of dentists became a double-edged sword. They did things in a certain way, and mentally I desired to break the mold.

Once I started moving in other directions that were not the norm for the industry at the time, things started getting better.

What is commodification? Commodification is a process in which goods and services become indistinguishable in the marketplace, the result of which the only difference to people is price. The price drops, which means that the business owner will have smaller margins. There are really only five places that money goes; taxes, living expenses, debt, giving or savings. When your margins get smaller, the fun things like saving money or being generous with your money go by the wayside.

Think about the milkman of days gone by. The dairy industry used to be able to afford a truck, a driver, his uniform and be able to deliver the milk directly to your door, along with cheeses, butter, ice cream and the like. All that is gone and the only factor now to distinguish one brand of milk from the other is price. The consumer opens the grocery sale flyer to see which store is running milk on sale or as a "loss leader" this week. Another example might be video stores. Renting a movie used to be the perfect way to spend a Friday night; now a person can stream movies live on the Internet. Who needs the video store or the service of a movie buff to advise on which movies are must-sees, when any online store will make recommedations for you based on your previous purchases?

I recently read that Walmart, the king of commodity purchasing, will soon be adding legal and tax/accounting services. The consumer will be able to purchase reduced cost legal services at the same time they purchase tires or their groceries. They have not ventured into the dental industry yet. How long will it be before they do? Adding insult to injury, television's portrayal of dentists as unethical, highways robbers who would advise for unnecessary dental work in order to make an extra buck is an unwelcome image we combat daily.

If your industry is becoming commodified, be ready by offering a superior service to your customers that will rival any low-priced competitor. Not everyone shops Walmart. Bloomindales and Nordstrom thrive because of the value-added service they provide. Proactive positioning of your business to add value to your goods or services ensures the survival of your business in any economy and despite commodification. At every opportunity, set yourself apart from your competition with ten simple steps.

1. Give More Service Than The Customer Pays For

Give more than what the client expects. Make every experience a wow.

2. Create A Customer-Based Practice of Business

We have instituted a series of activities in our dental office to distinguish our services from those of the other local dentists. When patients arrive at our practice for an appointment, we give them a wrapped gift. Now, this gift is not something a man is going to save to give to his wife for their anniversary, but it is usually something like a water bottle with our name on it that is useful. The wrapping shows that we gave forethought to the gift, and did not just unpack a gross of them in the storage room.

We employ a greeter who is dedicated to meeting the customer at the door to greet them, help them to complete the mandatory health paperwork and give them a tour of our office. During the tour, she recites a script that highlights pertinent details about our office.

Before the gift or the greeter, the scent of freshly-baked muffins wafting through our office welcomes the patient and calls to mind grandma's house, effectively obliterating the anticeptic dental office smell normally called to mind. When they leave our office, they receive a bag of muffins--with our logo and contact information. Most of our patients will be returning to work after their appointment, so we provide more muffins in the bag than they would normally eat themselves. Attached are instructions asking them to share not only the muffins, but also their experience with their co-workers. Also attached to the bag are coupons for $35 off their next exam for the sharer of the coupon and $35 off for the new patient at their first exam.

Referral contests generate a lot of support from clients when the contest prize appeals strongly to your clients' interests. In our area, giving away a four-wheeler is like giving away gold. Find what the big "thing" is in your area and use it to support your business.

3. Put Your Best Team In The Field

Hiring practices vary widely from industry to industry, but what does not change is the expectation your clients or patients have. Clients want quality employees who know the business, and meet the needs of the client and make the customer feel secure. Fielding your best team begins with the hiring process. Conventional thinking and hiring practices will net you only conventional employees, not top-notch, creative thinkers.

We test our potential employees without them knowing they are being tested, in an effort to assess their problem solving skills in a real-life setting. When we run an ad for an employee, we ask them to call a phone number for an interview. The recorded message they hear downplays the position and tells them the position requires hard work, no complaining, etc. The phone call weeds out many who are seeking a cushy job.

Next is a group interview during which we explain the position and the candidates have an opportunity to size each other up. The speed interview comes next and is much like "speed dating" in which the potential employee spends short periods meeting the current staff and being asked questions before moving along to the next interviewer. The process whittles down the group to the best of the employees; then we introduce the "cheeseburger test." During a typical cheeseburger test, we ask the candidate to get everyone's lunch order from the local sub shop that we have a secret arrangement with specifically for this "test." The employee takes each person's order and when he gets to mine, I order my sub with the ingredients in a peculiar order so the meat is on the bottom and the vegetables are assembled a particular way. I give the candidate a $100 bill that the restaurant has been instructed not to cash. The best candidates will figure out a way to get everyone's order and still get everything somehow. Speed interviewing works because everything in our world has speeded up and customers expect it too.

4. Speed Up Everything

Everything has gotten faster. Clients want to get in and out of their appointments and back to work or home as quickly as possible. "Waiting" rooms are no longer a welcome accoutrement of the office as the idea of waiting is so distasteful. That said, businesses that respect a clients time would be seen as superior to those businesses for whom timeliness is not a priority. To speed up what can be a slower or tedious process; we pre-set every treatment room so that when a patient arrives, the staff can focus on patient care and not facility preparation. A checklist ensures that each room is set with the items needed. Should we drop an implement or a new item be needed during a procedure, we utilize walkie-talkies to request a replacement. While this does require increased staff, the benefits to the patient far exceed the expense. If faster service reminds you a of a fast-food chain, be warned, the next barrier to commodification of dentistry— or any business—is facility improvement.

5. Facility

We are not a retail establishment, but we market ourselves like one. We patterned our office after a restaurant in Wisconsin and the locals sometimes refer to us as TGI Fornetti's. By design, the building looks more like an inviting restaurant than a dental office. Gone are the mint green walls and fluorescent lighting. Our sterilization area was composed for the efficiency of a tool and die shop. While we are busy wowing our clients with a more comfortable environment and faster service, we also make ourselves more accessible to them.

6. Convenient Hours

Our customers work longer hours and varying schedules; they need their dentist to be available when they are. The convenience of a business's hours contributes to the consumer's decision to frequent a business. Therefore, our dental office waved goodbye to "traditional" dental office hours of Monday through Thursday from nine to five. Instead, we operate our office with multiple doctors from 7-7 everyday and will soon add Saturdays to meet the needs of even more patients. To meet the growing demands of more patients, we also adjusted our infrastructure to include not only more staff but also purchased a city block to increase our parking and make convenience a priority all-around. Convenience makes it easier to do business with you, thereby bringing more people through the door, but how will your business increase the dollars coming in the door?

7. Increase Services & Increase Technology

Determining what, if any, additional services to offer your clients, involves weighing the potential increase of profits with the potential additional costs such as expansion or additional staff. Analyze your ROI. How much additional business will the new service escort through your door and how long will it take to recoup the initial investment?

The addition of new technology is slightly different. Labor costs are usually the largest espense of any business. Technology saves man hours by saving employees time or by eliminating employees altogether, obviously increasing profits immediately. Bringing the latest technological advancements to your office amplifies your business in another way; it keeps your office relevant. People assimilate rapidly to new technology and come to expect that everyone will have the latest and greatest. A business that does not keep pace with current technology is sure to lose customers. Consider that only a few years ago Blackberry virtually owned the market for smartphones. Now, their competitors' iPhone and Android technology owns nearly the entire market share once held in Blackberry's iron grip. Once you have satisfied customers, their friends become your natural next target market.

8. Master Referrals In Your Industry

Referral business comes with a guarantee, implied trust. The referral already trusts you based on their friend's experience. Client gifts net referrals. A feeling of reciprocity activates when the patient or client receives a gift; the client wants to do something nice for you in return, so they refer someone else to you.

9. Learn To Market To Your Industry

Customer appreciation events kill two birds with one stone; they increase your business's visibility and make your current customers feel special. Different areas of the country do prefer different things, so tailor your event to what your clientele will enjoy. Events with regional flavor, such as a clambake, will entice more people to attend. Build a business relationship with other local vendors while you make your customers happy. Collaborate with a local movie theater to offer your patients a free movie night complete with popcorn, soda and their friends. Yes, let them invite their friends to the event. The money you spend on the friend's ticket is far less than the cost of most advertising campaigns and is more likely to attain a pre-qualified, referral client.

Hire a videographer for your customer appreciation events and have him work the crowd. Your business will have great footage to use for promotions down the road, and you will often receive unscripted, unsolicited testimonials from attendees while they are relaxed and happy. Offering an incentive to your clients' guests who attend the event will bring new business, especially when an expiration date applies like "must sign up tonight" to receive a discount. Your goal is to create and keep satisfied customers who see your business as having greater value than your competitor's does.

10. Give People What They Want

As long as your promotions or techniques are moral and ethical, make every effort to impress. Dare to be different in your industry. Dare to be the best. When you practice the previous steps, your clients will be getting what they want.

Do not become concerned that if you resist commodification, you are "expensive" and priced out of your market. Arizona State University professor, Dr. Robert Cialdini extensively studied the marketing industry finding that if a business acknowledges their higher price and justifies it with better services, greater convenience, etc., the customer will pay more. The L'Oréal tag line "it costs more, but I'm worth it" was born of this philosophy. L'Oréal's line became synonymous with quality and value. Giving clients more in service value than the client pays in monetary value will increase your business today and safeguard it from the encroachment of commodification tomorrow.

About Dr. John

Dr. John Fornetti began his dental practice in 1983, but his roots had been planted many years earlier. Dr. John's father graduated from dental school in 1944 and returned to his hometown of Iron Mountain after World War II. There has been a strong family heritage of dentistry ever since. In fact, Dr. John's son, Dr. Dan, is now the ninth Fornetti dentist, all beginning with Dr. John's father.

Dr. John has been blessed with a powerful education which has helped him earn numerous diplomat and fellowship distinctions. He belongs to various dental organizations, is a public speaker on numerous topics and has privileges with both the Oscar G. Johnson VA Medical Center and the Dickinson County Healthcare System.

After graduating from dental school at Marquette University, he and his wife Terese returned to their hometown to begin their family. They now have four beautiful children and one daughter-in-law. Dr. John's favorite hobbies are hunting, fishing, and backpacking.

To learn more about Dr. John Fornetti and ways to prepare your business against commoditization or other subjects, visit Dr. John at: drJohnFornetti.com or call (906) 774-0100.

CHAPTER 27

YOUR POWER – YOUR RICHES – 7 Steps To Extraordinarily Release Your Powers Within

BY JUDY VAN NIEKERK

"The meaning of life is to find your gift.
The purpose of life is to give it away."
~ Pablo Picasso

'Good evening Ladies and Gentlemen, thank you for waiting, this is the first call for flight EI214 to London Heathrow...' I don't recall much of what she said after that.

My heart popping, my stomach churning, and my palms were sweating as I moved down the line to board. The faint odour of nervous energy surrounding me was keeping me going. There was no turning back. I had smelt that smell too often over the years at his hands to even consider going back. Diving into the black hole of the unknown was so much more appealing to me. In this case it was 'better the devil you don't know than the devil you know.'

I boarded that plane at Dublin Airport late on a Monday evening in November 1989, leaving behind everything I knew and possessed. I carried with me one single bag with some clothes and strangely, my First Holy Communion dress, the onyx stone from a ring my Dad bought me many years earlier, a copy of Wuthering Heights and a photograph of myself in my Communion dress with my Mom and Dad on the day of my Communion.

Sitting at the window seat that evening, the first time I had ever flown in a plane I was awestruck with our apparent proximity to the moon. It was in full bloom that night, shining bright orange, and the lines of the craters crystal clear. I felt such powerful energy from the moon and as I gazed at it, I was absorbed by it. I felt one with the moon. I knew then that I was on the most perfect path of my life. My mind calmed, my brain noise slowed down. All fear and doubt dissipated, replaced by certainty, wonderment, curiosity and excitement. I became absorbed in a knowing, trusting and powerful sense of being.

I pulled out the photo I had to look at my Dad as I relived the encounter I had with him just an hour earlier at the airport, I wondered if that would be the last time I saw him.

As I had walked away from him, I saw desperation in his eyes, I could smell his fear; hearing his pleading welled up such powerful conflicting emotions as I looked straight ahead without stopping to the check in gate – we were in a public place now and there was nothing he could do to stop me on my path.

I had not expected to see him at the airport, he saw me enter the airport at the same time I saw him sitting on a bench at the main entrance. As he saw me he stood up coming straight for me, speaking, I did not hear his words, only his pleading tone. My whole body wanted to yell and scream in desperation.

'HOW THE F___ DID HE KNOW I WAS GOING TO BE HERE?' It was only two nights earlier that I had escaped from him – finally after so many attempts. It was done with military precision, every detail checked. I had only this chance, if I left it any longer, I would die either physically or emotionally – lost forever in this mortal form.

It was raining and after he had gone to the pub, as he did every night, I packed my bag, petrified but excited, finally I had figured a way to get away from him, forever. After hiding the bag in the cloakroom under the stairs I went to the bathroom and looked into the mirror, a fix I needed on a regular basis, just to see me, am I real, to try and catch a glimpse of who I was inside, I would stare into my eyes – not seeing my physical form but into my soul. Searching.

Leaning my hot forehead on the cool glass, I knew it would be so much easier to break out now whilst he was at the pub than at 4 am but I couldn't, I had tried that often in the past and he found me and dragged me back. So each night now he made me swear I would be there when he got back and I would not 'do anything' meaning I would not take any poison or pills to opt out of this world as I had done on a few occasions. My only option was to leave while he slept and leave the country for good.

Longing for nights alone undisturbed, without the rapes, the beatings, being shot and threatened time and again, pregnancies and back street abortions. I tried to imagine what life was going to be like, what was London like, what will it be like to be with other people, what am I going to be like, who am I? What am I going to do? What will freedom be like?

Freedom. This was something I had never known after being enslaved by him for so long.

Weirdly my heart was sad, I knew I would miss him. I loved him as much as I hated him. He had such a powerful influencing effect on my 20 years of life. For the past 10 years he was all I knew – no schooling, no friends, taken away from my Mom and family.

As I sat on the plane that night, feeling relieved that I had got away the following morning at 4 am as planned. The taxi driver asking me, "Are you doing a runner, love?" made my heart stop. But I could not fathom how my Dad had found out where I was going and what plane I was catching.

I was to find out in years to come.

Today, over 20 years later as I reflect back on my life since landing in London that night, I feel in awe of the time I have had. London was euphoric, a heady time of learning to socialise, creating a career, boyfriends, parties and sports – the more extreme the better.

But it wasn't until I moved to Cape Town in 1992, after apartheid was abolished, did I feel I had a home, a base from which to start to settle and grow.

In those years between then and now, I have experienced enormous joy and extreme trauma. Being gang raped, assaulted and suffering a broken back, many drug overdoses, a divorce and for me, most critically was wandering lost in a wasteland in my mind trying to figure out what am I here for, what is my purpose, what am I 'supposed' to be doing?

In my search for the answer to this, I have experienced phenomenal diversity and achievements in sport, career and vocation. Having represented South Africa in SCUBA Diving at world championships, won major swimming competitions, competed in paragliding, water skiing, sailing, motor cycle racing, hiked the worlds' best sites including Mount Kilimanjaro, lived on three continents, had many businesses in many industries, winning the International Woman winemaker of the world, Brave Woman of UK, being a senior executive in major global corporations working closely with CEO's and CFO's, establishing pioneering business and winning national and global acclaim. I was responsible for the reporting of rape and incest incidents going up by 75% in Ireland after my Dad was sentenced to 15 years in jail and having the case held out of camera at my request, a first in history. Making fortunes and losing fortunes. And to cap it all, experiencing spectacular failure in business.

I am today completely clear on the answer to the question that caused me so much grief. I live in the Garden of Eden doing what I love and being phenomenally rewarded for it. And so can you!

The power lies within you to create and manifest exactly what you would love, and here are seven steps that I found myself using to get to where I am at today and which will guide you in becoming clear on your purpose, where your highest point of potential income lies, your bliss and experience, true joy and love.

1. **Connect to your source** – The first time I recall doing this was on the plane to London, where I felt one with the moon. The empowering effect of knowing that you are one with the universe is so exquisite that when you realise that, nothing can be missing – for if there was, the universe would not be the perfection it is.

We have a powerful inner technology that we have for the most part abandoned. When we consciously create from within and we do so knowing that the outer world will meet us and mirror that, we are choosing compassion, love and inspiration, instead of grief, resentment and anguish and we become powerful creators.

Own the phenomenal greatness of yourself knowing you manifest from within and you will be astounded by the miracles that show up in your life. What stands between you and miracles is tension. Dissolve this tension through loving yourself – unconditionally. The ancient Essenes say we find that place of love in our bodies through knowing peace in our minds, hearts and body.

I have found the most powerful way to do this is to align our conscious, sub- conscious and unconscious minds so they are working in unison. Our conscious beliefs and sub-conscious programming often stand in the way of achieving this state. I have a methodology to access the Theta mind to communicate with the unconscious mind using metaphors (as Carl Jung says: 'The unconscious evidently likes to express itself mythologically') that can shatter conscious negative beliefs and align the unconscious and sub- conscious with our conscious intentions.

2. **Your Loves and Talent**s – Your Loves come from your heart, you are inspired by them. There is a reason why you possess the Loves you do. Following these Loves will lead you to a fulfilled life on purpose and enrichment in mind, body and soul. You have heard the saying, 'Follow Your Heart'? This is so powerful yet so many of us do not do it. If you follow your Loves and not the thoughts from your minds your brain receives strong signals from your heart, your cells then receive strong signals from your brain – you are coherent, creating the perfect environment to develop your talents.

What are your passions?

What are you talents?

What do people comment on that you are brilliant at?

What did you love to do as a child?

Let yourself go. Find the answers to these questions. We all have an innate intelligence that is vitalistic, universal and from our source as well as an educated intelligence that is materialistic. Tap into that innate intelligence and there exists no limit to the extent of your talents.

Your Loves often uncovers your talent. Loves can also be the result of past experiences, particularly childhood. For me my Love of writing, learning and empowering others came from my inability to attend school and being overpowered and this Love has uncovered these talents.

3. **Gratitude for self and life** – You are interconnected and coherent with the universe. Take time to 'smell the roses', listen to great music, read great books, observe phenomenal art, gaze upon phenomenal architectural designs, go out into Nature, cast your eyes skywards and survey the night sky and stars. Appreciate from your heart the wonderment of this magnificent universe. You are energy, made of the same subatomic particles (which is basically energy) as the sun, the moon and everything around you and you are a magnet, you are the most powerful transmitter in the universe therefore your thoughts become your reality. Gratitude is the means to loving your life and growing from every experience you have.

You may have heard the saying, 'Be grateful for what you have and you will receive more to be grateful for.' This is so true and logical when you think that we are such powerful transmitters and our thoughts create our reality. At this stage it is generally accepted in the world of physics that we live in a world of duality and as we are interconnected with the universe – everything about us exists in duality; therefore it is impossible to be happy all the time. We will experience lows and highs to the same extent and the same amount. It is easy to be grateful when everything is going just grand but it is as essential to have gratitude when we experience challenge. Find the blessings in your challenges. Gratitude opens your heart and when your heart is open your mind is inspired.

Daily, physically write a list of everything you are grateful for, both in your life around you and just as importantly what you are grateful for in yourself.

4. **Meditation** – Our lives today are so intense, our normal consciousness being bombarded constantly – to the extent of sensory overload at times. It is in this conscious state where we live in Beta brainwave. This is where we remember the past and project into the future, but almost never in the NOW, it is in this state we live in duality and separateness, judgments and resentments. As a result there is a low sphere of influence in this state. Meditation turns down the brain noise and for the more experienced, turns it off completely. When meditating you are in the NOW, the brainwaves slow down to Theta and sometimes Delta tapping into the universe as a whole.

Meditation reduces stress and is a great way to receive guidance in your life from your Source leading to inspired ideas and increased creativity enhancing our Alpha state in consciousness.

5. **Visualisation** – A powerful tool for me has been to visualise mentally, through pictures on a self-made vision board and also daily affirmations to create the life I am experiencing now. The mind cannot distinguish between simulated reality or activity and real activity. You may have heard of great golfers visualising themselves taking each shot, exactly how it will feel, how they stand, how far the ball will go and where it will land and the subsequent effects on their game has been phenomenal.

"The act of focusing awareness is an act of creation;
consciousness creates"
~ Gregg Braden

The trick behind visualisation is to feel that what you desire has already happened rather than wishing for it. By doing this you thrust your hearts desires from a state of imagination to reality.

6. **Self Worth and Net Worth** – This is a crucial step, as it is our Universal Right to live well and be wealthy and by being

wealthy you become an expanded person of who you are. However you will only have what you believe you are worth. And this step automatically falls into place when the previous five have been accomplished or are being accomplished.

7. **Accept Failure** – This is possibly the single most important step. We all fail, I have, completely and spectacularly but as the old saying goes ' it is not the failing that matters but how quickly you get up, brush yourself down and continue'.

   Failure is not the end of the road but a detour, seed for your success. Walter Russell was once asked if he had ever failed and his response was, 'Oh yes, I have had my share of what one calls defeat, but I do not recognize these as defeats. They are but interesting experiences of life.'

These steps have powerfully changed my life, allowing me to live a life of love and abundance and I am certain they will do the same for you as well.

Love and Gratitude, Judy.

Judy van Niekerk © 2013

About Judy

Judy van Niekerk, is a Life and Business Strategist, Author and Researcher. She transforms peoples' lives around the world daily, mentoring, speaking and training as she ignites the Loves and Talents in people through her various programs. Globally she works with individuals, companies and groups across all markets including youth – guiding them to greater levels of empowerment and enrichment.

She has successfully and completely turned her less-than-Ideal childhood experiences into phenomenal opportunities, which she has capitalised on to empower millions around the world to see that the challenges we experience are stepping stones for us to grow from.

She demonstrates from her personal experiences that we truly do possess the power within to create the life we love and abundance – as she says 'it is nothing more than a choice, a simple decision that will irreversibly alter your life forever.'

She has reached the top of her game in everything she has turned her hand to in sport and business, winning major awards and medals. Although still young she has experienced an enormously wide spectrum in the business world from Accounting and Management Consulting, Environmental Care product development, developing Environmental training for ISO certification for diamond mines and wood mills, lobbying government to amend the Domestic Violence Act in South Africa to establishing a whole wine region in South Africa, working closely with government and creating much needed jobs in the under-resourced areas of the tribal regions of South Africa.

Having studied Social Justice at Strathclyde University in Glasgow, she now spends any free time studying Quantum Physics, researching all aspects of consciousness and accessing the Universal Intelligence.

Judy currently lives in the UK with her husband and soul mate, Tiny. They travel the world, hiking, sailing and SCUBA diving.

For more information on Judy van Niekerk, visit: www.judyvanniekerk.com

CHAPTER 28

HOW TO GROW BUSINESS KIDS *AGAINST THE GRAIN*

BY KATE CROWLEY SMITH

My family has a long history of being in business, with an interest in horse racing, so I was comfortable with having a little 'flutter' on horses. However, my husband's gambling was not minor. His addiction left us financially, socially and emotionally ruined and moving to the other side of the country. I saw it as an opportunity for a new start. In the end he took it as an opportunity for something more sinister.

My husband worked and I was an at-home mum who budgeted the family's needs on $50 per week, while the kids were young. A few years later we bought a home. But, his compulsive gambling worsened and his sociopathic behaviour escalated. Under the cover of a loud party next door, he tried to kill me. His reassurance was "you've brought this upon yourself." Somehow, we fought him off and got out of the house. The torment continued for nearly a year. We were in a refuge, he was in prison and we decided to move back to the east of the country.

As a jobless, homeless, single Mum, I drove across the country to get the kids to safety and to set up a new life. With support of family, friends and colleagues, we have successfully survived. My two wonderful entrepreneurial kids are now aged 22 and 19 years and their company is a growing million-dollar business. I want to share with you ten key elements of how to grow business kids against the grain.

1. TRUST

While young, my kids experienced no trust around money and a lot of broken promises. My ex-husband stole from his own kids to feed his gambling. To prevent this from happening again, I put the kid's money into bank accounts. One day, I was in line at the bank getting money for school shoes and chatting with school mums. While being served, the teller loudly told me there was no money available. I was very embarrassed and my excited kids were now devastated. Somehow, he'd accessed the accounts. Once again, at another bank, new accounts with special security requirements were opened. During these untrustworthy times I was dependable and honest. My boss said, *"So many of the things that you did really helped your kids. The main one for me was that your kids had someone that they could trust implicitly—you"*.

As they were growing up, I have had to borrow funds from the kids, but they got it back. When I have lent them money, they have paid it back. This trust has provided me with the confidence to provide some business start-up funding; they have a signed contract listing a repayment schedule. I taught my kids to trust me and themselves with money.

2. HARD-WORK

Speaking with friends and family about how I raised business kids, hard work was a common theme. They said I have "a strong work ethic… always trying new ideas" and "being motivated to put the hard work in to achieve goals."

I have worked hard at everything, my studies, relationships, family, job and my life. There were many times when I needed to work through the night or weekend to complete work for assignments, cooking, events, reports, whatever it takes to finish. The kids have watched me be knocked down and keep going until I succeeded.

It's not just hard work for you and your family, but also to give back to the community. My friend and I led a dedicated fete committee for 18 months of preparations and we included our kids. The hard work paid off, the school fete successfully raised the funds to air condition the school.

Many people will say to you. "You're so lucky to…drive a nice car" or "be on holiday." It's not luck! It is hard work, over time, behind the scenes. I role modelled the hard work, drive and determination it takes to successfully reach your goals.

3. SUPPORT

I have provided rock solid support to both my children. When my daughter was having a tough time at school, I tried everything to help her find her solution. Finally, after reading a short fable, she emerged from her room and through a wet chocolaty cuddle, I asked, "so what do you want to do?" Her response was 'change schools' and within one week she started in her selected school.

My son chose to continue the final school years, but he got in a rut and refused to attend. I did everything and found every support mechanism available to help him. He did not finish school, he left to work part-time and complete his certificate III in retail, and he had my full support.

When the kids decided to become franchise owners, they would come home from work at 1 am and hold business discussions. I would get up out of bed and join in their excited conversations for a couple of hours, only to go back to bed and go to work the next day.

Supporting the kid's business venture took a lot of emotional, creative, mental, physical and financial support. None of us had the capital. I was adamant about not using my house as a guarantee, which made it nearly impossible to secure financial backing. But it also forced us to be more creative. Yes there are risks, but it was also a great opportunity. We took on the attitude of build it and we'll find the money. This worked. In a bit over one year, they started their first shop in June, and will have four shops by July.

4. EARN MONEY

I have taught my kids the value of money; that you work for and earn money, not win it! I know it sounds tough, but I made them earn their pocket money and toys.

At first we had a job roster with the rule no jobs, no allowance. It became a battle to get the jobs done. I heard about the job-jar, which everyone agreed to try. The jar was filled with nice and really awful jobs. The funny thing was the kids wrote the worst jobs; like cleaning the toilets and picking up the dog poo. They laughed so hard as they wrote out horrible jobs, wishing someone else would pull out the worst job for the week. The job-jar worked because the whole family was involved in listing jobs, their value and doing the jobs every week. But it only paid around $5 per week, and they wanted more money to buy 'stuff' – which I refused to buy. Saving birthday money and pocket money was not fast enough. They were eager to try other ways to make more money.

5. HOW TO MAKE MONEY

Growing up, the kids saw how to make money, by going out to work and grandparents owning businesses, and the best lesson of all, making money for themselves.

When I asked my daughter how she learned to make money, she talked about her lemonade stand at age 11: "You always supported every idea we had, you asked a lot of questions about how we were going to do it and you never did it for us." For the lemonade stand: "you made us test a recipe, determine the quantity of ingredients, storage, cleanliness and attracting customers. We made our own fliers and letter box dropped them." I loaned them the start-up funds, they repaid the costs, filled in a balance sheet. Their stand was successful thanks to the support of family and friends.

A popular card trading game was very useful in teaching the kids the lesson of trading and negotiating. Eventually the school banned the game, but not before my kids learned successful trades and tearfully experienced losing their favourite cards.

My daughter also created and sold handmade cards. My boss ordered cards for the work volunteer program. The volunteers loved the cards and sent thank you notes. I came across her business files showing the key steps; product creation, customers, invoicing, branding and running a profit and loss sheet.

Next was the joint venture – Kidz Bizz with best friend and neighbour, both girls subcontracted work to their younger brothers. They developed fliers and business cards promoting the household chores they would do. Our neighbour was their best customer. They cleaned his filthy **ute*** for $10. He paid them everything in his pockets, often over $50. The

---

* A ute is Australian for a pickup truck, utility vehicle.

local real estate newsletter featured an article about Kidz Bizz. They spent their profits and also saved over $1,000.

In our new home, local shops were within an easy walk or bus ride. Both kids started in part-time jobs as soon as they could. My daughter had three part-time jobs while studying her final school years. My son was too young to be employed but still earned money washing windows and cleaning DVDs. When he was old enough to be employed, he submitted his resume three times for the job he wanted. Kids need to work for money.

6. HOW TO MANAGE MONEY

Growing up, I still remember a television show on how to manage your money by dividing it into velvet moneybags. I taught the kids to manage their money by dividing it into envelopes. My daughter remembers using the envelopes to save for her pink skate shoes and my son remembers saving for his console games. They saved and reaped the reward of purchasing what they wanted.

To securely save their Kidz Bizz money, they opened a join bank account. While opening the account, the Credit Union staff had the bank manager come out of his office to congratulate them, the boys were there as their employees and they all got a ruler, pen and a piggy bank.

I knew they needed to know more about money. In hard financial times, I spent $200 on a board game that taught them about the money rat race and a passive income. They were also encouraged to save money in a long-term savings account. The rule was to save for something big for when they left school. My daughter used the money as a deposit for a new car and my son bought a home theatre system.

Every week, I would budget my money using a spiral-bound notebook. My friend asked me about the book and wanted one for her budget. My spiral bound scribbles became the Budget Book©. Managing money is a lifelong weekly habit.

7. CELEBRATE

You need to stop and celebrate what you have achieved. 'Are we successful?' Well, it depends on your definition of success. But we are celebrating where we are now and looking forward with anticipation to where we are going.

We have broken free from a negative environment. We are building a happy trustworthy, supportive and encouraging environment. I'm celebrating having launched two kids who are employed; developing business skills, undertaking joint ventures, contributing to the economy, training and providing jobs to others and supporting community activities.

8. APPRECIATE

Truly appreciate everyone and everything that you have. This is hard. In my darkest moments, when I had driven across the country with no job, no house and I was wearing out my welcome with the people we were staying with, the wife handed me a book; one simple strategy from this book saved me from the depths of despair.

Just write down all the values you have left, everything you appreciate and all that you are grateful for. My first list was in a small spiral book and now I have an A3 sticky note on my wall. Every day, I say thank you for all the people who have helped us and everything we have. We are alive, together, with a home, food, clothes, cars and businesses that are thriving and family and friends to share it with. We are very blessed indeed.

9. REFLECT

It is easy to reflect and recall what has happened, only to ridicule what has been done and how you did it. Most people focus on the negative things and it has been no different in our family. Changing from being critical and negative is an ongoing process. It started while bringing up the kids and reading parenting books and putting into practice catching your kids doing something right, focusing on and rewarding the behaviour that you want repeated.

As the kids grew older, we had more midnight discussions that centred on questions like 'how did that go?', 'what went well?', 'what would you do again?', 'what can be improved?', 'any new ideas to make it better?' And then, let's not try that again - with a laugh instead of a self-beat up!

10. EDUCATE

We are on a journey of our lives and there is still a lot to learn. My dream is that my kids don't make the same mistakes I have. I would like them to take a short cut. I continue to try and teach them the lessons I have learned, without telling them how to live their lives or run their businesses.

They are still learning how to consolidate and maintain their business, how to work on and not in their businesses and how to have balance and stay positive. I am working on losing my fears so I can live my dream. You never stop growing, learning, improving yourself and working to keep your family and friends together.

SUMMARY

Are we the perfect family? Has this been easy? No way! We have heard every negative comment such as: 'fast food shops are a dead end jobs' and 'you're contributing to the obesity epidemic.' People truly looked down at my kids and me because they worked in take-away pizza.

It's depends how you look at it. When I have explained to the naysayers, that my kids are getting amazing skills, running multiple businesses, managing a turnover of over $1 million per annum, training and managing over 100 staff, they're amazed. So much for a dead end takeaway job!

We are real, the lawn gets too long, the house gets out of control, and there are days when we all get on famously and days when we don't. As Jack Canfield would say – 'don't focus on the problem, find a solution'. Do you know how many laundry systems I have put in place? I will crack one soon.

To grow business kids, create a **Trusting** (1) environment, show them that **Hardwork** (2) is important, have your support squad and provide **Support** (3) for their ideas. Teach your kids that money needs to be **Earned** (4), and how to **Make** (5) and **Manage** (6) money and CARE about everything you have. **Celebrate** (7) small and big efforts and wins. Truly **Appreciate** (8) everyone and everything that you have. Take time to **Reflect** (9) on how things are going, where you want to be and how you'll get there. Invest in **Education** (10) that will give you the information and the inner changes you need.

These ten base nutrients will help you grow *successful business kids against the grain.*

Max Simons. 2012. Day 2, Big Vision, 21 Day Money Breakthrough Challenge http://moneybreakthroughchallenge.com/21day/

1990 Norman Vincent Peale: *The Power of Positive Thinking,* Cedar Books.

About Kate

Kate Crowley Smith is a single mum, who has successfully survived, re-established her family and raised two entrepreneurial children aged 22 and 19, following a turbulent marriage breakdown due to domestic violence and compulsive gambling.

The rebuild was achieved through persistence, determination and a strong work ethic as well as staying gainfully employed by using her background in Nursing, Health Promotion, Injury Prevention and Patient Safety and Quality. As a Manager, Kate has experience in leading both work and volunteer teams, in organisational change and project management.

One of the key steps to rebuilding is managing your money well. Kate achieved this through the weekly/fortnightly habit of budgeting. She developed a book that makes budgeting easy. Due to the success of her own personal budgeting habits, Kate wanted to share her knowledge and as such has published the *Budget Book©*. This book is an easy-to-use guide focusing on the simple rules around budgeting.

Kate is co-author of falls prevention good practice guidelines, toolkits, checklists and journal articles, and she has been accepted to speak or Is often invited to present at conferences on this topic. She has been awarded the RoadWise White Ribbon Award for excellence in road safety initiatives and the Bishop Fox Trophy for all–round excellence in Year 12, the Highest Honour the College Confers.

Growing up, Kate was involved in her families businesses, during her marriage they had a business, and she has supported her children into their business. Now having launched her two children, Kate is developing the next chapter of her life; she is growing her Arbonne network marketing business and has plans in the near future to help others who have experienced domestic violence and compulsive gambling to rebuild successful lives.

For Budgeting information, visit the website: budgetbook.com.au or email: budgetbook@live.com.au

For Arbonne skin care: katecsmith.myarbonne.com.au

CHAPTER 29

EMAIL MARKETING, CELEBRITY-STYLE! — How to Create and Leverage Your List and Stand Out in Your Prospects' Inboxes

BY LINDSAY DICKS

Twenty years ago, electronic mail was first officially referred to as "email" – and, during those two decades, it has become one of THE primary ways we communicate with each other.

Yet, even though it is such a "youthful" communication method, many are poised to dismiss it as old-hat, ready to fall at the hands of social networking and cellphone texts.

Well, not so fast.

There are still over *three billion* email accounts out there – expected to grow to over four billion in the next three or four years. Approximately, 294 billion emails are sent *every single day* (that's a mere twelve and a quarter billion emails an hour).

Now you might say, "Well, so what? Most of that is spam that people ignore."

Not so fast again. Today, most emails are opened on a mobile device or a smartphone. And the number one influencer of mobile purchasing decisions, other than friends or family? Emails from companies and professionals – pointed to by 71% of mobile device users as the biggest tool of persuasion.

As you can see, there's plenty of life – and opportunity – left in email. So don't ignore this proven marketing juggernaut. Instead, go against the grain to create a winning strategy that will rock the socks off of everybody's inbox!

PLAYING THE NAME GAME

I've always maintained that building a strong email list is a critical part of growing your business. Yes, a well-crafted email marketing strategy leads to new clients, higher client retention, and ultimately higher profitability. But if you're not sending out those emails to the right addresses, you may be limiting, if not eliminating, your chances of success!

So how do you play "the name game" – and end up with a winning list of potential email leads?

Well, in the early days of email marketing, *purchased* email lists were often the solution. With this method, you could end up buying hundreds (or even thousands) of email addresses to use in your marketing campaign. It's easy enough to do, but a bad idea for a number of reasons.

First and foremost, sending unsolicited email (unwanted messages that get derailed to spam boxes) hurts your brand. It's not professional, and your recipients aren't going to appreciate it. More importantly, you might even end up with a "blacklisted" email address by being tagged as a spammer. And finally, you have no idea if the addresses you buy belong to anyone who would even be interested in whatever your business product or service might be. It's like shooting in the dark.

It's far more profitable, professional, ethical, and effective to build your own email list. Best of all, it's not that difficult – and only requires two simple steps:

> • **Step One: Set Up Your Site to Capture Email Addresses**

The first thing you need to do is create a website (or modify an existing one) for your business (or a specific product/service) that's specifically designed to get visitors to enter their email addresses for collection in your database.

There are several proven ways to motivate those visitors to give you their addresses:

First, **use attractive, easy-to-use forms on every page of your website.**

If your site is ugly, overloaded with confusing and/or hard-to-find information, and the opt-in forms are difficult to use (or relentlessly popping out at visitors no matter what they do to minimize them), you'll find few willing to give up their contact info. So make it easy for your audience to not only understand, in plain, attractive and well-organized pages, what you're selling, but also to enter their email addresses without too much effort – or anxiety!

Second, **offer freebies.** Let's be real – you and I both know we try to avoid giving out our email addresses as much as possible, simply because we don't want to be overloaded with spam. We all have overflowing inboxes as it is, without inviting more messages into our lives.

The best way to overcome this natural reluctance? Sweeten the deal!

Offer a free downloadable special report, white paper, or e-book to your visitors. Maybe even a downloadable video seminar if you're selling an expensive program or product and it's a cost-effective marketing tool. The giveaway strategy is a win-win: It provides your visitors with great value, and it gives you the opportunity to tell them more about your business and what it can do for them – while, of course, capturing their email addresses at the same time.

Third, **capitalize on "lukewarm" interest**. Undoubtedly, some of your website traffic will be "hot" – meaning, they'll be ready to buy immediately. On the other hand, some of the traffic will not be interested at all. But a *sizeable* percentage will be "lukewarm" - just intrigued enough to want to know more. Lukewarm leads will often convert into clients down the road – but that probably won't happen unless you capture their information and do some follow-up marketing.

So make sure that your lead capture forms appeal to these leads. Phrases like "learn more now" or "get the details" are a good way to grab their interest (and their email!) – and make it clear that they don't have to commit to anything beyond this right now.

One last word on this process—don't be afraid to make adjustments! Keep tweaking your site and your strategy until you find the approach that generates the best results.

• Step Two: Drive Targeted Traffic to Your Site

Now that you've hopefully created a better "email trap," you'll want to take every opportunity to drive as much targeted traffic to your website as you can to continue to build your email list. Here are some great ways to make that happen:

Start with **social media** channels such as Facebook, Twitter, LinkedIn and Pinterest, where it's easy to find members of whatever specific niche you're after. You can drive people to your site from these sites by posting links to your blog entries, sharing info about your products/ services and offering special deals and promotions. Start by highlighting whatever freebee you decided to give away on your site, with a link to the opt-in form.

Then there's **blogging**. A blog can be a tremendous tool for increasing website traffic. As I just noted, you can publicize your blog content via your social media pages. Not only that, but blog entries increase your visibility on Google and other search engines. Real and useful content is highly regarded by search engines and helps you rank higher in the results – which, in turn, also increases traffic to your site.

Article-writing works in a similar way to blogging. However, you can syndicate your articles across a variety of online sites and directories – and dramatically increase the exposure of your brand and your website. As long as the articles are well-written and provide value, you can count on many of your readers "clicking through" to your website in order to learn more about your business.

And then there's **video**. As sites like YouTube and Vimeo continue to grow in popularity, and videos become easier to create and distribute, business owners are finding that this is an awesome method to drive website traffic their way.

The premise is simple – create a video that focuses on the unique benefits of your product or service and distribute it via social media and other sites. When viewers see your video and want to learn more, they'll visit your website (through the link to it that will, of course, be featured in your video!). Just don't cut corners when it comes to creating these videos, as an "amateurish" or low-quality video doesn't position you as professional. Remember, you want to be regarded as a CelebrityExpert® - and everything you do must reflect that status!

Finally, there's **offline promotion**. Believe it or not, life goes on outside the Internet too – so why not spread the word in the so-called "real world," not just the virtual one? One great way to do this is by plugging your website while speaking or networking. Also make sure your site is listed on your business card and any other promotional materials. And don't just ask your audience to visit – give them a compelling reason to do so (like that amazing giveaway you came up with)!

Putting together a healthy, growing and targeted email list is vital to the success of your marketing – but it's still only half the battle. The other half? Read on and find out!

LEVERAGING YOUR LIST TO MAXIMUM MARKETING EFFECTIVENESS

As you build your list and prepare to create your next email campaign, there are four crucial keys to realizing the best results from your email addresses:

1. Understand your audience.
Who are you writing to? When it comes to the big picture, you probably already know the answer to this question. For example, a retirement financial planner wants to connect with those approaching retirement and those already retired.

But that's only the bare bones of what you need to know. One of the keys to an effective email marketing campaign is speaking directly to your audience, in as personal a manner as possible. Nobody wants to feel like they're just another name in someone's massive database – and, more importantly, if they do feel that way, your email messages will most likely be deleted without a second thought.

So learn more about your audience in terms of their individual traits.

Determine whether each contact is a business, or an individual. Identify gender. Identify age. Identify geographic location. Identify hobbies and other interests.

How? Well, simply ask a few extra questions on your sign-up forms, in addition to your request for their names and email addresses. But be careful - the more you ask a prospect to fill out, the more likely they are to opt out instead of in. Experiment and track your results to make sure you're not putting people off.

2. Segment your audience.
If you do have detailed information on your email contacts, forget about sending massive "one size fits all" email blasts to your entire list. You now have the capability to make it more personal – AND more success-ful.

And that's by *segmenting* your prospects. Break down your email master list into groups defined by common traits. For example, you separate the addresses by geographic regions or by age, gender, income level, level of education, or whatever filter works best for your business. That retirement planner I referred to earlier would likely start by segmenting email lists into "retired" and "not yet retired", as obviously these two groups would be interested in very different slants on how to handle their money.

Once your list is segmented, the next step is crafting content and offers that appeal to each individual segment you've created. Your list of those who aren't currently buying from you, for instance, could be targeted with special introductory offers designed to get them "in the door." Current clients, on the other hand, could be offered a rewarding referral program which offers an incentive for them to connect you with new leads.

The options are endless when you segment your list – and you're able to connect more directly with each segment's individual needs, making your individual email campaigns much more lucrative.

3. Be a "real" person.
Yes, I already know you're a real person – I'm assuming no robots are reading this! But most people don't regard spam as coming from a real person – they see it as a machine-generated annoyance. If the content

of your email blasts feels like junk mail, guess what? Your emails will be junked!

Here are a few hints to keep in mind when constructing your emails that will hopefully keep them out of the trash folder!

> **– Use your name in the "sender" field.**
> This is especially important if most of the list knows your name or you already have a good reputation.

> **– Send the email from a real address.**
> You don't want them to see the email came from something like do-not-reply@xyz.com.

> **– Greet your recipient by name.**
> Technology today makes it simple to set up your email blasts to begin with a personalized salutation, such as "Dear Mike" or "Hi Debra."

> **– Put your personality in the content.**

It's important to let your personal brand shine through in the body of your email. For some of you, that means humor. For others, it may mean "action photos" of yourself or your team hard at work. For myself, I like to keep my readers up-to-date on a variety of topics (especially the results of my shopping adventures!). Again, you want to come across as a person, not an anonymous salesperson. Be real, be interesting, be yourself…and your audience will be far more interested in what you have to say.

4. Always provide value.

Self-interest doesn't always trump everything else in life – but when it comes to a marketing campaign, it pretty much does. If your recipients don't have a reason to read your email – well, obviously they won't.

That's why your email must provide some kind of value.

Many businesses do it by attaching coupons and offering other savings opportunities – and a very effective approach. If you receive regular emails from your favorite local restaurant, and you know that they often include great coupons, you're going to open those emails every time… am I right?

But you can also provide value by offering helpful information to your audience. Going back to the example of our hypothetical retirement planner – he/she could share stock market forecasts, tips for saving money on taxes, an explanation of annuities, and all sorts of free and valuable information to an audience that already has an interest in obtaining it.

The best part about this approach is that it not only answers pressing questions for your audience, it also positions you as a leading authority in your market. It turns you into the celebrity-expert you are working to become, and it provides great value for your audience at the same time.

So take some time right now and ask yourself what type of information your audience is interested in. If you're not sure, ask them!

Yes, email is about to become an adult – and hit the age of twenty-one. But that maturity has its advantages – after all, email is now used virtually by everyone you want to reach (92% of Americans use an email account).

Not only that, but an email is still free to send. Contrast that with the cost of, say, direct mail, where you still have to worry about the costs of packaging, printing and postage. Email is an incredible bargain and an awesome marketing tool. It can not only be used to engage your customers, increase loyalty, and generate new leads… but it can also position you as the leading Celebrity Expert™ in your market.

So do some email marketing, celebrity-style – and become a superstar in your business niche!

About Lindsay

Lindsay Dicks helps her clients tell their stories in the online world. Being brought up around a family of marketers, but a product of Generation Y, Lindsay naturally gravitated to the new world of on-line marketing. Lindsay began freelance writing in 2000 and soon after launched her own PR firm that thrived by offering an in-your-face "Guaranteed PR" that was one of the first of its type in the nation.

Lindsay's new media career is centered on her philosophy that "people buy people." Her goal is to help her clients build a relationship with their prospects and customers. Once that relationship is built and they learn to trust them as the expert in their field, then they will do business with them. Lindsay also built a patent-pending process that utilizes social media marketing, content marketing and search engine optimization to create online "buzz" for her clients that helps them to convey their business and personal story. Lindsay's clientele span the entire business map and range from doctors and small business owners to Inc 500 CEOs.

Lindsay is a graduate of the University of Florida. She is the CEO of CelebritySites™, an online marketing company specializing in social media and online personal branding. Lindsay is also a multi-best-selling author including the best-selling book *Power Principles for Success,* which she co-authored with Brian Tracy. She was also selected as one of America's PremierExperts™ and has been quoted in *Newsweek,* the *Wall Street Journal, USA Today, and Inc.* magazine as well as featured on NBC, ABC, and CBS television affiliates speaking on social media, search engine optimization and making more money online. Lindsay was also recently brought on FOX 35 News as their Online Marketing Expert.

Lindsay, a national speaker, has shared the stage with some of the top speakers in the world, such as Brian Tracy, Lee Milteer, Ron LeGrand, Arielle Ford, David Bullock, Brian Horn, Peter Shankman and many others. Lindsay was also a Producer on the Emmy-nominated film Jacob's Turn.

You can connect with Lindsay at:
Lindsay@CelebritySites.com
www.twitter.com/LindsayMDicks
www.facebook.com/LindsayDicks

CHAPTER 30

A SHIFT IN NON-PROFIT FUNDRAISING

BY LYNN LEACH

Are you aware the economic climate affects not only individual households in our nation, but also the great non-profit organizations that take responsibility for improving our society? As budgets get tight, donations decrease, and organizations take in less to run their budgets with. This causes more organizations to compete for grants that are available through tax dollars and private foundations. The progression of creative ideas in raising funding for programming has been:

1. Face-to-face networking where the leaders and board members of an organization would go out and network with leaders in the Business Community and ask for donations to help the organization. Wealthy individuals and business giants looking to improve their public profiles would generously give to help the non-profits.

2. But more and more charitable organizations were formed and the trend moved towards event fundraising. Balls, auctions, dinners, luncheons, golf tournaments, etc. became an accepted way to raise funds for the charities. Volunteers were needed to organize and implement planning and physical tasks associated with a successful event fundraiser.

3. As the years passed and it became necessary for more families to have two incomes to run their households, volunteerism

decreased. The 20 / 80 rule factors in where we always see 20% of the people doing 80% of the work, and fewer people have been willing or able to devote that kind of commitment.

4. As foundations were established to manage charitable donations to worthwhile organizations, and government grants were set up to facilitate a fair and equitable division of tax dollars set aside to help non-profits, more and more boards of directors moved towards training individuals in grant writing.

5. As the number of non-profits competing for grants increased, creative grant writers began to partner with each other to increase their chances of being awarded funding.

6. The trend moved towards businesses partnering with organizations and giving them a "referral commission" for advertising their products or services to their memberships.

7. And now we see THE SHIFT or movement towards an awakening in understanding of the ongoing monthly residual income that is associated with network marketing / multi-level marketing partnerships. As individuals responsible for the decision making of funding proposals become educated in the distribution method known as mlm, we see more non-profit organizations embracing the concept and enjoying a continual stream of monthly income for their charities' programming.

This new trend in fundraising has its issues though. It goes against the grain for many people because of a lack of understanding. The history of network marketing has not been smooth. There has been a stigma on mlm / network marketing because of a few who ran scams, Ponzi schemes and pyramids. But direct sales, network marketing and mlm are legitimate business structures and effective distribution solutions for many companies. There are honest, ethical mlm companies out there that operate with integrity. So now it becomes a matter of educating individuals so they have full comprehension of the legitimacy of this powerful ongoing residual income that could be available to their organizations to help fund programming. As more and more non-profits move towards adding an appropriate mlm company to their fundraising portfolio, the negativity associated with this structure will dissipate and we will see a more open-minded and positive acceptance of this powerful funding option.

The fact is, building a customer base can be very lucrative if the mlm selected has a consumable product. When you have a consumable product, or reoccurring service charge, you have a built-in reorder business. You do the work once, and you get paid over and over again. And building a down-line of reps can also be lucrative because the non-profit now makes a little referral commission on each rep they sign and they continue to make money on everything that the reps produce. How easy is it for them to build a team of reps? Are you aware that there are over 175,000 people joining an mlm on the Internet each week? There is a new home- based business started every 12 seconds. The US alone has over 38 million home-based businesses. More than 2/3rds of Americans would prefer to be self-employed. 44% of home- based businesses are started for less than $5,000. Over $427 Billion dollars is made per year by home-based businesses. 70% of home-based businesses succeed within three years as opposed to 30% of the traditional brick and mortar businesses. Sobering facts. YOUR favorite non-profit organization or charity could be taking advantage of these figures by joining a network marketing company…not only for the fundraising aspect, but also to help that segment of the population that are seriously looking for a good company to join, and would appreciate being able to help their favorite charity out while they build a business and extra income for themselves.

I personally use network marketing as a ministry to help pastors, missionaries and non-profits raise needed funding for specific needs and programming. Most people may not be aware that some denominations and a lot of the smaller independent churches do not offer retirement programs for their pastors. This is also true for missionaries. In addition, there are pastors who make very little and must supplement their incomes with outside work. Many missionaries are also responsible for raising the money necessary to fund their ongoing work. My primary company, Q International, has more pastors and churches coming on board with each month that passes. There seems to be a conscious awareness of the wisdom of building a strong foundation with a company that will provide ongoing monthly residual income for years to come.

So how does this work for a church? There are several options. The church can join and let the congregation know of the opportunity to purchase the products or services through their website, a letter to the membership, or a newsletter. For those in the membership who may also be looking for a way to make a little extra money by working a side project from home, joining the company under the church would grow the monthly residual income coming into the organization. Some pastors join and then have the church join under them. Other pastors have the church join and then join under the church. Some missionary groups join and use the funds generated to support missionaries in the field, or to fund missionary trips. If they have a school, food bank or outreach ministry, they could sign up that entity under the church. Another option is for the national or parent group to sign first and then have the individual churches sign under them. If you have a denomination that has state and regional structures, funding for all groups could be accomplished with a little forethought and planning. If it is an independent church, sharing with other churches in a ministerial association would help several groups.

Secular organizations are also beginning to understand the power of the mlm structure for funding programming for their organizations also. It is so simple to place a link on the official website that connects their membership to the products or services and also affords those individuals looking to generate an extra stream of income, the opportunity to join under the organization. This now allows the non-profit to benefit from everything their member builds. Again, this would be an ongoing monthly residual income. It would take a little work to get set up initially, but once you get a customer base and/or a down-line established, then the money comes in month after month after month. Again, a little wisdom in laying down the foundation could pay off in raising monthly residual income for several organizations. If the organization has a national, state and/or regional structure, have the top organization join first and the other organizations join under them. If there is no structure and the non-profit stands alone, they can share with other non-profits they are associated with from Chambers of Commerce or other associations.

Exactly how does a non-profit organization select the right mlm to join? The same way an individual would select a company to join or a company to invest in. They would need to have open minds and listen to proposals. They would need to research and follow some established guidelines their committee sets up. Just know that there are many good choices and one can be found that would be a good fit for just about any charitable organization I can think of.

EIGHT STEPS TO SELECTING A COMPANY
TO PARTNER WITH:

1. How long has the company been in business? Companies in pre-launch or new start-ups offer excellent foundational positioning, but are a gamble and a lot of work. 95% of new start-ups do not make it past the first year. Most tools and resources are not developed yet, because it is the pioneers in a company that usually develop those. Young companies under 2 years are, in my opinion, not for the weak of heart and definitely not for non-profit organizations. I would recommend a company that is past their second anniversary and has had the opportunity to stabilize themselves.

2. Are you comfortable with the owners and management team? Do they have the experience to take the company into the future? Are they ethical, honest, and committed to working with integrity? Would you be proud to associate your name with theirs? If you have the opportunity, try to have a representative or your committee group visit the corporate offices to get a feel for the company, products, management team and owners.

3. Take a look at the product line or the service they provide. Is the quality there? Does it have real value? Most mlm companies have good quality products, otherwise they would not last. Remember, this is word of mouth advertising, and if the products do not deliver, they cannot stay in business. If you have a great product or service to offer, it is much easier for your membership to have belief in the product line. That belief is crucial to everyone sharing so the business grows and commissions are earned for the charity. But the belief factor goes beyond just the product line. Everyone must have belief in not only the products, but the management team, the comp plan, the owners, the resources, the tools, the training…in essence, belief in everything about the company. If you can accomplish that belief among your membership – then you will have something solid to build with.

4. Are there established marketing and sales resources available? Young companies usually lack in this area, so do investigate

what is available to aid you in building. If the company is strong in this area, then it is a plus for your organization. If not, and other things are in place, then you would want to try to see if you have members who have talents in that area that could pitch in and help design some things for you to use.

5. Is training and guidance available to you? Investigate the training that will be made available to you. Is there corporate training? Will you have strong up-line guidance and training that you will have access to? Will there be someone to help you design a plan of action for your organization?

6. Does the company provide good customer service? This is crucial. You need to know how they handle problems and issues. When is customer service available to retail consumers and also to reps? Do they have the right attitudes toward customer service?

7. Is the product or service backed by a solid guarantee? How much belief does the company hold in their product? What is the return ratio?

8. Is the company committed to being legally compliant in all jurisdictions they open in? This is a commitment that you want to make sure the company is willing to be steadfast in.

Researching and partnering with the right company will ensure success in your endeavor. Traditional fundraising companies are rarely able to provide an ongoing residual income from a one-time sale. The benefits of setting up the residual income with a good mlm company is that the orders will continue to come in on a monthly basis for years to come, providing ongoing funding for worthwhile programming that will benefit our society in many ways.

As the paradigm shift begins, and more and more non-profits begin to embrace this fundraising opportunity, I foresee charitable organizations being able to enjoy stability in funding that will enable great and wonderful achievements that will advance the quality of life for many people.

About Lynn

Lynn Leach has been married to her husband Norman for 42 years, and they have 3 sons and 6 granddaughters.

She has been involved in direct sales / network marketing for 45 years. She also has 13 years of experience in restaurant management. Her 44 years of ministry include serving on the board of directors in leadership positions for 8 large organizations and also 3 national secular non-profit organizations. She served as pastor of Mars Hill Baptist Church and was a gospel clown and had a puppet ministry. She now uses network marketing as a ministry to help families, ministers and missionaries, and as a fundraiser to help non-profit organizations and churches.

Marketing and teaching are two of Lynn's strengths, and she has developed her own training program to help people understand how to build their home businesses. She has authored *CALLING ALL LEADS* – The 10 Minute Interview, which is the first book in her Mentor With Lynn Series. It is available on Kindle. She is also a co-author of *NEW RULES FOR SUCCESS* with John Spencer Ellis, and co-author of *DARE TO SUCCEED* with Jack Canfield.

Because she understands what a toxic world we live in, she has embraced the Q philosophy of maintaining our life essentials -- our air, water and nutrition. She was the first to achieve the rank of Premier, the highest position in Q International, Inc.

Lynn is passionate about all natural healing -- on all levels: physical, emotional, relational, spiritual and financial. She owns Common Scents Health Research & Wellness Centers and is an aroma therapist and massage therapist. She specializes in essential oil science concentrating on emotional release, all natural pain management and all natural first aides.

You can reach Lynn at: pastorlynn@comcast.net. 724-292-8481

Her training website is: www.mentorwithlynn.com and her corporate site with Q International is: www.qinternational.com/lynn.

CHAPTER 31

WHERE IT ALL WENT WRONG, AND HOW TO MAKE IT RIGHT!

BY MATTHEW ELMER

"It's not what you know, but who you know."
...If only that were true, I'd have been a millionaire
since the day I was born.

Clichés are great, and occasionally true, but I've found most of them to be clever half-truths, like the "truth" we always hear about growing up: that going to school, working hard, and being honest will result in success.

Ok, so raise your hand if you work hard...(No, really go ahead and do it.)

Now, keep it up if you are independently wealthy (meaning you don't have to work tomorrow or any other day after that and you will not lose your cars, houses, or toys.)

Don't worry if you put your hand down; you are not alone. In fact, less than 1% of Americans could have kept their hand up! Clearly, there is more to success than just hard work and honesty.

Maybe the answer lies in your connections, or "who you know." For me, this was not the answer either. I came from a successful family, yet at age 30, I was still broke; in fact, I was in massive debt. How could

I have close connections with loving, caring people who were wealthy and still be so far from personal success? My question lingered, "How do I become successful?"

Drilling down into the question of what creates success can take one on an incredible journey and can result in some amazing stories. For me, this journey began at a relatively young age.

INAPPROPRIATE QUESTIONS

"Mrs. Schmidt, so why do I need to know this again?" I asked with my hand raised, but before I was called on by my 7th grade teacher.

"Shush," came the soft voice from the friendly blonde sitting behind me, "you're not supposed to ask questions like that, you'll just get into trouble."

"Don't shush me! I think I deserve an answer if I'm going to spend 40 plus hours of my life over the next year in this class." I replied so the whole class could understand my rationale for the question.

"Mr. Elmer, you know the answer to that question." the teacher vaguely replied.

"No, Mrs. Schmidt, that is why I'm asking it." I retorted, pushing against the grain with my tone.

"It is part of the curriculum." she replied.

"Curriculum? Who chooses this crap? I'm never going to use this to run a company some day," I replied.

"Maybe not," Mrs. Schmidt admitted, "but it's what you are supposed to do, and supposed to learn; it's important."

"Important to who?" My voice now faded into a mumble as I finally gave in and realized that bucking the system wasn't going to change anything at this point, and asking questions was simply futile.

And so the process continues. *We grow up, we listen, and we learn, hardly recognizing the pattern that the only questions being asked...are the ones directed at us.*

Onward and upward the path leads, from elementary, to middle school, on to high school, and then to college (if you are "smart," that is). Statistics show that the more education you have, the more money you make. The statistic less often shown is that the more education you have the more money you tend to owe. With the price of education increasing, and the job market having taken a significant dive, too many graduates are finding that once again, something is missing. What's missing is the answer to the question…What if I don't find a job?

Now, those with college degrees are statistically less likely to be unemployed, so isn't that enough proof that the system is working? It comes back to the question you are asking. Was "having a job" really the goal we all set when, as five-year-olds, we dreamed of being fighter pilots, firemen, or movie stars? Or does success mean security, freedom, and living a life of value?

Is security found in the path toward higher education? Students are now borrowing sometimes more than $200,000 to go to college. The majority are paying these loans back into their 30's (and 17% even into their 50's).[1]

Sadly, it's not necessary for you to verify if this statistic is true, because in the back of your mind, you can recall how you have seen the truth all around you. Still worse, you may ask the harrowing question: What if somehow I did beat the system, paid off my debt, and even saved a bit of money? Why isn't what I have enough? How will that retirement I dreamt of even be possible?

Why do I feel "Don't die with your music still in you?" may be the one cliché I ought to believe.

THE RIGHT QUESTIONS IN THE RIGHT DIRECTION

It wasn't until years after my inappropriate question to Mrs. Schmidt that I realized I wasn't the only one asking this question, "Why do we have to learn this?" I was just the only one willing to voice it. Although I censored the number of questions I vocalized, I never would tame the questions in my head, especially the question, "How do I become successful?"

---

1 (FRBNY at libertystreeteconomics.newyorkfed.org/2012/03/grading-student-loans.html)

I had a whole list of other questions such as, "Why were tests so hard for me?" "How can I use my skills to make money without a degree?" "Where do I go to learn the important stuff?" "How does money really work? Who really knows how to create money?" "Who really knows how to create results, or is everyone just committed to good test scores?"

This whole process of questioning others, instead of them asking me, felt a little unnatural. I'd been taught not to talk to strangers, but how could I even make connections if I didn't go against this counsel? "Respect your elders" meant "Shut up and listen, don't question, just trust." But I wanted some deeper conversation. So, I questioned my elders. I'd ask question after question to almost any person older than me. I was hungry for answers.

It soon became clear that people like to talk about their opinions, and outside of a traditional schooling system, people would tell you the real story of how to create success. All it required from me was the one thing I felt traditional education was stifling in me: curiosity.

It was on this journey of curiosity that I learned the power of questions.

RESULTS-BASED QUESTIONS

As you ramp up your curiosity and learn to ask creative questions, you will quickly learn there are some rules for asking effective questions:

Rule #1 – The questions must be open-ended.

Rule #2 – The most effective questions have no agenda.

Rule #3 – The most insightful questions are those you ask yourself.

It's time to start asking questions, not just to get answers, but rather, to get results. It's time to move past the need to be right to the need to be fulfilled. A life of fulfillment comes from a daily exercise of powerful questions.

THE MOST POWERFUL QUESTIONS

After coaching hundreds of business owners, I am often asked, "Are some questions more powerful than others?"

Now, that is a great question, though it does break Rule #2.

Powerful questions can help you forge your path toward an exciting destination. Like a lighthouse acting as a constant focal point for the exhausted sailor, these questions should be constantly held as a guide to us in our own voyage.

Three Types of Breakthrough Questions

<u>1. Launching Questions</u> – The answers to these questions will start you on the journey of becoming a creator.

- Why am I in the situation I'm in?

- If anything were possible, how would I describe my ideal life?

<u>2. Shaping Questions</u> – These questions, once answered, will shape your journey into the most ideal path for your life.

- What excuses do I allow myself in life?

- What is weighing on my mind most at this moment?

- What are the 3 most valuable things I can accomplish in the next seven days to experience more success?

<u>3. Acceleration Questions</u> – These questions are geared to accelerate the speed at which you experience the success you are striving for.

- What in my life is creating friction, distraction or interruption? (Think of 5 answers.)

- What do I do in my life that creates friction, distraction or interruption?

- What one thing can I do in the next 24 hours to eliminate that friction, distraction or interruption?

- What are the three activities that create the most immediate value in my business?

WHERE GREAT QUESTIONS LEAD

Now, after all of this talk of questions, it would appear that they may be able to unlock the answer to my original question, "How do I become successful?" Great questions unlock the door to the vault, they stir an inspiration in us to do more, be more, and experience more. Questions, once answered, can empower one to go against the grain. Still, something more is required.

My questions have led me to a realization that the greatest gift I've been given in this life is my agency, a freedom to choose my own course, and to become whoever I want to become. It has led me to question my purpose in this world. It has led me to discover how experts found their purpose.

I have found the consistency among great people is the principle of creation. They are creators of business, creators of inventions, creators of confident children, and ultimately creators of legacies, emulating all along the way the greatest creators.

Yet, creation, whether it results in a family or a business, has its continual challenges. And so, in my pursuit to engineer faster processes for growing my own companies and those of my students, I went beyond questions and discovered Four Pillars used by the massively prosperous in order to take quantum leaps in their success.

FOUR MUST-HAVE PILLARS OF ACCELERATED SUCCESS

The Parthenon was completed in 438 BC, yet its structure is still standing today 2,451 years later. At the core of its strength are 69 pillars. You don't need quite so many pillars when securing your own stability.

Specifically, four pillars are needed:

1. Result-Based Education
2. Cutting Edge Systems
3. Expert Mentor's Guidance
4. Mastermind Community

The future of education is one that combines the pillars used by the greatest successes of the past and the present including the Rockefellers, Henry Ford, Tiger Woods, and many more.

1. Result-Based Education

A Result-Based Education (RBE) is focused on results as opposed to simply scores on tests. Results include actual revenues and profits generated. Students are forced to view their time and cost of education as an investment which will render not only a Return on Investment (ROI) over the next two to five years, and Result-Based On Investment (RBOI) within 90 days of entering the curriculum.

In general, Result-Based Education is focused on the entrepreneur's journey. Three elements most common among the highest quality of RBE programs include:

   i. Visual Methods of Teaching

   ii. Detailed Step-by-Step Instruction, and

   iii. Entertainment mixed in with Education

These three elements capture the entrepreneurial brain's attention more effectively than traditional education, which attempts to belittle and correct the sometimes distracted, creative brain.

Result-Based Education, when applied to business models such as Real Estate Investing, has been proven to work incredibly well. However, it is anticipated that RBE will be built around many business models which can be operated by five employees or less, and can produce $100,000-$300,000 in profit by year two of operations.

2. Cutting Edge Systems

Ever since Henry Ford's assembly line process, cutting edge systems have been a critical piece of bringing greater value to the market than your competition. Without a system for taking care of mundane activities, precious time is wasted that could better contribute to the bottom-line. Today, it is critical for us to seek out, utilize, and improve the most dynamic technology, personnel, and training systems in order to maximize the results experienced in creating our own businesses.

3. Expert Mentor's Guidance

Research well-documented in the book *Outliers*, by Malcolm Gladwell, discusses the consistency of 10,000 hours of focused effort required in becoming a Master. However, additional research by Mr. Gladwell, along with Geoff Colvin's understanding in *Talent is Overrated*, provides a secret into expediting mastery. It comes from adopted hours. Mr. Colvin un-earths a key to how many geniuses become masters in their field. They had mentors or fathers whose own experience, when taught to the student, could shorten the time to mastery by several thousands of hours.

The point? Seek out experts, ensure they have other students who have obtained results, and pay them what they charge. It will save you years of your life, and may just be the key to surviving long enough to see your creation come to fruition.

4. Mastermind Community

The final pillar, a mastermind network, is preached in the greatest books, such as Napoleon Hill's *Think and Grow Rich*. Additionally, it was re-confirmed by Rick Sapio, a member of my own mastermind network.

Rick Sapio interviewed twenty billionaires in an effort to discover similar traits. One distinguishing characteristic is that the majority of them were part of a mastermind or community of some sort, in which they were held accountable to their peers. Effective accountability is hard to find, but appears to be essential if you wish to diminish the time between business launch and 'out of orbit' profits.

Truly, Your Network = Your Net Worth. Hang out with broke people, and you will continue to think and become more like broke people. Hang out with wealthy people, even if you don't fit in at first, and your mirror neurons will naturally start adjusting your behavior to match the success around you.

Doubt the power of these little neuro-processes? I suggest you take a flight to Australia and New Zealand for a couple weeks like I did a few years ago. While you're there, try a little experiment where you make every effort not to let "G'day Mate" or a "No, Worries" escape out of your mouth. It's nearly impossible.

Be aware of who you are subconsciously becoming and resolve to get involved in a community of successful, like-minded, result creators.

The educational programs of the future will be held to a higher standard. They will operate with not just one or two of these pillars, but rather all four. A long-awaited alternative to the emphasis on test scores and speed-reading will have arrived, and the creation of an entrepreneurs' world will cut hard against the grain of tradition.

The greatest fulfillment comes from the greatest effort. Your invitation is to inspire first yourself, and then others to live a life of fulfillment.

So, ask the questions, find your path, and implement these Four Pillar's to support your journey. Let your answers guide you to an exciting exploration as an inspiring creator. And remember:

"All men die, but few men ever really live."
~ William Wallace, Braveheart

About Matt

Matthew Elmer is a best-selling author, real estate investing specialist and serial entrepreneur who is regularly sought to consult and speak because of his systematic process for creating entrepreneurs success. Matthew Elmer has been seen on NBC, CBS, ABC, and FOX.

Matthew has one simple focus, "How do I create more results for those I train?" He calls his four-pillar approach, "Result-Based Education." Result-Based Education (RBE) creatively meshes rebel culture with business principles to create a hype-free following. His combination of training, support, connections and systems produce results for entrepreneurs looking to quickly build a profitable real estate investment business.

Matthew has proven his Dallas-based company's model is working by providing a systematic formula that has supported his students in completing over 220 real estate deals in their first 2 years of business. More importantly, these results were spread over 71% of his students and include all of his students that have been in the program for 60 days or more.

His passion for identifying a "better way" has been consistent in his real estate flipping business, Skyward Properties, LLC, and with his brokerage, Simplified Realty. He's personally negotiated over two million dollars of debt down to create the necessary equity for profitable real estate transactions in his own business.

Matthew's journey, however, was not an easy one. At the age of 22 he found a beautiful bride. Having been diagnosed with Hodgkin's disease, he watched as his dear wife passed to another life in that same year.

The journey from this experience led to him dropping out of college and later taking a job working in a sewer. It was those dark days that led to the drive he has today to assist others in overcoming their own challenges.

Matthew is now remarried and has 3 kids. He loves coaching his kids in football and basketball and will tell you he feels as Job is described: having lost so much, yet been given so much more.

To learn more about Matthew Elmer:
Visit: www.therealalliance.com or call Toll Free: 1-888-640-7325

CHAPTER 32

THE PRODUCTIVE EMPLOYEE PROGRAM (PEP)

BY MATTHEW T SOILEAU

Did you know that music and cows have a great connection, it seems that they give more milk if you play it for them? Somehow, my father figured this out in the early 1960's. He categorically dismissed conventional wisdom to try something new. He got a radio and played music every day for his herd in an effort to encourage them to give more milk. Dad had the best herd in the county. He had only 21 cows, but he could get more milk out of them than any of the neighboring farms could, and most of them had 75 cows or more. He got a better return because he took better care of his biggest asset and with individual attention got them to produce more than any of other dairy farms in the area. He gave his cattle the best feed he could get; and in the middle of the winter or blinding rainstorms, they came first and they took priority over other things. He advanced the individual animal as much as possible; in a way he removed the obstacles for them so they could do what they do best. I do not mean to imply that people are anything like cows, but I am saying that, to dad, the cows were his staff; he made sure that they were happy so he and his family could be better off. My father's example became my manifesto in business: give people the tools they need to advance while removing the obstacles from their path. Sometimes my approach went against the grain or was deemed foolish by my colleagues, but the success rate speaks for itself.

After the farm and then college, I went to work for a national garbage company in Houston, Texas. It was founded by an entrepreneur who started the business with one truck that he drove and collected the neighborhood garbage because no one else could do it as good as he could. In the late 1980's and 1990's this unusual company grew rapidly and became very successful for many reasons. One of the reasons was it was willing to take care of the people who worked there. They believed that if you nurture the soul of the individuals that make it happen, the individual would give something back. I directly benefitted from and was a student of that philosophy.

As a testament to their progressiveness and belief in building human capital, during my tenure there, the garbage company even began paying for my MBA at a private university in the city. They also sent most of their staff to Dale Carnegie programs, Toastmasters, and began a Quality Program long before it was popular. Their employee input committees and programs were highly successful and achieved many layers of success for the company. The company even had a gym in the building, which was virtually unheard of in any industry at that time.

Although I did not originate any of these programs, they inspired me and coddled me to success. I was able to finish my MBA and advanced my career by getting the education and experience from leaders who understood that to amplify their own success they had to cultivate their greatest assets, the individuals that make it work day after day. From my father to the chair of the board of the garbage company, they understood the necessity of fertilizing a growing crop to enrich the individuals' lives, and therefore producing workers who yield more for the company. Most of the people who came from these environments became very successful in life. When the garbage company sold, every employee found a very easy path to their next level of success. At this time, I had completed my MBA, had several progressive education and training programs under my belt, and was ready for the next level.

I joined a beer distributor in 1993 and quickly gained success as Vice President of Operations. In a short period, we grew this company to the largest distributor of its kind in the world. The progressive owner and his wife understood the principles of growing staff with incentives and making their world a happy place in which to become top producers. The owners are also products of this type of "giving more until you get more" programs.

The main program the distributor used was something called an EAR. EAR was a contract with each executive of the company that is known in other industries as Employee Appreciation Rights. Since this was a privately-held company, stock was not available to earn as an incentive in the salary programs. The owners created a virtual "right" (virtual stock) and as the company grew and the company met select parameters, the "right" grew in value. At the end of a specified period, sometimes five years, the "right" was cashed in and paid out to the employees over time. The company based the required parameters on profits, EBIDAT, paying off debt and market share. Each executive had jurisdiction in certain areas of the business, and agreed upon goals for a specific timeframe. At the end of the period, the measures were verified and a set pay out was established to be paid quarterly for the next five years. Some of these programs were worth millions in payout dollars.

"Rights" had two effects: earning them incentivized employees to excel at their jobs and propel the company forward, and during pay out they enriched families' lives.

Even though money was comparatively not as lucrative to the employees as music was to the cows, it had powerful impact on the leaders of the company. It kept them motivated while feeling like they were participants in the company's growth and the growth of their personal wealth.

At about this time in 2005, I created a company that owns a gym in the heart of a residential area that had no other fitness facility within miles. With its great location and a lot of luck and hard work, it has become a local establishment known for its customer service and happy staff. We help people live healthier and happier lives right in their own community. My staff is a great set of people who are very dedicated to what they can do for people and the local community. My role as a leader is to facilitate each person's life including those of the gym members. We are part of their growth, their path to the future and, hopefully, to a more fulfilling future of health and happiness. Through an employee care program, I have retained more customers, reduced complaints and increased revenues by establishing goals tied to monetary incentives for our employees. My company even offers a health insurance program with both medical and dental benefits, which is uncharacteristic for a company of its size.

As president of a company, you are president of employee care. Establishing a happy employee care program is a multi-step process.

STEP 1 – SELF EVALUATION

To do this right you have to be able to evaluate yourself. You have to know who you are, and you have to be comfortable with that end. It is difficult to help anyone, let alone run a company when you cannot see the real you inside. I learned long ago that you have to sit down alone and figure out what you need to make the best of your world before you can help anyone else achieve the best in theirs. It's a little like the safety measures on an airplane; put the mask on yourself first. Grow your personal education; read, go back to school, and seek counsel of others. Find as many personal flaws as you can possibly admit to yourself; and then fix or find ways to mitigate as many of them as you can before you begin this journey. Then you need to evaluate and be willing to do it repeatedly until you feel like you can go out and teach it to others. Unless you find and address your weaknesses, your weaknesses will become other's weaknesses. You want to be the best owner/president/manager you can be as an example to your employees. If you play only the music you like, and not what the cows like, you may miss opportunities to propel your business forward. You have to be willing to step out of yourself and your comfort zones and see what others are seeing and what they desire. Helping your employees grow will require this level of empathy.

STEP 2 – MAXIMIZE INDIVIDUAL PREFERENCES

As president, I have found maximizing individual preferences to be especially challenging. I really put a lot of effort into it and came up short. I interviewed every employee and asked a myriad of questions about where they want to be and what they desire out of their lives. The results were surprising. Most individuals really want to be at peace with the world around them, not everyone wants to own and run a company of their own. Most only want to live the best they can right here and now. They want to party or go on vacation, or just eat and rest and live a simple, healthy life. It took me awhile to see this, and it took even longer for me to understand that not everyone wanted to be like me. Subsequently, setting their goals and meeting their needs suddenly changed from what I wanted for them to what they really wanted.

All management has to do to create a happy employee care program is to remove the parts of an employee's life that are hard to deal with on a daily basis. Removing complications such as health care, dental care and retirement savings makes it easier to live and share their lives with their families. Once a manager removes the obstacles that frustrate an employee, the employee will gladly give the company what it needs to succeed.

STEP 3 – SEE A FUTURE FOR SOMEONE

See the employee's future for them. Sometimes I sit with people who do not see any future for themselves. I once asked someone where he saw himself in six months, in six years, etc. The answer he gave me was surprising. He said that he saw himself alive and working at the gym. He really meant what he said. He saw no progression, only that he was alive and happy. He is a great person and employee. So sometimes, I have to promote education to him and push him to try things in an attempt to find his passion. Sometimes it works, sometimes it does not, but it shows that you really walk your talk and see the world as a place with opportunities for everyone.

STEP 4 – DON'T MAKE IT THIS...A SOCIAL PROGRAM

A happy employee care program is not a social program; it is a loyalty program. We all share one goal—to make the company the best place to work so it can take care of the employee and the founders and/or investors. However, this is not a commune, and everything is not equally distributed. The ultimate goal is still profit and capitalism. It just begins and ends with the true assets of the company, the people who work there every day without fail. When employees are happier, the company and your customers are content. Additional content customers will increase profitability, so you can return at least some gifts to the team.

STEP 5 – GROW YOUR EMPLOYEES, AND THEY WILL GROW YOUR BUSINESS

Grow each person for who they are and what they can be. Everyone has limits to how much they desire to grow. It is not that they cannot do something; they lack a deep desire to do it. Some people are blessed to know what they want to do with their lives and have the passion to do it and push for it, others have to search for it and sometimes never find it. As a company leader all one can do is provide the music for the life and see if they find their way. Sometimes they will give you more, sometimes they are lost and stay there until they find themselves.

STEP 6 – EXPECT THEM TO LEAVE, AND THEY WILL BE LOYAL

Expect that at some point every one of your team will leave you for a better place and job. At least that is what they will think at first when they find the "perfect" position in another company. It is your job to see to it that the job they are going to or the place they leave you for is never as good as where they came from, your company. If you begin with their interest in mind, your best employees will stay with you. You provide a comfort level they cannot find anywhere else. You are on their side until they make the breakthrough for themselves one day.

Although devising and implementing a happy employee-care program within a company can be a lengthy process, the rewards for the employees and the company are worth any investment of time and money. There are some additional things to consider when building your business's program. Programming yourself as a leader so that you can program your employees begins as a journey of self-discovery, during which the best leaders will recognize that not every employee has the skillset or the desire to become a leader. In fact, not everyone can be a leader, but every employee can be encouraged to improve his or her own performance. Subtle team-building games to train for greater efficiency or group trips to encourage a team to get along better are bonus tools company executives can use to further build happy employees.

Regardless of the details of an employee program, the goal remains the same. Happier workers, like the happy, music-soothed cows on my family's farm, produce more for the company.

Just make sure that if the cows prefer jazz, do not play Rap music for them even if you love it!

About Matthew (Matt)

Matthew T. Soileau is currently the Vice President and Director of Internal Operations at Silver Eagle Distributors, the largest private Budweiser distributor in North America. He is in charge of warehousing and loading for the distribution of some 50 million cases annually in the Houston and San Antonio metro areas. He began his tenure 20 years ago when he became Silver Eagle's Director of Information Systems. After converting the company software system to current technology, he added branch operations to his area of responsibility. Matt was also Director of Construction and completed Silver Eagles Headquarters building on I-10 and Washington in 1995 along with several other projects in Rosenberg and Cypress.

Prior to joining Silver Eagle he spent 10 years as Project Lead (MIS) for Browning Ferris Industries where he installed landfill management systems. Mr. Soileau began his career with CECOS International, a division of BFI, as an accountant in Livingston, Louisiana before being promoted to BFI corporate offices in Houston.

He also served as Chairman of the Montrose Clinic Board of Directors and was member at large for the foundation. Montrose Clinic, now Legacy, is a multi-service community service organization.

He received his BS from Louisiana State University in Baton Rouge, Louisiana and his MBA from the University of St. Thomas in 1994.

Matt is also President of SMC Inc. and the General Partner of KPOD Limited Partners in Houston, a real estate and fitness facility management group of companies. The group purchased a franchise from Anytime Fitness in the Friendswood area and Houston Heights. SMC Group is also currently operating a few apartment complexes in the same area.

CHAPTER 33

FROM NORMAL TO EXCEPTIONAL

BY RORY CARRUTHERS

"Difficulties mastered are opportunities won."
~ Winston Churchill

It happened in the blink of an eye, but for an instant, time slowed as the cold steel hit bone. Then time raced back to normal as I could see the blood pouring down my hand.

I could feel the intense surge of energy rise up in me like a generator powering on. But this time the generator in me was wired wrong and in an instant, an explosion of sound, raw and powerful, exploded into the room.

The walls vibrated as the guttural roar came out of my mouth. My body oozing with pain and frustration. I looked back to see my wife standing there with a fearful expression on her face in reaction to my unexpected outburst.

I dropped the knife that had caused this outburst and ran to the bathroom. The sink started to turn red as I turned on the tap. The cold water came down on this newly formed wound in my hand. Relief for just a moment.

She rushed in to the bathroom to find out what had just happened. She could see me getting pale and all the blood swirling down the drain. I took a deep breath as I explained that a knife had slipped while cooking and had gone full force into my hand. She helped me clean the wound and bandage up my hand. As she did this, I thought back to what had just happened and how it would impact my future.

For 10 years, I had been a professional recording and touring musician, playing various instruments from guitar and bass to piano and keyboards and many others. In my line of work your hands are your livelihood and in this moment I was faced with the striking fact that my career could be over. I thought of what I could have done differently in the moments leading up to the knife slipping. I could have been paying more attention to the task at hand. Maybe not so focused on my thoughts. I could have chosen something else to eat. I could have decided to eat later or earlier. The list is endless but the reality was that, at this moment, I truly didn't know if there were going to be any repercussions to the incident. All I knew was the pain I felt in my hand and I was scared.

As it turns out, it was bad. Not horrible, but nonetheless it was bad. I had cut through some muscle and due to a one in a million condition where I heal really fast, a ton of scar tissue built up under the skin. That caused a lump to form under the skin at the site of impact. To this day that lump is still there. To this day I still have some pain in my hand. To this day I still can't play bar chords on an acoustic guitar.

So what did all this mean for me and my career? It meant I had to relearn how to write music. It meant I had to figure out how to play my instruments while accommodating the injury. It meant I had to find tricks to make it easier to play parts that I could previously play, but could no longer. It meant that in the face of watching my passion disappear, I fought back and did not let a seemingly career-ending situation get in the way of what I have to share with the world.

At times I felt as if I would never overcome this obstacle. Because of something as simple as a slip of a knife, I could lose everything I had worked so hard for. At the same time, I knew I couldn't give up. I couldn't give up on my talent, passion, and dreams. I knew that I owed it to myself to find a way to heal and continue with my work. Little did I know that I would do more than get back to where I was before the slip of the knife, I would push myself far beyond that. This injury gave me the opportunity to challenge myself. To see myself as an artist and musician in a new light. To tap into my unrealized potential.

As I put time and energy into physical therapy and practice, I realized how committed I was to continuing my career as a musician. This passion, energy, and intent allowed me to become even more successful than I was before facing this physical and emotional challenge. In the time since, not only has my playing improved, but it has affected every aspect of my musical career. I have vastly improved my songwriting and production skills. I have released more albums in a shorter period of time, while being more technical and complex than I ever had before. I also have been able to have my music played on the radio all throughout North America, something I had not been previously able to accomplish. I have been able to make an impact in numerous lives by sharing my message through music. And I've been able to write music that I truly enjoy playing and listening to.

What does this all mean for you? You may not ever have a knife slice through your hand; however, you will face obstacles. You will be put in positions where your commitment to your goals is challenged. Some might give up and say it is not worth it. Well, if you are reading this, then I bet you are a lot like me. That means that when it seems like the end, you know that it is really a new beginning. Maybe things haven't gone according to plan, but you have a passion and desire in you to make the impossible possible. It is this quality that makes you a rare breed. It's not an easy path to take, so let me guide you through these treacherous waters and give you the tools you need to bring forth the potential in you.

First off, this is not about getting you to set goals or pump you up or start you on your journey. Not at all. This is about what happens when you've been striving hard for a long time. You've been working hard toward your goal, but you're facing unexpected challenges. It is in these moments when you have three choices. You can give up, try to just stay where you are, or you can use this opportunity to flourish. I hope that you will choose to use these challenges as opportunities to flourish.

My job is to be honest and upfront about the journey you have embarked on. There are many out there that will tell you that if you just do this and this, that you will just magically achieve your goals. You are going to have an unrealistic perception of what it will take for you to become successful and you will quit because you don't know what lies ahead. The road is long and battles are hard won. Anyone who becomes successful knows that there are going to be failures. Tough times are part of the process.

This is going to be a hard pill to swallow. Going from horrible to normal is easy. Going from normal to exceptional takes at least ten times more strength, passion, and determination than you think it will. With that said, let's dive into what it takes to become exceptional.

The first thing I realized is that you have to absolutely stop comparing yourself with others. When you're facing a challenge, it's tempting to compare your situation to those around you. You may think about whether or not you can meet their expectations or experience their level of success. We all embark on a journey, but we all have different journeys to experience. You need to free yourself from the shackles of living up to someone else's ideal. Comparing yourself to others is a major pitfall because your best will be different than someone else's best. Once you realize this truth, it becomes so simple to comprehend because you realize that you only have to be better than you were, not better than someone else. This becomes the foundation of all your achievements. Every day you are given the opportunity to be just a little better than you were, at whatever it is you choose to focus on, so make the most of this wonderful gift you've been given.

Another realization I've found to be true is that you have to be stubborn. This does not mean being inflexible, it means being firm in your vision. Don't let anyone convince you that the temporary obstacles you are facing is the permanent end of your dreams. Remember that others may not be able to envision your full potential. Refuse to give up. Realize that by committing to your goals, you will make sacrifices. Know what sacrifices you're willing to make and don't allow others to dictate your limits. Be willing to give up something you want, for something that you want more. I can be unbelievably stubborn, just ask anyone who's worked with me. I push people past their limits and I hold myself to an even higher standard. When I face a problem, I allow myself to be stubborn and say, "I won't let this get in my way. I am going to find a solution or die trying." You owe it to yourself to reach your full potential. You've put in so much time, effort and money to achieve your dream, why stop now?

William Barclay said "Endurance is not just the ability to bear a hard thing, but to turn it into glory." If you want to be exceptional you will have to develop endurance. In the beginning, things are exciting and you are motivated by passion. But after a while that passion fades to some degree because we can't always by going 100% all the time. The further you are from your goal, the easier it is to start and build momentum. The problem arises when you are already doing well but you aren't "there" yet. The closer you get to your goal the harder it gets to achieve it. When you start, you may receive a lot of support, especially if you are starting in a bad place. However, when people don't see the immediate results of your labor, they begin to question what you are doing. Support and enthusiasm may wane as time passes. Do not let this lead to self-doubt. Realize that you will have hard-times, setbacks and failures. That's part of the process, and when you can comprehend that, you can see the traps ahead of time. Be vigilant in the pursuit of your goals and know that hard times are the stepping stones to greatness.

Keep in mind that society is designed so that achieving success is hard. If it was easy, everyone would do it. Now is when you have to realize that you need to dig deep within yourself, understand yourself, and focus on your strengths in order to bring out your truly exceptional self into the world. When you start doing that, you start to see things change in your life and in the lives of people around you. My wish for you is that you will learn to trust yourself and develop a deeper understanding of what you have to offer the world. You will be a more effective person and better equipped to reach your potential if you really pay attention and figure out who you are at your core. Use these new-found understandings to help guide you on your own unique path and to keep you moving toward your goals.

Remember, becoming exceptional is harder than you imagined. But simply knowing that there will be difficult times will prepare and hopefully encourage you to keep going. Be bold. Make things happen.

THE 3 KEYS TO BECOMING EXCEPTIONAL:

1. Stop comparing yourself to others. Free yourself from someone else's ideal and live the life you were meant to live.

2. Be stubborn. Be firm in your vision. Remember that others can't always see your true potential.

3. *Develop lasting endurance. Understand that becoming exceptional takes time and you will face difficulties and failures along the way.*

About Rory

Rory Carruthers is an author, professional musician, and audio engineer. He is also a songwriter, record producer, record label CEO, and a local and mobile marketing expert. In addition, he is also co-founder of the You Are Enough movement, a collaboration between music and resources, dedicated to suicide prevention.

Rory has been running businesses since he was 12 years old. However, it wasn't until he was starting high school that he found his passion for music. He began playing in a band with friends first learning the bass. Over the next few years, Rory taught himself how to play multiple instruments.

In 2001, Rory attended Audio Engineering School where he built the foundational skills to become a highly sought after Recording, Mixing and Mastering engineer. After school he co-founded the internationally recognized record label, The Gaia Project, which focused on helping bands who otherwise wouldn't have a chance, get their music out to the world.

Rory spent the better part of his 20's using his music talents to record and tour the country with various bands. After a potential career-ending injury to his hand, Rory reevaluated where he was focusing his time. After rehabilitation he formed a band where he writes all the music and plays all the parts, except main vocals. Since then he has dedicated his musical career to helping people overcome difficult situations and improve their life situations.

His band, Forever Yours, has gained popularity and extensive radio play throughout North America due to their positive message and sound that fills the listener with optimism and enthusiasm. Rory hopes to inspire readers with his words, the way his music has done for so many others.

Rory lives in beautiful Santa Cruz, CA with his wife Carly, dog Marley and cat Speech. For more information on Rory, visit: www.RoryCarruthers.com/bonus

CHAPTER 34

THE OPPOSITE

BY DR. RUDY BRAYDICH
& DR. MARK BRAYDICH

In the TV comedy series Seinfeld, there was an episode called "Opposite." George decided that his way of thinking had only brought him misery, heartache, unemployment, and a pathetic life. He decided to adopt a new philosophy by which he would do the opposite of what every fiber in his body was telling him to do. The results are that George gets a girl, a dream job, and numerous other opportunities because he quits thinking like the old George.

Could it really be that simple? Do the opposite? In 2007, rumors had already started about the changes that were going to affect the economy. Planning forward into the new economic reality, we decided to invest some money to hire a coach to give us suggestions on not only how to maintain our practice, but also to continue its growth in the predicted tough times ahead. Our coach helped us to realize that we had been operating our practice "doctor centered." We had decided what hours we would be open based on our preferred schedules, and we had made assumptions that patients and potential patients knew about our capabilities.

Many people hire consultants; it is always a good first step. It took us two years, however, before implementing the consultant's suggestions. Realistically the implementation determines success or failure. Since implementing these ten steps, our business has double over the last four years. Sometimes the changes were the opposite of what we would normally have done; some were just minor tweaks to processes already in place. All of them apply to any business.

1. BUY A SIGN THAT GRABS PEOPLE'S ATTENTION.

A business with no sign is a sign of no business. We had a sign, a standard, ground level, lighted sign with bushes around it. In two years, the overgrowth of bushes sorely in need of manicuring covered half of the sign and obscured its visability. We installed a new, elevated LED sign. The third day after its installation, an operational person from across the street who had worked there for years came in and announced that he had not known our office was a dental office until our new sign went up! The new sign cost $20,000, but it generates an average of $9,000 per month in revenue from new patients who schedule appointments because of our sign.

If you cannot change the entire sign, due to city codes or because it is cost prohibitive, consider adding something to the existing sign. In our case, a large toothbrush added to the top of an existing sign will give it a new and different look that will cause people to take notice.

2. TELL PEOPLE ABOUT YOUR BUSINESS.

People do not know what you do and what services you offer unless you tell them. We began direct mail marketing to existing patients and cold contacts. Our investment of $5000 per month has a ROI of $22,500 per month. Our office sends a newsletter to educate our patients and potential patients about our services.

Look for opportunities to tell people what you do: attend events to make new contacts such as "Do Business with a Member" at the local country club, or go to a Chocolate Expo and hand out toothbrushes. Place imprinted pens in every restaurant in town (the wait service always need pens). Use email campaigns to educate clients on new products or procedures. Every opportunity utilized to put your business name in front of someone new will pay off.

3. GIVE THEM MORE VALUE THAN THEY PAY FOR.

Never be stingy. People want value when they come into your business. Some are looking for discounts, but most are looking for the most 'bang for their buck.' Offer monthly incentives--we have monthly patient giveaways. A couple days each month, anyone who comes in gets a free something. In December, it was a window ice scrapper. In March, we gave a small green tin with mints in it. Father's Day week, men receive a sleeve of golf balls imprinted with our logo; for Mother's Day, each woman gets a rose.

Take time to listen to your customers. We are here to offer solutions to problems and to make people feel better after they leave our business. Kind words, a gentle touch, a card of thanks, or birthday recognition are inexpensive ways to insure customer loyalty. Customer feedback remains one of the best ways to build a business; your customers or patients know what appeals to them and what does not. This is your best market research. Consider sending monthly surveys to your client base and offering an incentive like a gift card toward their next visit.

Through our surveys, we learned that our customers wanted more hours on evenings or weekends to come in for appointments. Although the "opposite" of a doctor-centered practice, we trudged forward and hired staff to offer evenings and weekends to our patients. We did not realize before that many patients felt as if they were paying twice for our services, once when they paid for the appointment and a second time because they had to take off work to come in. One of our catch lines is "if you call us in the morning, we will see you the same day, guaranteed."

4. ASK FOR REFERRALS THROUGH CONTESTS.

Over 60% of our new customers are referrals. We encourage referrals by gifting our customers each time they refer a customer to us. Our initial offering is a thank you note right after the referral has been to our business. We follow up later in the month with a small gift with our logo and cards to hand out to other potential customers with an offer. We have a progressive referral reward system. The more clients refer, the better the gift they receive. Gifts range from coffee mugs to personal organizers to gas cards. We also offer quarterly referral drawings for big items. Every client who refers a patient gets one entry into the drawing for a 50" flat screen TV or a BBQ grill. A business might even offer a car as an incentive for the drawing, but with any large drawing, it is best to consult with state officials first for legality.

The difference between a potential patient or customer and a referral patient or customer is that potential patients are shoppers looking at services; referrals are buyers who have already decided where they intend to buy. The person who referred them already completed half of the selling process for you.

5. BE ABOUT THE CUSTOMER.

Get off your high horse. People do not want you telling them how great you and your product are, they want to know if you are the right person from which to buy. I tell my employees that if a customer knows more about you than you know about the customer, you messed up. Focus on the customer's needs, wants, interests, families, and friends; and you will have a customer who buys, pays and refers others to your business. Tell the customer all about you, and how great you are, and they will vote with their feet. What does that mean? …That they will leave and never come back.

Make extra effort to improve your customer's experience. We hired a greeter to offer the client coffee, give a tour of the office, point out certifications, and show them rooms like our sterilization room. The tour demonstrates our office's cleanliness and we have nothing to hide. Consider asking your clients what they suggest you make changes to or do differently in the office. Our patients have even mentioned to us the need to repaint walls; scuffed paint is something often overlooked by the people who see it everyday.

6. HIRE QUALITY PEOPLE AND TRAIN THEM WELL.

In the past, we relied on a hit-and-miss hiring system. We asked existing employees what they thought of a new hire and proceeded from there. We let the employees do the training. We got very few star employees by using that process.

It is only natural for existing employees to make sure new employees are not as good as they are. That is job security in their minds. Eventually, we developed systems within our business, which allow us to measure a person's progress as they develop within the organization. We measure progress, not by subjective opinion, but with statistics and knowledge of the systems in place. Then we continue to train and go over the basics. Just as football's foundation is repetitive tackling and blocking, each business has basics that require review. We never arrive; we just get better every day.

7. UPGRADE YOUR PLACE OF BUSINESS.

Get a fresh set of eyes to offer you perspective on your business's image. Do the grounds need maintenance or new landscaping? Is the carpet worn in spots or the wallcoverings dusty? Take pictures in and around your business. The camera will capture the "real" view that your clients see each time they frequent your office or business. Again, this is a perfect time to ask your clients what they notice first about your office.

8. INVEST IN YOUR COMMUNITY.

Establish a policy whereby every organization who asks for your time or a donation gets something. If the local cheerleaders ask for a donation of $200 toward their travel costs for the season and you only have $20 in the budget to give them, give them $20. The point is never to miss an opportunity to make a connection within your community.

Find out what your customers or patients are doing. Most will readily tell you about charity events they participate in or local non-profits they assist. Take an interest and help as many of these as you can. When you do so, you send a message that you care about your customer and the organization they support. Train your staff to gather information for you about what your customers are doing. Your staff is the eyes and ears for your marketing program.

9. TRACK EVERYTHING.

We track everything! Each marketing piece has a different phone number to contact our office. By having this we can determine if a piece is effective for us or not. The calls we receive from a marketing piece determine if we continue with that piece or make changes to it. We track our sales and who made them. We tape our calls received, which enables us to review our employees' telephone answering techniques. We have established procedure protocols for our services and sales people. How well they follow protocol determines their success in our business. When an employee is slipping within their job duties, it is usually because they have fallen off the proper protocol. We have a daily goal sheet which every employee receives that gives us information on how we did the day before. The goal sheet tracks: total and individual sales presented, sales closed, the number of new cutomers seen, the number of new customers who rescheduled, how much money we collected, and how we collected the money. Daily goal reviews by everyone keep our organization on track. It is amazing how a written goal that is reviewed constantly is always achieved. Tracking your marketing helps a business gauge its return on marketing investment in every area.

10. HAVE FUN DOING IT.

Show enthusiasm. You and your staff should love coming to work. Create an atmosphere of teamwork and fun in your office. Office contests work brilliantly to enhance employee morale and participation. Consider establishing a goal, say 200 new customers this month, and make it a contest in which every employee earns a $200 bonus when you meet or exceed 200 new clients.

Customer appreciation events also make it more fun to do business with you than with the company next door. Host customer appreciation events such as a bowling night or a movie night, or offer tickets to a sporting event and have a special section reserved for your customers. One event that our office has hosted for years is a bowling night. We invite our customers to attend a special bowling night at a local bowling alley and bring friends. Each customer must respond via email or telephone to RSVP because space is limited. They must then stop by at another date to pick up their bowling pass. We serve every guest pizza, soda and desserts and every participant receives a t-shirt for the event. During the bowling party, we hold a trivia contest for additional prizes. Free bowling and being able to invite their friends thrills our guests. The friends likely think to themselves, "My dentist doesn't take me bowling." The event fosters team building as our staff work together to plan it, and our customers get to feel loved and appreciated. We all win.

About Dr. Rudy

Dr. Rudy Braydich graduated from John Carroll University in 1973 and received his dental degree from Case Western Reserve in 1977. He and his wife, Jayne, started the practice in 1977 in Hubbard, OH. They have four children, Rudy, David, Phyllis, and Sarah.

Dr. Rudy and his brother Mark annually provide three partial scholarships to deserving students enrolled in the Choffin School of Accredited Dental Assisting. Dr. Rudy also is co-sponsor of an annual fundraising drive, Smiles for Charity, for local organizations that help children in the Youngstown-Warren area. They also provide an annual "free" dental care day in October that is co-sponsored by the "Dentistry from the Heart" organization.

He is a member of the American, Ohio and Corydon Palmer dental associations. He is also a member of the Dental Network Committee for Case Western Reserve University School of Dental Medicine and chairs the Advisory Committee for the Choffin School of Accredited Dental Assisting.

Dr. Rudy is an avid reader, enjoys teaching Sunday School, and loves spending time with his family.

About Dr. Mark

Dr. Mark Braydich received his undergraduate degree in Biology from Brown University in 1987 and his doctorate degree from Case Western Reserve University in 1992. Dr. Mark takes great satisfaction in making all patients comfortable. He has extensive implant education from the Misch Implant Institute and the IMTEC Sendax Mini Dental Implant System. Dr. Mark is a firm believer in continuing education and has trained in advanced cosmetic and implant dentistry during the 17 years of practice.

He and his brother Rudy annually provide three partial scholarships to deserving students enrolled in the Choffin School of Accredited Dental Assisting. Dr. Mark also is co-sponsor of an annual fundraising drive, Smiles for Charity, for local organizations that help children in the Youngstown-Warren area. They also provide an annual "free" dental care day in October that is co-sponsored by the "Dentistry from the Heart" organization.

Dr. Mark and his wife Rose were married in 1992. They have a son, Nicholas. Dr. Mark is a member of Holy Family Parish where he participated in the Men's Renewal Program.

Dr. Mark maintains professional associations with Corydon Palmer, Ohio, and American Dental Associations. These organizations allow Dr. Mark to converse with other dentists and provide high-level service to his patients.

CHAPTER 35

THE VICTIM'S LEADER

BY MONIKA BRUNSCHWILER

For 17 years, I was employed by the Zürich City Police. My job was, for the most part, that of an investigator. On the 3rd of August 2011, I was beaten severely by two Zürich city cops; both of them former co-workers. This violent act resulted in my hospitalization and I had to undergo surgery several times. However, I decided not to be a victim, especially not the victim of my former colleagues at work, whom I knew quite well. I felt humiliated though, and perceived my situation as very harmful. As a basically introverted person, I had to learn how to fight for my own personal rights, to find out the right position, and stand as tall and firm against my attackers as a rock.

I was one of very few females in a job with a 0.2% percentage of women; a member of a minority; a female David facing a Goliath. Hence suddenly, my former employer, the police corps of Zürich, was the cause of my massive physical suffering.

I was forced to take legal steps against these former colleagues, some other policemen, and even the Zürich City Police. This proved to be the greatest challenge of my life. Anyone reading this, who had to file charges against illegal actions committed by state employees in the past, is aware that one needs excellent leadership capacities in order to set this kind of thing in motion. I filed charges against five cops, and so far, the court has opened an inquiry and given authority to the prosecutor's office to investigate all but one of them. A success rate of up to 80% now is a really good result in a situation like this. Now where did I get the power, wisdom and knowledge to achieve such a high rate of success? How did I manage to switch from victim to leader?

Well, I did something quite unusual. I learned how to comprehend and apply the most effective leadership qualities that has and still does, make the world go around like nothing else.

The greatest challenge for a leader is this: Accept being a victim! Isn't that "against the grain?" "I'm just an amateur about the Bible,"– says Jim Rohn, "and I am asking you: isn't it interesting, that after Jesus asked God at the Lake of Gethsemane before He went to the cross: whether He could die in another way other than being crucified? And I think that God's answer can be reflected on as: You are free to do as you wish; however, if you aim to achieve that the entire world counts their calendar years after you and a lot of other world-changing influences that I wish to grant you, you must pay the proper price. And the price for this special place in heaven is to die on the cross. And if you do not wish to pay that price, then do not choose this path, do whatever you like to do. But I seek to exalt you. Do you seek that too?"

No other leader has ever had such an impact on the world as Jesus Christ, whether you believe in Him or not, whether you believe He ever lived or not, is that not unique? And He sacrificed himself, not just once, His whole life was a sacrifice and then at the very end, He made the greatest sacrifice in His life: He went to be sacrificed Himself on the cross.

In Switzerland, a mountain guide threw himself in front of a falling cable car and prevented a number of people inside from dying by sacrificing his own life. However, people don't often speak about this sacrifice-aspect of leadership and they do not even like to mention it.

Looking from the point of a mountaineering leadership philosophy, in which we perceive the mountain guide as a group-leader, one must mention that these mountain guides in the Swiss alpine regions usually walk behind their groups when going downhill – exactly 50% of the way. So it is clear that as a leader, one must give 50% of one's time to help stumbling, falling and weak members of one's group instead of being in the front at all times.

I had just turned 50, just been beaten up by my former policemen-colleagues, just moved to a new home and was just then learning how to go about defending myself against government employees, in order to obtain justice. I achieved this by using my own concept, the **Leadership 4Human Beings**®, which I had developed. It looks at people's talents in four main directions: *Headintroverts, Headextroverts, Gutextroverts, Gutintroverts*, and I named these directions: *MMLJ*® *Profile* (after Matthew, Mark, Luke and John). I named the system to improve oneself and the interaction between human beings that I put in a mindmapping system, the *PPI-System*© (Personal Performance Improvement System).

Leadership 4HumanBeings is very efficient in extremely challenging situations. I worked out the foundations for these techniques in seven years of research and by analyzing the speech of individuals **during tough situations and under severe pressure**. It's interesting to note that there are mainly four ways of communication used by people under pressure. My observations encompass adults, children, managers as well as leaders, business-peoples and families. And especially people in relationships.

When facing big overwhelming challenges, pressured hard and really "on the edge," the Headintroverts (Matthew) will try to be silent, and, if forced to speak, will do that in an informative, strategic and precise manner.

Put in the same situation, the Headextroverts (Mark) will not hesitate to talk, quickly summarize the issues in a results-oriented way, and will **not** pay attention to the details.

The Gutextroverts (Luke) though, when pressed to talk in a difficult situation, will speak without hesitation, and embellish his sentences, and express himself enthusiastically.

If the Gutintroverts (John) finds himself in difficulties, he will try to be silent. Persuaded to speak though, he will talk in a calming, caring and diplomatic way.

Now due to my heavy injuries, despite the fact that I wanted to flee the scene, I was forced to face the offenders. To go and confront extrovert authorities while being an introvert myself, represented a really tough challenge for me. I had to go and file charges against them and their unlawful behavior, knowing that they most probably would lie and try to make me appear as the guilty party and not cease to attack me. My research though had clearly shown me, that the only way to win against these cops was by not going into a position of defense. So in order to obtain a conviction of the perpetrators, I had to attack. Can you imagine just how uncomfortable you feel, as an introverted person, to assume the role of the extrovert? Charging, staking one's territory, charging again, keeping an eye on one's conquered territory before charging once again and securing the newly conquered grounds! During trial, those opponents, those authorities, officials, and their lawyers will not leave you any choice. And the good old game of the extroverts who charge the introverts by nature; and the introverts who retreat or run away as is their nature, plays a very important role during any trial; actually even before trial, during investigation. However, during trial all parties are really challenged and provoked.

And so each of the four talents has got their very own linguistic particularities, as well as specific strengths and weaknesses!

When using the PPI System you draw a mind map or an organizational chart and enter each person in their appropriate position. On the sketch, you finally mark, in chosen colors, our own position and main-talent (Head-Introvert, Head Extrovert, Gut-Extrovert, Gut-Introvert). You then add our co-workers, colleagues or members of our group. You check each person for the way they speak about personal or touching issues, under time-pressure or when in a dangerous situation.

When the atmosphere is loaded with tension in such a way that our nerves tingle, and everyone present is working hard on being understood, You will find out that it's actually impossible to understand each other.

> *"When the going gets tough, the tough get going"*
> ~ Brian Tracy.

Any conversation that has arrived at a dead end will stay there and spin on the spot until a continuation has been reached somehow. But how?

As soon as the Headextrovert becomes more accurate and listens more, the Gutextrovert reduces his enthusiasm and listens more, the Gutintrovert dares to confront and speaks more, and the Headintrovert harmonizes words more and speaks more, the tension ebbs away and the air becomes breathable again, the fire is extinguished and discussion once more has arrived on a factual level.

MMLJ® PROFILE

My MMLJ Profiling Concept is about talents and how people put together a sentence speaking from their heart and the behavior part is less focused. This is probably its greatest difference from other personality profile-methods currently existing on the market.

It took me 14 years to work out and complete my profiling concept. The first time my name was mentioned with regards to this system was in 1997 in Dan Korem's bestseller: The Art of Profiling, which was published by International Focus Press in Texas in 2001. On page 215, Dan Korem describes an event during which he and I totally unprepared and without prior communication ran ahead in support of the Winterthur police during the arrest of a thief. At that time, I was rather interested in the question of "which personality is the most likely to go on a rampage or killing spree." I have not found an answer to this until today. What I found out though, is the fact that since ancient times not a lot has changed with regards to general human interactions, and the way they treat or mistreat each other.

DISG® and Insight MDI® are based on the philosophies of C.G. Jung and American psychiatrist William Moulton Marston. The latter is not well known in Europe, but under the pen name of Charles Moulton, and in his further professions as inventor and comic-book writer, and in collaboration with his wife, he created the comic character "Wonder Woman." In some ways these models may help you to understand the MMLJ® Profile.

My findings have led me to religion. The interesting part about this is that religions too indicate 4 different basic types or talents, which have been given to us right at birth. The way to establish a profile based on this might even be a world first at this time, even though the method is, in fact, ancient as reflected in the name of my full-length MMLJ® profile: Matthew, Mark, Luke and John Profile.

According to my MMLJ® Profile, the head-introvert has been gifted at birth with Matthew's talents.

According to my MMLJ® Profile, the head-extrovert has been gifted at birth with Mark's talents.

According to my MMLJ® Profile, the gut-extrovert has been gifted at birth with Luke's talents.

According to my MMLJ® Profile, the gut-introvert has been gifted at birth with John's talents.

TWO POWERFUL QUESTIONS TO FIND OUT YOUR MAIN TALENT IN MINUTES

When you are unjustly verbally abused, what is your first verbal reaction? Reply or remain silent?

When you are unjustly verbally abused, how does your body react? Do you rather think or move?

Your answer could for example be this: If I am unjustly verbally abused, I immediately launch my counter-attack by verbally assaulting my opponent. In doing so, I definitely talk without great physical movement, concentrating on the most important issue. If this is your reaction, you are a head-extroverted talent with the gift of talking in a concise way which makes for fast results. Even though what you say may lack in evidence, and this can bring about trouble in the case that you should be forced to prove what you say. Long-term projects might be likely to collapse due to insufficiently funded templates. This reflects the Mark-talent.

If you have answered for instance: In the case of me being unjustly verbally abused, I immediately launch my counterattack not only verbally, but also by using body language and by emphasized speech with high and low intonations. If this is your reaction, you are a gut-introverted talent. Yours is the gift of gab and you are able to excite people just by talking to them. However, you easily run out of breath and lack concentration when planning on the long run, as you get distracted. This reflects the Luke-talent.

If you have answered for instance: In the case of me being unjustly verbally abused, I take one step back, gather my feelings and be silent or talk soothingly to the aggressor. If this is your reaction, then you are a gut-introverted talent. You have the gift of speaking in a harmonizing way and hence are able to calm down people very well. You handle yourself beautifully during long-term projects, as you are on friendly terms with all involved, but due to your consideration of the harmony among the people's feelings, they might be too time-consuming. This is the John-talent.

If you have answered for instance: In the case of me being unjustly verbally abused, I take one step back, think hard and be silent or present my findings in the form as evidence during my counter-argument, you belong to the group of head-introverts. You have the gift of verbally making sense, talking strategically and can inform people very well about complicated facts. However, due to your consideration of all the facts, others may be confused not seeing the read line in a project.

One of those four reaction-speeches is a match! Which phrase suits you best?

So if you have found out the reaction-phrase that best suits you, you will know how to improve yourself, especially when facing tough situations under severe pressure.

TWO "DO'S AND DON'TS TO IMPROVE YOUR SELF-ASSURANCE, SELF-BELIEF AND SELF-IMAGE

In a relationship like a couple, when he is extroverted and she is an introverted person:

– To the extroverted talents, let me say the following: Do not chase your introverted partners; do not attack them too often, stop overstepping their boundaries! Because if you keep doing all this, the time will come when you stand there empty-handed and your partner has left or will leave. Such behavior weakens both parties.

Hint:
Don't cross the border so often. Do not enter into the neighbour's garden without permission. As soon as someone pulls back, you immediately cross the border.

– To the introverted talents, let me say the following: Don't run away from your extrovert partners, do not leave them "standing in the rain," and stop ignoring them. Because as you continue to act like this, the extroverted will insult you, and accuse you of not listening, of not loving them, and ask you to change. As an introvert-talent now, you will go on soul-searching trips to find those mistakes and only blame yourself. This weakens the self-assuredness of both parties.

Hint:

– Establish a fence around your house and ask anyone that has entered into your garden without permission in a nice charming manner to get out of your garden.

About Monika

Monika Brunschwiler, is the founder of the MMLJ® Profil, PPI-System and the Leadership 4Human Beings. She has her own company in Zürich. She worked sixteen years in private industry and seventeen years in the police force of Zürich. The first time her name was mentioned with regards to this was 1997 in Dan Korem's bestseller: *The Art of Profiling*, which was published by International Focus Press in Texas in 2001. In 2012, she was in a Swiss TV Show, *Time to do*, where she talked about the work of the police, violence and rights as a former police investigator. This was a life stream shot and now is available on YouTube. Having seen a lot of extremely challenging situations, she recognized that there are mainly four ways of communication used by people under pressure.

The way to establish a profile based on words and language focus might even be a world first at this time, even though the method is, in fact, ancient as reflected in the name of my full-length MMLJ® profile: Matthew, Mark, Luke and John Profile.

To learn more about Monika Brunschwiler, the founder of the MMLJ Profiling System,

visit: www.monikabrunschwiler.com or call: +41 43 931 72 85.

www.monikabrunschwiler.com

Monika Brunschwiler,
Rudenzweg 74,
8048 Zürich, Switzerland.
Tel. +41 78 655 04 94 and +41 43 931 72 85

CHAPTER 36

MINDSET OF A SUCCESSFUL ENTREPRENEUR GOES AGAINST THE GRAIN

BY SHOMAIL MALIK

It was 10:30pm on December 30, 2009, my wife was at home pregnant with our first-born and I was sitting on the edge of a sofa in Hector's home, the brother of my client, Anna. Anna found it comfortable to meet with me at her brother's house, not because she was afraid to meet with me at her own house but more so out of sheer necessity. You see, she only spoke Spanish, and although I knew at least two more languages besides English, Spanish wasn't one of them. And when we spoke to one another, it was all in some concocted sign language. So whenever a meeting was needed to make progress in our deal, her brother would ask me to meet her at his house so that his son could translate what I had to say to her and vice-versa. For the past 6 months, I had been negotiating with her foreclosing lender to allow me to buy her house as a short sale so that I could do some light renovations and then sell it to a retail buyer. The bank was going to be losing a tremendous amount of money, but was willing to play ball so that they could take that money and go invest it elsewhere. After all, Anna had stopped making payments on her mortgage over a year ago after she went through a rough divorce. When she first called me to help her avoid foreclosure and buy her house directly from the bank, I could tell that this deal was going to take a LOT of work. My weekends no longer existed as I worked tirelessly to get the house in shape in order to re-sell it once I eventually was going to buy it. I even got my dad involved one weekend and gave him a bucket of spackle and asked him to patch up the ceilings. We picked up garbage around the yard, had to tow a deserted vehicle left on the driveway, and even evicted a squatter. And then there was the rodent problem, and ... oh yes, the illegal basement that the town would use as an obstacle to keep us from closing. And now, after all of this work, the day before we were going to close on the deal and make a nice fat five-figure check, she was threatening to back out. Aside from the divorce, her only son was disenfranchised after acknowledging his parents wanted nothing to do with each other and was planning a move to Florida to start anew.

As I began to explain to her, or rather to her nephew (the translator), all of the benefits of going through with the deal rather than throwing in the towel and accepting the bank to foreclose on her, which would be devastating to her credit and would make it impossible for her to attain finance at any point within the next few years, she revealed to me that the bank was not going to forgive the entire debt. They were still coming after her for $30,000 in order to release her of her mortgage lien--$30,000 that she did not have. For someone that only worked for under-the-table cash, $30,000 may have well been a million dollars. She began to sob profusely as we communicated in a triangle format, with our trusty translator reminding me that her husband left her and now her son was moving out of state and that this house was all she had left, and even that was now being taken away. She would rather prolong the process and frustrate the bank even more, not to mention waste the last six months of work that I had put in to this deal, rather than give her lender a single penny more. When I realized this conversation was going south and I was on the verge of losing this deal—the solution to came to me. I knew I could get the bank to settle for 10-20% of that amount—I just needed to convince her of it. I told her that I would buy her big-screen TV along with some of her other belongings in the house in order to give her half the money for her settlement. She had been working three jobs for the past year, and so, I assumed that she would have some of that money saved up and could contribute the other half. She knew I had the ability to get the number we wanted because I negotiated her primary lien down from $375,000 down to just $180,000. After some long deliberation, she agreed to our deal where I as the buyer, would help pay half the amount to have her mortgage lien released so that she could start a new chapter of her life absolutely debt-free. Our three-way conversation ended abruptly as Anna quickly lunged across the table to hug me and in the little English that she knew, with tears still in her eyes, she gathered her strength and said "Thank you." I guess emotions are universal, so there was no longer a need for a translator. She repeated that sentiment a few more times as I exited the door, knowing that we had both created a win-win situation for everyone involved. We made good money on that house, but unlike other closings when I was just happy to cash in the check, this one brought me to a few distinct realizations. Of all the people that I knew in my own circle of influence, less than a handful would have been able to close this deal from end-to-end. There were so many moving parts, so many different negotiations to manage, I quickly realized that had I approached this deal with an employee mindset, I would have been 'dead in the water.' The challenges that came with this deal brought out my survival instincts, and with it came out my entrepreneurial mindset.

The mindsets of the employee and the entrepreneur are, in fact, mutually exclusive. Although the employee may aspire to be an entrepreneur, the entrepreneur would never want to become an employee. Interestingly enough, if you look on the exterior, both of these types of people look about the same—both have eyes, lips, arms, legs, nose, and a mouth. So then what gives? I'll tell you—it's what they have between their ears and the lens that they see out of. You see, both an entrepreneur and an employee can have the same opportunity and be faced with the same situation, but the way in which they respond could be totally opposite. There is the age old story that talks of two partners with a shoe business that go to an island where they meet the local people and find them all to be bare-footed. One partner says to the other, "We are doomed! No one wears shoes on this island! How are we going to sell any shoes now?" The other partner, while perplexed at his partner's comments, ecstatically rejoices, "Are you kidding! We're going to be rich! No one on this island wears shoes! We're going to make shoes for all of these people and sell them a pair or two!" It's the SAME situation, yet two very DIFFERENT responses. Through my years in business and from practical life experiences, I've been able to boil these differences down to five Critical Lessons. If you are an aspiring businessperson, irrespective of the industry that you go in to, there are some paradigm shifts that you should be willing to embrace wholly. That shift has to first occur in the mind—if you lose that battle, the war is already over. And once you win that battle, half the war is already won.

1. TIME

For an employee, time is something they kill. For an entrepreneur, time is EVERYTHING.

Entrepreneurs acknowledge that time is absolutely the most precious commodity that they have at their disposal. Money can be made and money can be lost, but time is something that will never return. Each breath that a person takes is one step closer till their end. As the late, great Steve Jobs said, "Almost everything—all external expectations, all pride, all fear of embarrassment or failure—these things just fall away in the face of death, leaving only what is truly important, Remembering that you are going to die is the best way I know to avoid the trap of thinking you have something to lose. You are already naked. There is no reason not to follow your heart." While employees watch the wall clock from the cubicle waiting for it to strike 5pm so they can be relieved of their burdens, the entrepreneur is using every second wisely to either work in their business, or on their business, or on their own personal growth.

The entrepreneur embraces the fact that the day may not end at 5pm, heck it may not end at 10pm, but he or she has to make progress towards the goals that were set at the beginning of the year. He or she strives to find the highest and best use of his/her time by outsourcing what can be done by others and not wasting any time on menial tasks themselves. They understand that just as much as they need to plan out their day and account for every activity within every hour, they also need to make a list of things NOT to do in order to make progress. The entrepreneur has no time for tangents—they are laser-focused on what needs to be accomplished. Employees attempt to get through a day while entrepreneurs look to find what is the best utilization of every hour of the day. Employees wait for the "perfect time" to start a new business or project, whilst the entrepreneur fully understands that no such event exists, and so, the entrepreneur acts NOW. There will never be a time when every little aspect of your life will line up to your liking and comfort, and so, most people end up procrastinating their dreams away. Instead, take inventory of your resources and time and then begin to move forward in actualizing your dreams. Friend, if you want to be a successful entrepreneur, you absolutely must embrace the fact that time is EVERYTHING.

2. MINIMUMS AND MAXIMUMS

The employee approaches his job/career with a minimum mindset. As a colleague of mine would often say, "An employee will do just enough so they don't get fired, whilst the employer will pay just enough so the employee won't quit." The entrepreneur's mindset is one of maximization—whether it's making a calculated investment to grow the business, seeking best avenues to increase their investors' ROI, allocating resources to the most lucrative projects--the entrepreneur realizes that they have to set the bar for their business, and it has to be set super high. The entrepreneur is constantly competing with his/her best self, looking to outdo what he or she was yesterday with what he or she could be today. When it comes to service, the entrepreneur seeks to give the client an unforgettable experience by going the extra mile. As Michael Jordan once stated when asked in an interview regarding how he got to the top and stayed there, "I just had a higher level of excellence for myself than anyone else could expect of me." Friend, if you want to be a successful entrepreneur, switch off the "just get by" attitude and enter into a maximization mindset. And remember, how you do anything is how you do EVERYTHING. In case you didn't get that the first time, I will repeat that—how you do ANYTHING is how you do EVERYTHING.

3. VISION

Employees have just enough vision to get them to 5 o'clock every single day. They often live in the past and try to get through their present. Entrepreneurs, on the other hand, learn from the past, but live in the present and future. An entrepreneur must have the vision of charting an entire course for their company. Without vision, the company is doomed to failure. As the saying goes, "If you don't know where you're going, then you won't like where you end up."

Employees depend on the vision of upper management to provide them a roadmap and then simply plug into that vision, many times half-heartedly. The entrepreneur, however, is the captain of the ship. He or she knows that how they steer the ship impacts every single element of their business—their customers, their employees, their product lines. The entrepreneur has to be able to visualize what the future could look like and then draws up the strategies and game plan to go and execute on that vision. Friend, if you want to be a successful entrepreneur, you must develop a vision for your company and then work your tail off each and every day to bring it to reality.

4. STATUS QUO

The employee looks for ways to stay under the radar and is okay with doing things as they have always been done. The entrepreneur will look for ways to disrupt the status quo in every area of his/her business. How else will he or she stand out from amongst their competition? While employees are figuring out how to **survive**, entrepreneurs are strategizing how to **thrive**. Entrepreneurs are constantly inculcating within themselves a desire to be the very best in their industry.

When Apple created the iPhone, camera phones and mp3 players already existed. But the idea of combining all of these elements plus adding a unique design and incredible aesthetics allowed them to make a quantum leap ahead of all of their current competitors at the time. As the old adage goes, "Watch what everyone else is doing, and then do the opposite." There is so much wisdom to be realized from this saying. If everyone else is doing it, then chances are that a level of mediocrity has been reached and no one is looking to rattle the cage in order to make massive progress. Friend, if you want to be an entrepreneur, harness what has always worked, but always keep your eyes and ears open to try out new things by disrupting the status quo in every facet of your business.

5. INVEST

Employees look at investments as a cost or even a gamble, whereby once it is gone it is never to come back. Entrepreneurs understand that investing is like sowing seeds—not all of the seeds will sprout, but if it was a calculated, educated investment, the ones that do sprout will bring them back multiple-fold of that which they put in. Entrepreneurs are not afraid to seek out the best mentorship and deploy the best resources within their business in order to reach their goals. Most importantly, outside of just investing in their companies, entrepreneurs invest in themselves. They are avid students of personal development and are consistently looking to better themselves. They invest in books, in seminars and conferences, and in tools that will help them stay on the cutting edge. They realize the more knowledgeable and more plugged in they are, the better they are in terms of leading their companies. They understand that personal growth will translate to company growth, because after all, the speed of the group is determined by the speed of the leader. Friend, if you want to be a successful entrepreneur, then you must invest in yourself and you must invest in your company. And as your company grows, re-invest for perpetual growth and expansion. If you are not growing, you are shrinking.

About Shomail

Shomail Malik, like most Pakistanis and Indians, was conceived to be a doctor. Where they come from, you're either a doctor or an engineer—or you don't exist and no girl will marry you when you get older. While on that pre-med journey in college, he started his own distributorship for an Internet service provider and became one of the top distributors in the country, and yes, he did it from his tiny college dorm room. He told his parents that he would no longer be pursuing medicine because his heart was not in it, and being that this was the dream they wanted for their son when they came to the United States, you can imagine the mushroom cloud explosion that he had set off when he broke this news to them.

Around that same time, he was introduced into the world of real estate by a friend and went on to get his real estate license. He was privileged to be trained directly by the master franchiser in the state of NJ for Keller Williams, Mohammad Abbasi, from whom he not only learned the business of real estate, but daily habits of success and leadership that he implemented into his life up to this very day.

Upon graduation from college, Shomail started his career in healthcare sales, with increasing responsibilities in training and sales management. While he was working at his job, one of his clients introduced him to the notorious world of multi-level marketing. His 3-year stint in MLM gave him the gift of an incredible work ethic and a tough skin to endure the harshness of rejection that is often found in the world of business. In 2008, while still employed, and as the economy began its downward spiral, he started Strategic Realty Solutions (www.strategicrealtyllc.com), a real estate solutions and residential re-development company dedicated to helping homeowners avoid foreclosure, and buyers find great deals on and off the market. Along with his success with SRS came opportunities for him to teach what he had successfully done in real estate investing to new and upcoming investors, which gave birth to the Real Estate Wealth Academy (www.rewacademy.com), a premier teaching company that teaches and provides support to real estate investors all over the country.

Shomail is an avid supporter and leader of various Muslim American organizations and in helping his community contribute to our society. He serves as the Project Manager for the Muslim Youth Community Center (www.myccnj.org). Through this organization, he helped to found and co-organize the Annual Halal Food Festival, which drew a crowd of 4,000 people in 2012. Shomail is a certified speaker and trainer for the New Jersey Islamic Speakers Bureau (www.njisb.org), and co-organizer and co-founder of MYCC Sports (www.myccsports.org). He is also the Lead Volunteer

Coordinator for the Ramadan Orphan Drive for the Northeast Region of Islamic Relief, which has helped to sponsor over 300 orphans over the last two years. He can often be found giving the Friday sermon at various mosques or speaking to Muslim students at universities and Sunday schools throughout New Jersey and Pennsylvania.

CHAPTER 37

TURN OFF YOUR FAT SWITCH FOR EFFORTLESS WEIGHT LOSS

BY SUSAN KANSKY

Do you see yourself or someone you know in this story?

"Every time I go on a diet, restricting certain foods, and restricting calories, I feel deprived. About all I can think of is food, all the foods I can't eat. I crave food almost constantly and feel hungry most of the time. I can't keep this up indefinitely, so I go off the diet. All the weight comes back and then some. Then I feel like a failure. It's not that I don't have a lot of will power. It takes a lot of will power to just go on a diet. Why can't I lose weight? My doctor and my friends keep telling me I should lose weight. What is wrong with me?"

Why do calorie restriction diets fail so often?

There is usually a short-term benefit from dieting and that is because you initially burn the energy that is stored as glycogen, (a chain of glucose molecules), in your liver. You burn that up within 9 to 10 hours. And then you start burning stored fat.

Then as you stay on the diet longer, you burn fat up to your Fat Set Point. After that, you begin to burn muscle tissue. Then your body says, wait a minute, that's not good. Then your body starts storing even more fat. You go into fat storage mode if you continue with a diet past reaching your Fat Set Point.

Going on a calorie restriction diet is deprivation. It causes your body to think you are experiencing a food shortage, a time of scarcity or famine. The body thinks, "There is a shortage of food, a famine. I've got to store more nutritional reserves so that I can survive these hard times." This turns on the body's Fat Switch, which puts the body into fat storage mode. When your body thinks there is a famine, you are going to store fat even more. This is why when you go off a calorie-restricted diet, you often gain all your weight back and then some.

Your initial weight loss on the calorie-restricted diet leads to a grand illusion and misperception that to lose weight, you need to eat less. Actually, after going through a "famine" you gain more weight than you had before. Each time you go through another "famine," you gain even more weight. You end up gaining more weight in the long run as a result of calorie-restricted dieting.

There is a new paradigm. If you are too thin and you want to gain weight, then go on a calorie- restriction diet for a month to turn on your Fat Switch. Then eat plenty of food, and you will gain weight. To lose weight, have plenty of nutritious high quality food around and eat whenever you are hungry. This is the opposite of being in a famine. Counter to what you would think, or what you have been taught to think, when your body thinks there is plenty of food and there is no scarcity, and your body is not starving for nutrients, you actually lose weight. When there is plenty of food around, your body doesn't have a need to store nutrition for a later time.

When there is a famine or when you put yourself into starvation and scarcity mode, your body stores food for when there might not be enough later. Your body thinks, "I've got to store up food now, because there might not be enough food tomorrow or the next day."

When there is plenty of food with the nutrients your body needs, then your body turns off your Fat Switch and you can start losing weight.

If you want to lose weight, turn off your Fat Switch and stop storing fat. Make your body think "there is plenty of nutritious food; I don't need to store nutritional reserves." Eat whenever you are hungry, as long as you eat healthy foods, avoiding the Food Fat Switches, the few foods that turn on the Fat Switch.

There are two parts in the program for turning off your Fat Switch. The first part involves eating nutritious food when you are hungry, so that you don't turn on your famine programs. This approach works better when you avoid the Four Food Fat Switches and you also exercise.

Making a change in your diet is one way you can turn off the Famine Fat Switch. By adding in nutritious whole foods you will no longer be starving for nutrients, and then this Fat Switch will turn off. The principle is - add before you subtract. If you just cut out foods from your diet, you are going to be craving food. So add in whole foods, healthy foods including organic fruits, vegetables and legumes, healthy fats such as organic extra virgin olive oil, coconut oil and organic butter, healthy salt such as Celtic salt or pink salt, and organic grass fed meats that have not been finished off with grain. Adding raw foods, whole food supplements and super foods such as super greens and fermented foods will help you lose interest in unhealthy foods. That's the easy way to go about making a change in your diet. You can eat as much of these nutritious foods as you want. This will turn off your starvation famine program caused by starving for nutrients or by starving for enough food when dieting. When you add these foods into your diet, your cravings for sugar, refined carbohydrates, fruit juice, beer and alcohol and fried foods will just fall away.

The Four Food Fat Switches to avoid are: 1) refined sugar, corn syrup, high fructose corn syrup, fruit juice, soda, artificial sweeteners, whole fruit is okay, 2) refined carbohydrates including baked goods made with flour, 3) trans fat, fried foods, margarine and 4) alcohol especially beer. If you are exposed to refined sugar for 1,000 meals, which is three meals a day for a whole year, that will switch on insulin resistance and also lead to weight gain. Sugar consumption switches on a fat program that does not involve a stress event to trigger the fat switch to turn on. We are especially sensitive to fructose in our diet because it is metabolized in such a way that it causes you to store fat.

Exercise regulates our metabolism, reduces insulin sensitivity and improves our ability to feel satiated by the food we eat, helping us eat less.

The second part of turning off your fat switch involves using modern stress reduction methods to clear the stress events that turned on your Stress Event Fat Switch. Choose an approach that appeals to you. Some effective methods are hypnotherapy, Resonance Repatterning®, Recall Healing™, Advanced Clearing Energetics™, Emotional Freedom Techniques, and EASY™ – an Emotional Acupressure Self-care for You™ system. Obesity is just one example of a survival program that is turned on by specific kinds of stress events according to the Recall Healing system. Other diseases have specific events and situations that trigger the disease to switch on the Stress Event Disease Switches.

There are eleven stress events that turn on the Fat Switch. To burn fat automatically and easily clear the stress events that turned on your Fat Switch. You may have one to three or more of the triggers in the list below to clear. Fat storage is something we can adjust, when we understand how our Fat Switch and our survival brain works. Fat storage helps us survive. Once we clear the emotional upset around the Stress Events that trigger our Fat Switch to turn on, then our body doesn't need to use fat storage for our survival anymore. The fat will just fall away once your body feels safe to be thinner.

Have you experienced any of the following eleven types of stress events in your life? If so, you may have activated one or more of your Stress Event Fat Switches.

1. To store nutrition. Fat provides energy. We store fat for nutritional energy reserves. A real or virtual event that we perceive as a famine or scarcity can turn on the fat switch. Anything that our survival brain reads as a threat of famine or scarcity can turn on our fat switch.

Here are some examples of famine and scarcity issues to clear:

- Losing a job, the threat of losing a job, or living pay check to pay check.

- A stock market downturn and the loss of personal resources. Oh no. Am I going to have enough money to buy food? Will I be able to survive?

- An infant who is abandoned for a short period of time feels a huge threat to being able to get food on its own. So it stores fat so it will be able to survive longer when alone.

- You can be nutritionally starving, yet well fed or over fed and overweight. In other words, you can be eating fast foods, refined foods, and a regular American diet with bread and refined foods that are missing essential nutrients. Within 72 hours of grinding, grain has lost most of its nutrients. It's a dead food at that point. People are eating so much dead food that a lot of people are nutritionally starving even though they may be eating enough calories. Being in a state of nutritional starvation switches on the Fat Switch and causes people to store fat.

- It is known from the study of epigenetics that if one of our ancestors went through a famine that the progeny will be much more likely to turn on their fat switch. These programs can be easily cleared with modern healing approaches, such as those mentioned above.

2. Protection. We store fat especially in our middle. That provides protection to our internal organs. After a woman leaves an abusive relationship, she gains weight to make herself unattractive to men to emotionally protect herself from abusive men in the future.

3. To insulate for warmth. Fat has a lot of functions in us and in animals. If cold weather is coming, we tend to put on fat because it insulates us and keeps us warm. I have a friend who lives in Canada. Every winter she puts on 10 pounds and every spring she loses 10 pounds. You can also gain weight for symbolic warmth, for instance, when you live with someone who is emotionally cold.

4. To float. I know someone who nearly drowned. After that, she gained weight, because fat enables you to float. She will be better able to survive in the future if she is in water and possibly in a situation where she could drown.

5. To be seen. Some people put on weight in order to be seen and have more of them to be loved by others.

6. To slow down. Some people put on weight to slow down, because they feel they are moving too fast.

7. Looks. (a) To fight. I have to be bigger in order to be the dominant one, to fight and win the fight. So if there is competition in

the workplace and there is no possibility of running away and escaping, and if it is a very aggressive adverse environment, then you will gain weight until you become dominant. Just like animals fluff their feathers or raise their fur, because whoever is biggest wins, we can gain weight to be more imposing, so that we win the fight. (b) You may feel that you look too thin and feel in danger of dying. So you will gain weight to feel safer. (c) You may feel that if you're big and imposing, that you will be safe from danger, so you will put on weight until you feel imposing enough. (d) You may be ashamed of how you look or you don't like the way that you look. You may feel safer hiding the way that you look under fat.

8. Abandonment, separation. I know people that were put on a feeding schedule and fed every two hours a set amount of food, and left to cry and cry with hunger and not picked up when they cried out. They tend to carry weight on their hips and thighs – and struggle to reduce weight from their hips and thighs. When their stress of abandonment is cleared, then the weight on their hips and thighs just dissolves by itself.

9. Don't have what you want. You may feel you didn't have enough contact with your mother, enough nutrition, or enough mothers' milk. So you store nutrition in the form of fat which gives you the unconscious feeling of having enough.

10. Identity issues. You may feel you don't have the right to exist, the right to express yourself or the right to your own territory. Fat storage gives you a bigger presence which increases your right to exist.

11. Daily life stress is another Fat Switch. Chronic stress can lead to insulin resistance and metabolic syndrome and obesity. Metabolic syndrome is a collection of diseases which all relate to insulin resistance, where the body doesn't recognize the insulin very well. This syndrome includes weight gain, diabetes, hypertension, cardiovascular disease, cancer, dementia and Alzheimer's. All of these conditions are linked to insulin resistance.

The fat programs for people are similar to the fat programs that animals have. It is more complicated for us because the event that triggers our fat program can be a real event or the way we perceive an event. In other words, a virtual famine will switch on our fat programs in just the same way an actual famine will. Stress Event Fat Switches are the reason why your body must store a certain amount of fat. In order to effectively lose weight, these Stress Event Fat Switches need to be cleared.

So we all have a set point of how much fat our body wants to carry based on the experiences we have had in our life. Whether we were abandoned, whether we were attacked and decided to stand and fight or run and flee, and whether we experienced times of scarcity, are all examples of Stress Events that determine our set point. We all have our own unique set of events that have led to our having a unique set point for how much weight our body is comfortable having. If we do something, like go on a diet to try to change our weight without changing our set point, we will reach a certain point while on a diet where our body will do whatever it can to maintain that set point where we feel safe. There is a certain weight, at the survival level, that our body feels comfortable with.

These new discoveries mean that it is possible to change our Fat Set Point by clearing events in our past that triggered our Stress Event Fat Switch. In addition, we can support turning off our Fat Switch by avoiding the Four Food Fat Switches. Using modern stress reduction methods, we can turn off our Fat Switch and lose weight effortlessly.

About Susan

Susan Kansky helps people get to the reasons behind their weight gain and resolve them for effortless weight loss. She is a Resonance Repatterning® practitioner, and expert in Energy Psychology and stress reduction methods for resolving the patterns that turn on the Stress Event Fat Switches. Susan helps frustrated overweight people lose weight effortlessly, by helping them turn off their Stress Event Fat Switches, to switch off the fat storage mode in their body. She is passionate about helping people gently and effectively clear their specific cravings for foods, and their food and dieting traumas and issues.

Susan offers sessions and self-care emotional acupressure products to members of her Private Membership Association called Optimum Wellness PMA. Susan brings her 30 years of experience and a vast depth of understanding and knowledge to her work with overweight people. In individual sessions for her members, Susan quickly identifies and clears the specific issues that switch on fat storage. Susan developed EASY™—an Emotional Acupressure Self-care for You™ method for her members to use to clear Stress Events and other food issues on their own. Members report losing weight without even trying to, and without going on a diet. Others report having their food cravings disappear and stay gone.

For more information on Susan Kansky, visit: www.wellnesspma.com or call: 928-925-3426

CHAPTER 38

FINDING HOPE AFTER ADDICTION: MY LIFE-CHANGING TRUTH

BY LAUREL HURST

Living a life based on prior bad choices can easily undo us – just as much as a single childhood experience can easily be pivotal in forming our future.

This will be an unusual chapter in a book that, I am told, is filled mostly with business advice. Mine is *life* advice – a result of lessons learned as a result of adversity, much of it brought on by myself. The fact is this: Twenty-three years of addiction almost took all of my adulthood from me. Eighteen of those years I struggled to break free of the grip cocaine had on my consciousness.

Let me tell you how I found my escape.

IN THE BEGINNING...

I am the oldest of six children. My parents didn't do drugs and never exposed me to them. Nor did I just wake up one morning and think, "Today I'm going to make an absolute mess of my life" – and then go out and become an addict. I don't believe most people who create their own personal train wrecks do it knowingly.

No, the thought that began my troubles was I somehow began to believe that God created me to go to hell. I misunderstood the teachings of the church when I was young and I was certain that the Creator had nothing good in store for me.

Of course, when you begin to think that way, when you begin to think the All-Powerful One has rigged everything against you and you're helpless to do anything about it, you feel hurt – a tremendous hurt. That hurt gradually transforms into anger, resentment and then finally, hatred.

At the age of 13, the transformation was complete. My subconscious, my instinct, whatever you want to call it, directed me to destroy myself and get even with the God who hated me. Senseless rebellion was what now defined my future. At the beginning of my addictive period, I dreamt of my own death through drug overdose (I would have two more of those nightmares over the years).

When I locked down my heart and turned against God, when I began to use and sell cocaine, it was, of course, hardest on those who loved me. Of that dark period, my sister told me, "I was always waiting to hear that you were dead."

A TURNING POINT

As I mentioned, I was an addict for twenty-three years – and my feelings of anger against God were what set me down that deadly, dangerous path. The ironic part was that, less than a quarter of the way into my years of addiction, I was suddenly freed of that anger.

It was 1984, in a town outside Edmonton in Alberta, Canada. I had already been a hard user of coke for five years – and many of my user-friends had already OD'd. I was hitting bottom. I remember there were three of us outside in the thirty-below temperature – in our bare feet, fighting over a base pipe. Two days later, one of the other two would be dead.

That shook me to my core and in August I finally convinced my boyfriend that we should go north and get straight. But he spent all our money on dope – so he had to siphon gas from another car so we could make the trip to Whitehorse, the capital of Yukon, with our five-month-old puppy. Once we got there, we were arrested for possession for the purpose of trafficking – and the police impounded our car. I was finally released on the condition that I stay at a Whitehorse church shelter, where someone gave me a New Testament.

God was now back in my life.

But so was my boyfriend. I had made up my mind to leave him, but he made bail and I thought he could get me back home. Little did I realize how horrible that trip would be. He stole a canoe – and I found myself with him, our puppy and a large bag of dog food, headed north in October with only a nylon pup tent for shelter. I read my new bible furiously, from Matthew through Romans – and I had plenty of time to do that, since we spent eleven days on water for a trip that would have taken us two hours in a car.

Finally, we made it to a truck stop restaurant, where we got a ride back to our hometown in Alberta. I left him and went back to live with my parents, because I had been having some bad health problems. A specialist told me I had five cysts that were all the size of large eggs inside me, leaking blood. I was scheduled for surgery in two weeks.

Before that, however, on the Thanksgiving Sunday, I went to church with my mother and sister. An evangelist was preaching – and he gave me a physical healing in the name of Jesus. He began by putting his hands on my mother's – and then she placed her hands on me. He proclaimed that he was casting out the cysts in Jesus' name – and my mother and I both felt something like an electrical current pass through us.

In that instant, I knew I was healed.

I was examined again before surgery – and the doctor just kept saying over and over, "All the cysts are gone!" I never told him what happened. I just promised God that I would buy a Bible.

I was changed. The anger, the hurt, the resentment and the hate were all gone. God was suddenly with me, because I reached out and opened a door that I didn't believe I was allowed to walk through.

ACCEPTING GOD, FIGHTING ADDICTION

Now that I was through that door, I had made a decision to accept God. I had to change the decision I made for my destruction. I had to decide and want to live. It would take me eighteen years to beat it – with the longest period I was able to stay clean from cocaine during that time being only a four month stretch. I was caught between the two worlds of darkness and light.

I developed an intimate working knowledge of Jesus' Word through the Kenneth and Gloria Copeland Ministries. My heart held no distance from God. Sin is what steals, kills, or destroys life in us or others. That is why sin is judged to bring death.

Addiction brings the user a kind of gratification they can't get anywhere else. Cocaine, for example, stimulates the central nervous system and works on the pleasure centers of the brain.

Even though cocaine's addictive effects are considered only psychological, it still can have a physical basis. A psychological dependence exists when a drug is so central to a person's thoughts, emotions and activities that it's extremely difficult to stop using or even stop thinking about using it. Regular users, like I was, develop a physical tolerance and require more to get the high they want. That causes them to adopt a lifestyle that's outside the norms of society and riddled with habitual crime. Because of this difficult and endless situation, addicts begin to only identify with failure and struggle.

So I was caught between the two worlds of darkness and light. Before church, I would smoke joints in our car.

It was 1986. I was living with a few of my friends and in a new relationship. To make money, we grew and sold pot. I attempted to kick the cocaine habit for the third time – when someone told me that marijuana was also a sin and was preventing me from becoming truly clean. It never occurred to me – I was so focused on cocaine being the true evil in my life.

I knew once again I had to get out of the place I was in – and away from those I was associating with.

Fear plays a huge part in cocaine living. I flushed jewelry and everything that I associated with that old way of life. Immediately after I heard groaning voices coming from underneath the trailer I now lived in. I was overcome with fear and called my mother in a panic. She gave me some Kenneth Copeland cassettes to listen to on the topic of fear – and I listened to them over and over again, for three months, all through the day. Once again, I felt relief and I felt God all around me. As I step off a city bus, I felt fear step out of me; it left.

But still cocaine wouldn't let go of me. In 1989, I saw what I thought was a vision – someone who looked exactly like me walk away from me and then cross the street. I learned later our guardian angels look like us.

During those dark days, I felt like every time death came close to me, God intervened in some way to save me. His patience rescued me repeatedly. I remember doing lines of cocaine once while reading my Bible. I thought, "All I have to do is ask God to forgive me – and he will." What came into my mind was "Be aware of your wrongdoing." I entered treatment and spent six weeks trying to be cured. They told me I had a zero chance for recovery and that all my pleasure centers were dead.

I continued to use for another 11 years.

THE FINAL VICTORY

I found myself in jail again, thinking to myself, "Thank God this is over. I couldn't stop myself." In October 2003, I listened to the minister Jerry Savelle's audio sermon on "Breaking Habits." And he said, "Everything – and I do mean everything – that's connected to your old way of life? Get rid of it. And do it now."

And I spent a year with God. I refused to let any memory of cocaine usage into my mind. Instead, I was determined to live out the words of 2 Corinthians 10:5 and 6 – "Cast down every thought and imagination that puts itself higher than God." I continued to listen to The Message and to the Kenneth Copeland ministries audio files.

In 2003, I stopped using and began working. I got straight on the same block where I had last got high, and lived there for the next three and a half years - in the Victory Foundation transitional housing in Calgary, founded by Pastor Don and Colette Delaney, along with Co-Founder Administrative Pastor Vic Lappa.

My story continued to be positive as I continued to heal. A Federal coordinator told me, "Laurel, everyone is watching you. You had so many obstacles and you overcame them all." I was flown to Ottawa in Ontario, where, along with two others like me and eleven Canadian service workers, I met with the Head of Corrections Services and the Head of Research for woman offenders.

There, I attend a workshop entitled "Factors - What Works?" In other words, what will help the someone who I used to be become the someone I am today? My answer? Jesus the Word works. Whatever I hear or read that contains God's message works. Hope follows and brings you new life.

Two weeks after that workshop, I returned to my hometown. My memories had banished cocaine from my consciousness. I had no 'using cocaine' memory, no flashbacks. I was familiar with the area, that's all. Yet I can remember my little sister taking her first steps, when I was only four years old. I wanted to feel good, not remember the bad.

And I followed a principle I call a "Law of Life." All of us know that life is governed by various physical rules – gravity, physics, math and so forth. We all know that two plus two always equals four. To me, God's Word is a Law of the Spirit that is just as immutable and unavoidable.

The words we use on a daily basis affect how we feel, think and act – they are carriers of either good or bad things. Words that have the Law of Life behind them bring health to our bodies, minds and spirits. Spiritual laws are more powerful than physical ones – and they work for all of us in the same way. When we defy them, we create our own troubles.

When people tell me that God brought me out of my addiction, I disagree. God didn't take me out of my life, he brought me into the life I enjoy today. He delivered me to health and well being.

I took myself away from God. He brought me back home.

Now, there are others who suffered as I did who have found the same success as I have – and in less time. They have discovered the Law of Life as I did. I'm a forerunner. It's all fast tracks after me.

WHAT'S ONE YEAR WITH YOU, GOD?

If you or someone you know needs help the way I did, I suggest trying a year with God. In two years, I became a clean page because I did commit myself to that goal.

If you are hesitant, just start by asking, "God, what's one year with You?" Think about the answer He would give – or just stay still and silent, and see if the answer comes to you on its own.

If you are still reluctant, compare what a year with God would be to your current dismal and difficult reality. Could it really be worse to try the Law of Life?

When you are ready to begin, cut yourself off from all the world's noise. Listen as I did to those who speak God's Word – and to the Bible itself. Eugene Peterson's The Message spoke to me the loudest and it may do the same for you.

As you continue, you will find yourself at a point where you must make a decision to genuinely commit. You must allow God to overwhelm you and lead you.

Once you do that, the final step will be to open your heart – and God's love and joy will fill it. Don't try to figure everything out. The mind's questioning can block the gate to our spirit.

Remember to ask God to forgive those who won't ask themselves. Stay focused and stay strong. Remember that God will be with you no matter how long your struggle goes on. Mine went on for over two decades.

And I am here to tell you that He never abandoned me.

About Laurel

Let me introduce myself. My name is Laurel L. Hurst.

I experienced God's supernatural power in all areas of my life. I wrote this chapter for you and others to receive life as I have. God went through it all with me. And he made it possible for me to live his Word.

I went through as much as anyone could in my life – and now I want to reach as many as I can for God. Two years I searched for a certain kind of passion. The passion I was looking for is to help others to experience God's great goodness. Life is connected.

I'm: www.icitc.org facilitator and a motivational speaker for youth. I aspire to write about God in an easy-to-understand manner. Jesus' gift to me is to be able to teach others and, through my faith, believe in the miraculous for others.

I am in my 10th year listening to *The Message*, the New Testament God gave to me. Jesus said the Word of God is the wisdom of God. The Word is Spirit and gives life to us all. I experience God in my need for God to be involved.

Our will, our doing they can't separate. We make a decision when the situation arises. That decision made is what we will do.

> *"If we'd just be alive right now, we will see great things in God for us."*
> ~ Francis Frangipane (author of: *In Christ's Image Training Center*)

I hope you will access the following life change and Christian resources online at: www.nume.ca. Thank you.

For more information on Laurel. L. Hurst, write: lrllhurst@gmail.com
Or visit: www.nume.ca

CHAPTER 39

STACKING S-CURVES FOR HYPER GROWTH

BY KEN COURTRIGHT

<u>The following is a based on a true story:</u>

It's 1968. You work every day behind a spacious dark walnut desk. You are the head of sales for the North American division of one of the most stable, well-known, kitchen cookware companies in the world. Your product is not only carried in every state and province, your brand is showing up in two new countries, each and every month. Your product seemingly has no competition. Life is "Great."

A large coffee, a pack of Camel cigarettes and a one-inch thick stack of the last 30 days sales reports are dropped with a thud on the right side of your enormous desk, every Monday morning at 9:15 sharp. Under your directorship, you've held weekly meetings to discuss the successful "growth" of these reports for the last 12 years.

This particular Monday you sit at your desk and notice the coffee and cigarettes, but the large stack of sales reports is nowhere to be found. Thinking nothing of it you peruse the copy room, the break room and even the reception area looking for anyone that may know the whereabouts of the report. Not only can you not find the report, but you notice the lack of the normal commotion and sounds of activity. For a brief second you wonder if it's actually Sunday. You are brought back to reality as one of the few people at a desk, in a very uncomfortable and soft-spoken manner says, *"you may want to look in the conference room."* With your curiosity at its highest level, you make your way to "Conference room B".

As you get close to the door it becomes obvious that there is quite a ruckus going on behind closed doors. As you reach for the door, thoughts race through your mind...*we've been sold, we bought our competitor or our stock took a hi*t. As you open the door the room becomes completely quiet. As all eyes turn to you, the president of **Corning Cookware** looks at you and says, *"We have a serious problem."*

Within 5 minutes you are brought up to speed that not only have sales **not** grown for the first time in history, it has become clear that there are now 3 competitors that are within 6 months of having shelf space next to Corning in every store. To make it worse, the competitive products are high quality at half the price.

You know immediately that life is no longer "Great." Worse, you know of no conceivable sales model or method that can compete successfully against such an ominous obstacle. In your heart you know Corning is cooked. The meeting in the conference room lasts for hours. It becomes clear that Corning can't make glass cookware any less expensively without sacrificing quality. If they can't lower their cost, everyone realizes death may be inevitable.

Although the actual setting of the above story may have been slightly different, this is an accurate snapshot of the fateful day when Corning Cookware came face to face with the reality that their days might possibly be numbered.

From 1968 to 1974, in one of the most dramatic business success stories of all time, Corning did a complete pirouette, going from the global leader in glass cookware, stopping for a moment at a state of "near bankruptcy," to the global leader in a completely new and different industry. The Corning success story is considered one of the greatest business turnaround stories of all time.

Having unsuccessfully navigated a similar situation in one of my own businesses, I could not sleep until I understood exactly how Corning rose from the ashes to not only, once again, become a global company, but to do it almost overnight in a completely different industry. I had to find out exactly how they did it.

The principles and methodology that Corning used to "Immediately Increase Revenues," and moreover, to "Re-invent themselves" is a lesson that any company or individual can put into practice today. The method that was used is now known as "Stacking S-Curves." If you or your company is in need of either a quick burst of cash flow or sustainable secondary revenue stream, you may want to follow the three action items that Corning pioneered and begin stacking your own S-Curves.

Stacking an S-Curve, defined: An S-Curve is a visual chart or graphic of the annual revenues over the course of the life of a company. In almost every case, the chart will closely resemble the shape of a slanted letter "S".

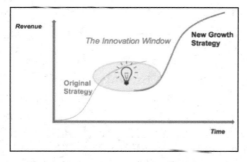

Every company has a life cycle that goes through three phases; beginning, growth and maturity. If you track the annual gross revenue of a mature business, the chart will almost always look like a slanted letter "S". The bottom of the S is the beginning years of the company when revenues are typically smaller. The vertical stem of the S is the growth phase of the company leaving the top of the S to represent when the company matures and sales plateau or drop.

The principle of "stacking" S-Curves is to keep an eye on your companies "S" and when signs of maturity begin to show that signals the need to develop another revenue stream, or "S-Curve". Jack Welch of G.E. was a master at stacking S-Curves. He was a master at researching and developing new revenues streams that used existing resources.

To understand exactly how Corning tiptoed around collapse by stacking an S-Curve, let's go back to their story...

It's now the very next morning. All management, sales staff and engineers are in an early meeting. This meeting is held on Corning's factory floor with all workers present. Corning's C.E.O. stands on a platform and says, "As I'm sure you've heard by now, we are in a bit of a pickle. We have about six months before our sales dip so low that we will no longer be able to function. We need every factory worker and engineer to set his or her mind to the task of answering the following question…

What other products can our equipment be retooled to manufacture?

The C.E.O. restated,

"We need to find at least 30 different items we can make that will not take any extra equipment, manpower or capital expense."

We will meet back here again in 30 days to see the ideas everyone has come up with. Our management team will pick two of the 30 options and begin diversifying our business. Thank you for your time.

A month later, back in Conference room B, 30 different products were laid out for all of management to study. A heated discussion broke out as to which of these products carried the most potential.

One person held up a small thin item that had been proposed and asked, "What is fiber optic cable?" An engineer stood up and explained that it is a thin glass cable about the size of a human hair. It was invented to be an alternative means of carrying voice and data packets as good or better than the traditional copper wires the phone companies currently use.

3 short years later, Corning was the global leader in the manufacturing and production of fiber optic cable.

Corning did not stop there. They continued to stack S-Curves. They continued to ask the major legacy question of "what else can we do or make that will not require any extra equipment, manpower or overhead?" 15 years later Corning invented Gorilla Glass and is now the largest global supplier of glass to smart phones, laptops and flat-screen TV's.

So what, exactly, did Corning do that everyone reading this can apply?

They did 3 things.

1. They asked what I call the "Legacy Question."

   "What else can we make or do that does not require any extra equipment, manpower or overhead?"

2. They brainstormed "Multiple Options."

   They asked hundreds of employees to come up with a total of 30 quality options.

3. They "Acted."

   When they made the decision, they immediately converted a small percentage of their equipment from creating glass cookware to glass cable. Those workers worked nights and weekends during the test phase of production. They began immediately.

So what is the lesson? How can a company, or an individual, put these into practice today? What can someone do to ensure their personal income or company never comes face to face with a financial disaster, and more importantly, sets a course for increased revenues each and every year, *regardless of the economy.*

I can best explain how to Stack S-Curves and add additional revenue streams through my personal story. I have a testimonial that speaks to the power of Corning's 3-step growth method. At the time of writing this book, my company, "Today's Growth Consultant," is filling out paperwork to see if we made the Inc.500 list as one of the 500 fastest growing U.S. companies.

Two items make our 20 year-old company's story fairly interesting. First, our fastest 4 years of growth came over *the last 4 years*. To some, these last few years are considered to be the worst U.S. economic climate in decades. Second, we only experienced hyper-growth after stacking our own S-Curve and repeatedly applying Corning's 3 Step Process. The true irony of our story, as we've been "growth consulting" since 1992, is that our real growth began when we stopped all forms of consulting in 2009. Here's our story and how I fell in love with the letter "S".

I started my first small business, a growth consulting company, in 1992. As a young business owner I was not afraid of long hours and backing up my marketing and growth concepts with 100% customer satisfaction. After a few years of good growth in the consulting industry, I decided to put my growth techniques into practice and open a business with a storefront. I decided to branch out into the video store industry. Three years after the decision, my wife and I owned and operated a small chain of video stores. With multiple video stores and both companies well past 30 full time employees I felt 10-foot-tall and bullet-proof.

As quick as Corning felt the pressure of 3 global competitors, I felt the sting of Blockbuster, Hollywood and Family Video moving right next door to every video store we operated. All three competitors moved in over a 9-month period of time. In less than 9 months we went from profiting $10,000 per store per month, to losing $3,000 per store per month. It was the most hopeless and suffocating feeling I've ever felt.

As I had not yet been privy to Corning's resurrection success story, our office became very somber very quick. Every week we walked into sales reports that were worse then the week before. Stress and financial pressure were at an all time high, so much so, that we even lost an employee to a heart attack during a sales meeting. We eventually lost everything in our video store company, selling off the final inventory to pay down debt.

After these dark times I vowed to never put my family or one of my companies in that position again. I attacked our consulting business with a vengeance. A few years later I heard someone share Corning's success story. I read everything I could get my hands on about how they did it. I had never before heard a company story that sounded as hopeless as the one I had went through. Not only did they make it, they grew 50 times larger over a 10-year period of time. What hit me the hardest was that in 1968 Corning had one revenue stream. Today, they have dozens. I became consumed with a plan to apply the principles that Corning, to this day, applies on a regular basis.

Here's what I did.

In 2008 I took stock of where we were. In 16 years we had helped grow 2700 businesses. I charted our annual sales and drew out our lifetime S-Curve. In the beginning we had grown sales year after year. The last few years our chart was showing very flat at the top, with similar sales each year. It was clear that it was time to reinvent for two reasons. First, the top of our "S" was perfectly flat and second, we dangerously had only one source of revenue.

I started at Step 1. I asked myself the legacy question. What else can I or we do to add an additional revenue stream without adding any extra manpower, equipment or overhead? After coming up with and reviewing many options, one item (Step 2.) kept jumping off the page. One option was to begin partnering up with industry thought leaders to create authoritative revenue-generating websites. It would be like creating mini-versions of the website WebMD.com. I found that this site was generating hundreds of millions per year in ad revenue. I felt we could train part of our staff on nights and weekends to learn how to build large websites, modeled after WebMD. We would partner up with industry experts, we'd build, market and monetize the site, they'd write the content, and we'd split any revenues we created. I loved the idea because it didn't cost anything to try.

One challenge, at this point, our company had never built a website. To me, that didn't matter, as Corning had never made fiber optic cable. I also knew that necessity is the mother of all invention, and it was necessary to change. I had historical personal evidence that no company is bullet proof; I was determined to add another revenue channel.

It was now time for Step 3, action.

It's been an incredible ride as we have built and own hundreds of websites all over the world. Our revenues have doubled four years in a row. Most importantly, however, is that I will never forget that all companies mature. To state it differently, all companies are mortal. In 2011 we stacked another S-Curve. We asked exactly the same 3 questions.

Due to our new experience in large website building, our answer to the legacy question was completely different. In January of 2012, part of our existing staff got trained in a completely new area of "buying" websites. We started another company, Income Store. Income Store buys existing revenue generating websites for individuals and fund managers. Once we buy the website for them, we split the revenues. Income Store is outgrowing Today's Growth Consultant in only one year. I will be stacking an S-Curve every three to five years.

Every person reading this can stack an S-Curve on top of his or her current job or business. S-Curves eliminate most new business start up obstacles because the S-Curve's inherent formula is simply based on time.

I challenge everyone to take the first step and ask yourself the legacy question...

"What else can I / we make or do that does not require any extra equipment, manpower or overhead?" Then, of course, review multiple options and take action.

About Ken

Ken Courtright is the author of Online Income: *Navigating the Internet Minefield*. Ken is the founder and CEO of Today's Growth Consultant (TGC) and Income Store. Over the last 20 years, Ken and his team have helped grow over 2700 businesses. Re-Inventing itself in 2009, TGC now owns over 200 authoritative websites, each site partnered with industry thought leaders, executives, authors and people of influence.

Recently, Ken launched another company, Income Store. Income Store buys "revenue generating" websites for individuals and fund managers. Ken's (group of) websites are seen by just under 100 million people each year and are referenced and featured in all forms of media.

Ken's companies have doubled revenues each of the last four years allowing them, after 20 years, to submit paperwork to apply for the Inc.500 list as one of the 500 fastest growing U.S. companies.

After losing nearly everything in a separate business venture over ten years ago, Ken vowed never to allow himself or his companies to have just one form of revenue. Currently Ken and his team manage over 80 different revenue streams in over 30 industries.

To learn more about Ken Courtright,

visit: www.MeetKenCourtright.com

Or call: 877-627-1213

CHAPTER 40

MINDSET TO SUCCESS

BY TOREY EISENMAN

Business and life are about positioning and strategy. Have you ever had a great idea and have someone tell you that you will never succeed? How about "You will totally fail at that venture?" I have had multiple people tell me this. I understand that we all have different strengths and are willing to experience different risks. There was a time in my life that I really wasn't sure what my purpose was. I felt lost and wasn't sure if I should listen to the naysayers and go back to corporate America or proceed forward as an entrepreneur. I am going to share how I got to where I am today.

I had a challenging twelve months in my life that commenced in December of 2006. I lost my mom to cancer in December of 2006. In May of 2007, I lost my dad to undiagnosed heart disease and in November of 2007 I was laid off from a 15-year home-building career. I must admit at that time I questioned a lot of things, and I often asked "Why me?"

I had a choice. I could feel sorry for myself or I could start moving forward. This sounds easy. However, when you have a lot of bad things happen at once sometimes it is a challenge to see light at the end of the tunnel. I started to write down on a daily basis what I was grateful for. I must admit that initially I could not think of one thing as I was consumed with negativity. I started with stating I am grateful to have my health. I am grateful to have my son, Zachary. After several days and evenings on focusing on what I was grateful for, the process became much easier. The list became longer daily, and frankly, my mindset began to change.

I decided to take six months to spend time with my son. I was a single mom at the time and with the recent loss of both of my parents, I felt as though I had just lost a large part of my support team including a large part of myself. This time allowed for a substantial amount of self-evaluation and time to seriously consider my options going forward as I needed an income- producing career of some sort. After several months, I decided to open my own business.

I am sure you can imagine the feedback I received as I asked friends and peers what they thought about me opening a real estate company. Keep in mind, we are in the Spring of 2008 and the real estate market has crashed. People are getting out of the real estate industry as times are tough. I had to agree that it was a tough market. I assessed the market and realized it may be tough; however when things get bad, there always tends to be an opportunity. I spent several months getting educated on the short sale market. I made appointments with attorneys and accountants, and I interviewed them and asked as many questions as I could, relative to real estate and the effects of a short sale on the consumer. I spent months researching the Internet and taking classes specific to obtaining loans and eliminating debt. I joined the local real estate association and I learned how to write residential contracts and joined committees to get educated on the residential real estate industry.

I was educating myself. I am a third generation realtor and a second-generation General Contractor. However, I worked in the home building industry from an operations perspective with no experience on the sales side of the business. I understood the power of knowledge.

It was great that I was able to educate myself and get a strong understanding of processes. Now it was time to go help people. What I didn't realize was that no one knew who I was. I again felt frustrated. I had a plan to understand all aspects of this business, which was great; however, I failed to plan to market myself. I hired a coach and some Internet consultants to later find out they knew less than I did about marketing. They had no problem charging me a considerable amount of money and not performing. The one thing I learned about getting into business was to trust but verify. You can't always believe what you hear.

This is where my journey began. How do you start a business and what do you do to get society to know who you are? Honestly, this was my biggest challenge. I had several marketing entities tell me they would bring awareness to my company. I literally spent tens of thousands of dollars on marketing programs that did not assist me in my business. You can imagine the amount of stress and frustration I was experiencing.

Life always has challenges. How we handle these challenges is called choices. Every misfortune has an opportunity. I say this because, had I not been taken advantage of by these marketing companies, I would not have take the time to truly understand the Internet and how to market a company. Society in general will tell you if they are looking for information they now turn to a computer, or more often than not they turn to a cellular device.

I now spent months researching and understanding social media marketing and website development. This allowed me to understand the importance of blogging and creating videos. This then led me to form a marketing company. You may think, that is strange - What happened to the real estate company? The real estate company is successful today. We actually opened a property management company to complement the real estate company. We realized in the first couple of years that there had been a shift in consumers looking for real estate. Consumers are now researching homes online. Some actually purchase homes online without ever physically viewing them.

In order to continue growing the real estate company we needed an online presence. Our real estate company was built from online business and continues to grow by the Internet business and referrals from our amazing clients. Yes, those clients that are reading this book know I am referring to them. I am grateful for each of you. Relationships are so extremely important.

I was, and continue to be, very passionate about helping others. There is a huge sense of satisfaction in knowing I personally made an impact on someone's life in a positive manner either emotionally or financially. Many people saw me as a target when I started my first business and they sold me a lot of junk. It was sad and I was angry. I refuse to remain angry, and I tend to find a way to make something good out of bad.

So now we proceed forward with a marketing company. It is extremely important in business today to understand the importance of an Internet presence. When you are out and about, take a look around. What percentage of people are without a cellular phone? Even the younger generations still in school down to the elementary level have cellular phones. Since this is an ongoing trend, would it be beneficial to have an online presence? I believe it is fair to say absolutely.

I truly believe that you need to become an expert at what you do. Stay on top of the trends within your industry. You also need to understand how other industries may directly affect you and your clients. This may not always be available in a classroom. You may wonder how I can do so many things as I am only one person. The answer is you leverage people. This is where I recognized the importance of strategic alliances.

The development of strategic alliances is not a difficult task. However, finding the appropriate successful people with a high level of integrity may be a bit more challenging. You can either adopt an advisory board or create a team of professionals to meet with monthly. Two teams are actually better than one. Each group should be comprised of successful business professionals. An example may include a business broker, an accountant, lawyer, financial planner, real estate agent, and mortgage broker, website design professional and marketing specialist. This group meets monthly and is your safe place to share business ideas and obstacles.

These relationships develop over time. A few things are achieved here. First, you are learning about another industry monthly. In addition, you are developing relationships. This forum is intended to be strictly confidential to not only discuss business needs but personal issues. This meeting enables everyone to recognize that we encounter similar circumstances although our businesses may be much different. We all have clients and most of us have employees. This is the safe place to discuss all activities and learn from others to avoid loss of time and revenue.

This was an amazing opportunity for me to learn faster, and in addition and probably more important than that, obtain credible referrals. It wasn't just someone I met at a networking event that may take months for me to get to know and hope to trust. I now have a group of trusted successful business professionals that have experienced a lot of trials and succeeded.

We all have different experiences that allows for faster growth within our companies and we can get solid advice within our group. In addition, we have solid experience with other business professionals that have a high level of ethics and we are able to refer competent professionals to each other to enable us to proceed forward faster and with more success. Growth has to do with quality. A company may grow fast, however, lack of quality will eventually create a failure. These types of strategic partners allow for quality and speed which are the best of both worlds.

In order to grow a successful business you really need to become well-rounded and understand a lot about not only your own business, but also other businesses that may directly or indirectly affect your client base. These strategic alliances allow for you to hear about these changes monthly. You now have several successful business professionals as mentors and colleagues. Remember knowledge is power.

It is very important to understand there are good and bad in every profession. We want to be the best. This is achieved by maintaining knowledge and successful execution. Think about this word "execution." It either means putting to death or putting into effect a plan. It is your choice what the outcome is.

Follow the nine steps below, and in tough economic times or times of emotional stress, you are sure to succeed and move forward regardless of what you are faced with.

1. Define your purpose.
Why do you do what you do? My purpose is to make sure that my son Zachary is always financially secure and debt-free. In addition, I have a sister that can't work. I am determined to make sure that she remains financially secure. These are the things that drive me to remain focused. Once you understand your purpose, there is no stopping the road to success.

2. Gratitude.
Write down the things you are grateful for on a daily basis. Share your gratitude with others.

3. Write down your goals and categorize them.
Write down personal, family and career goals. Review your goals weekly at a minimum.

4. Create a plan and evaluate it often.
Once your goals are defined you need a daily plan. It is like

a road map. This is a step-by-step guide that will define how you will accomplish your goals. Sometimes a daily plan is overwhelming. Start with an annual and quarterly plan and define the plan further as you mature with your business.

5. Online Presence.

You must be able to be located on the Internet. Create an amazing presence online. Remember people are using mobile devices to capture information.

6. Strategically Partner.

It is extremely important to align yourself with successful business partners. Remember to choose positive people. The choice is yours.

7. Choose your environment.

Yes you can. It is extremely important to surround yourself with like-minded people.

8. Educate yourself.

You must understand your industry. Just as important you must understand people. In order to truly become successful you must be able to integrate personalities with your expertise. Know who your clients are, understand their needs, and produce. These three items are critical to success.

9. FAITH.

You must understand that you are not in control. There is a major difference between control and accountability. We must all define our goals, review, and execute. This is what makes us great, better than good. We are accountable and we define and complete our goals. We do this because we have a purpose.

We maintain the highest level of integrity. This is what makes us great. What allows us to do these things and do them successfully? Our understanding that there is something GREATER than us. We are all different. That greater something in my life is GOD, our creator. I know that not only do I have a purpose I have defined for myself, but also God has a purpose for me. Once I truly understood this concept, setbacks became opportunities. Every setback now became an opportunity to excel.

You might say that sounds crazy. I thought so as well until I evaluated my life, the experiences I was blessed to have, the experiences at one time in my life made me angry and resentful. Once I understood I am here on a journey and it isn't always my own. I am now able to view my setbacks differently. Instead of frustration and anger, I experience excitement. I ask myself what is on the horizon. I pray for answers and I quietly wait. This process sometimes and many times takes much longer than I like. However, the more I practice this asking, remaining quiet and waiting, the easier it becomes.

I now look back over my life at my life tragedies. Yes, there have been several with true emotion and pain. The hurt and pain doesn't go away. However, my mindset has changed. This is no longer a negative experience. This is an opportunity to help others. People are not always honest with a high level of integrity. We will experience negative things. It isn't the experience we need to focus in. It is the opportunity it presents.

You see, we are all human. We all have experiences. It is what we do with them that matters. Your partner steals from you. You are angry and hurt. These are valid emotions. Feel them and grieve. Now it is time to ask questions. Why did this happen? Avoid the blame game. This is difficult to do. Ask productive questions. What can I learn from this? What opportunity is this experience providing me to help others ? In time it all becomes clear. Perhaps you make changes to who you are. This is a great opportunity for self-evaluation.

You will be a success and be able to overcome any obstacle you choose.

Get it Done. Be Grateful, and make No Excuses.

About Torey

Torey Eisenman is an entrepreneur, a best-selling author, and a leading expert in hyperlocal marketing. Torey was recently chosen as a guest on the "America's Premier Experts" Television show to speak on the importance of Hyperlocal Marketing for businesses big and small.

As a graduate of Florida Atlantic University with a degree in Marketing, Torey took her skills into the home building industry in 1991. By the time the real estate industry was ramping up in 2001, Torey had 10 years of experience in the Luxury Home Market, a general contractor's license, and a brand new company called Benchmark Real Estate Group, Inc.

She quickly found that her success in the corporate world for seven years was a detriment to focusing on her business. As job offers came in from various companies, it was hard to branch out on her own and walk away from perceived security. As life would have it, there came a period of time when the real estate market crashed, she lost her job, and sadly lost both of her parents. It was at this low point that Torey made one of the most significant decisions of her life. During what was perhaps the worst possible time to start a real estate company, she turned these losses into strengths as she drove full throttle into starting her company.

Eisenman quickly realized that starting a business was not easy, especially in this market. It became clear that although she was very well known in production homebuilding, the general public had no idea who Torey Eisenman and Benchmark Real Estate were. Eisenman started marketing her real estate company utilizing the Internet as a low cost, high reach tool for building her brand. She learned the in and outs of not only marketing online, but connecting online with prospective clients.

This proved immensely valuable considering that over 90 percent of homebuyers search online for properties. Torey just couldn't keep these online marketing strategies to herself and saw a business opportunity in helping other businesses. The next logical question for Torey became, why only real estate? She expanded her hyperlocal online marketing business to all industries and began showing businesses the profitability of not only having an online presence, but a social presence. Her hyperlocal marketing business has expanded dramatically since 2012 and she continues to have major success in the real estate profession – having acquired expertise and new perspective in her years as a successful entrepreneur.

For contact information for Torey Eisenman: Call: 407-230-6836
Email: toreyleisenman@gmail.com

CHAPTER 41

BUILD YOUR BRAND THROUGH REFERRALS IN A DOWN ECONOMY

BY TONY SIDIO

Author's note: Although this story is about my local Chamber of Commerce, I have successfully used these principles in public and private companies as well as non-profit clubs and organizations. Whether it is a Chamber of Commerce, Rotary or Optimist Club, not-for-profit Association, Society or any group of like-minded individuals, these principles can work for you too. Enjoy the story and visualize how you will apply the principles you learn in this chapter to your specific situation.

You may already know that we tend to find what we expect to find in life. Our expectations precede us. When you move to a new town, start a new job, or join a new organization, you will likely find what you are expecting to find. If you are expecting to meet cheerful, interesting, friendly people, you will probably find them. If, on the other hand, you expect to find grumpy, unfriendly, or uninteresting people, that is also what you will likely find. Same town, job or organization, but different results from different expectations.

Just as Henry Ford said "Whether you think you can, or whether you think you can't, either way you are right," you will tend to find what you expect to find in life. Not what you want and not what you need, but what you expect!

Of all the chambers in all the towns, in all the world, I walked into this one!

Little did I know, that this would be the beginning of a love affair. A love affair with the members and staff of my local Chamber of Commerce.

On a mild December day in 2006, I walked into my local Chamber of Commerce. I did not know a single member of this chamber or any member of the staff. In fact, the only business owner I knew in town owned a restaurant. He was not then and still is not a member of the Chamber.

So, why was I here?

Two years earlier I started a computer consulting business. The computer company I had been working with for 10 years had been put up for sale. My daily commute was 60 to 90 minutes each way depending on the traffic and I now wanted to work closer to home.

One of my first decisions as a new business owner was to talk to an established, successful, computer business owner. We had met at a computer vendor seminar a few months earlier.

I prefer to work with small business owners who have 5 to 25 computers in their office(s). So it made sense to find some strategic partners who worked with bigger companies. We could work together on some projects or pass the lead to the other partner depending on the client's needs.

During our conversation, I casually mentioned that I was thinking about joining my local Chamber of Commerce. I was surprised at his immediate response. "The Chamber would be a waste of your time. Go out and knock on doors and get your new clients that way," he said. So, I took his advice and went on my way.

Fast forward two years and my clients were still scattered around the western suburbs. It was time to go Against The Grain (professional advice of successful owner). It was time to meet the local business owners.

I wanted to build my business by referrals, not cold calls. I wanted my clients and friends to recommend me to their clients and friends. Of course, for people to do this you must deliver outstanding service and/or products. Think about it. If you are a business owner, professional, sales person, etc. you only want to recommend people that you know will do a good job. Otherwise, it will reflect poorly on you.

I found that when I receive a good referral, I really don't have to "sell" potential new clients. They were "presold" by the person referring me. I often find that the potential new client is ready to do business with me before we even meet face-to-face. The business is mine if I chose to accept it. That is the power of good referrals.

Now that you understand why I love referrals, you may wonder how do you get more of them? In my case, I decided the best way to meet local business owners, my primary prospects, was to join the Chamber of Commerce. You may decide to join a Rotary Club, Optimist Club, Kiwanis or any other group of like-minded individuals depending on what is available in your area.

Before walking into the Chamber office that December day, I committed to go all out. The Chamber membership is an annual one and I would make the most of it. I would attend every possible event and meet as many Chamber members as quickly as I could. I would volunteer to work on committees where they needed help. I believed this was the right decision and I would do everything possible to prove it. I immersed myself in the group.

Within six months I knew all of the members who attended Chamber events and they all knew me. As you may know, some members do not attend events. I did not meet them. In fact, there are still a few of our members that I have not met after 6 years.

I also joined a Leads Group. There are many kinds of Leads Groups with varying structures and rules. Some are associated with or sponsored by local chambers, clubs, or associations. Others are affiliates of National organizations. The Leads Group I joined was sponsored by the Chamber and met weekly for lunch. We were limited to thirty members max, each exclusively represents their industry. One realtor, one insurance agent, one banker, one computer person, etc. and they pass leads to each other. The realtor may have a new client who needs an attorney or an insurance agent. The insurance agent has a client who needs a CPA, etc.

Each Leads group takes on the persona of its leader and the format of the weekly meetings vary considerably. I recommend that you visit several Leads groups before you make your decision to join one. Pick one where the people are friendly, have a good time and, of course, pass leads every week. After all, the reason you join a leads group is to build relationships and pass leads. It is a lot more fun when you like the people in your leads group.

When you join the leads group, look for possible power partners. These are people with whom you can work very closely on a regular basis. For example, if you are a realtor, you probably work with attorneys, banks, mortgage brokers, insurance agents, home inspectors, etc. When you build your power partner team, you can increase your leads and your income dramatically. You should strive to work with all of the members of the leads group, but most of your business will probably come from your power partners.

People do business with people that they know, like and trust. The leads group gives you the opportunity to get to know many other people and for them to get to know you. When you do this correctly, you end up with many other people who are selling you and your products and services too. It's like having your own personal sales force of 15 to 25 people on the street referring their friends and clients to you.

Many leads groups provide the opportunity for you stand up in front of the group and deliver your personal commercial each week. This commercial, sometimes referred to as your elevator pitch, is typically 30 seconds and is very important. It is your chance to tell your story quickly and effectively. It should be carefully crafted. You should be able to deliver your commercial to a stranger and in 30 seconds he will know who you are, what you do, how you do it, and why he should do business with you.

Meanwhile, some of the chamber leaders had been watching me and asked if I would consider taking over as Chairman of one of our major fund-raising committees. This was quite an honor and a great responsibility. I was flattered and of course, agreed to do it.

I was also extremely pleased to be asked to sit on the nominating committee. This committee is charged with selecting candidates to run for the Board of Directors. I consider this committee to be one of the most important committees in the chamber.

Some of my colleagues might disagree. I know that the fund-raising committees are important. We can't operate without money. However, I submit that the organization cannot properly grow and thrive without a good Board of Directors. If you have a dysfunctional, inept or inexperienced Board, you are headed for big trouble. A great Board of Directors will make things happen!

By now, the Chamber was like family to me. I knew and loved the members and staff of this chamber. I looked forward to attending each event. We have some really great people here and it was fun to network with them and just be with them. When the economy changed in 2008, some of our members were hit hard and lost their businesses. It was a challenging time for all of us. On top of all of this, the Chamber had suffered high turnover in the top staff position, Executive Director. Many of our members were upset, angry and concerned about the chamber's future.

While all of this was playing out, I was being mentored behind the scenes by some of the leaders who wanted to take the Chamber to the next level. I agreed with their vision of a professionally-managed Chamber rather than a Chamber micromanaged by the Board of Directors. To succeed, though, we would have to get the right people in the right places, and make major changes that some current board members would vehemently fight.

So, once again, it was time to go against the grain. I knew that I could help guide the Chamber through the challenging times. I also knew that I could get elected to the Board because virtually everyone knew me, liked me, and trusted me. There was no question in their minds about my loyalty to them and the Chamber. The election to the Board at this time was still a popularity contest. If we needed to fill 6 seats, we would ask 10 or 12 candidates to run. With the approval of the nominating committee, I put my hat in the ring. I was elected.

In my first year on the Board, I was able to implement a major, much needed change. It was a hard-fought victory that required a special, heated, "Emergency" Board Meeting, but we prevailed. I served as Vice-Chairman for my second 2-year term and we implemented many other changes. Today, our Chamber is one of the few in this country that not only has survived the down economy, but has also thrived. We have a record number of members and provide more networking opportunities for our members than many Chambers twice our size. We encourage our members to do business with each other. Our members give and receive great referrals!

I started a new business in a town where I did not know anyone. My initial clients were not near my home. I wanted to build my new business as quickly and solidly as I could. I also wanted to find good clients closer to my home.

In a relatively short period of time, I met many good prospects who became friends and clients. I now have many clients close to my home. My business has prospered from great referrals even in a down economy!

Here is what you need to know and do to duplicate my success with your business in your area.

The events that your chamber, club or organization sponsors, are where you will meet the people you want to meet. Treat the events just like your other business appointments. Enter them in your calendar and attend as many as you possibly can.

A positive mental attitude will do wonders for you and everyone who comes in contact with you. When someone asks me how am I doing, the answer is always, "Great!" It makes me feel good and it lifts their spirits as well. People will enjoy spending time with you because you are always in a good mood.

I have always been a "people" person. If you are not one now, become one. I take a personal interest in the people I meet. I let them talk about themselves and I listen closely. I remember what they tell me and I remember their name.

Dale Carnegie said that a person's name is to that person the sweetest and most important sound in any language. Remember it and use it. He also said you can make more friends in two months by becoming interested in other people than you can in two years by trying to get people interested in you. Do this too, you will like the results.

Don't be afraid to stand out from the crowd. From the beginning I decided to stand out and be recognized. Blending in was not an option.

I redesigned my business card and added my photo. I wanted people to recognize me as quickly as possible. I put my logo and my name on all of my shirts. My logo and business cards consistently presented my brand information. It was different and it was memorable. I used them in everything I did. Email specials to the membership worked well for me. People who had not yet met me saw my picture, often several times. When they finally met me in person, they would say something like, I recognize you from your picture in the email blast, or wherever they had seen it.

People are more relaxed and comfortable talking to you when they can readily read your name. There is no pressure for them to remember your name if it is right there in front of them. So make sure that you have your name on your shirts, or have a name tag, always. Then, the pressure is on you to remember their name, as it should be.

I selected yellow shirts for my brand identity and put my logo on all of them. Why yellow? Simple. The yellow color represents sunshine. It is a constant reminder that my most important job is to brighten the day of everyone I meet. If they are looking forward to our next meeting, it is working.

About Tony

Tony grew up an "Army Brat." He lived in Japan and France as well as in eight states in the U.S.A. The lessons he learned traveling the world and constantly meeting new people have proven invaluable to him. He developed a **passion for people**.

In the fourth grade, Tony was introduced to science fiction and technology when he read Robert A. Heinlein's *The Star Beast*. He went on to read virtually every book Heinlein wrote, and, of course, many other authors as well. He developed a **passion for technology**.

He was an avid athlete and graduated in the top ten in his high school class. He attended Purdue University where he majored in science, psychology and math.

He was introduced to the concept of personal growth while working part time in college. Earl Nightingale's "Lead the Field" audio series taught Tony valuable lessons which helped him become one of the Top 10 College Dealers in the U.S. for Wear Ever Aluminum, Inc. He was hooked. He developed a **passion for personal growth and development.**

Tony has worked for Fortune 500 companies, medium-sized companies, and small companies. He is a serial entrepreneur. He has succeeded in multiple industries including direct sales and marketing, radio and television, and information technology. He has worked in New York City, Chicago, Philadelphia, Indianapolis, Fort Wayne and other cities.

Tony Sidio Consulting, his computer consulting business since 2004, was born from his passion for technology. He recently announced his Personalized, Professional Growth and Development™ company that helps people break through their barriers to success using the latest neuro-scientific techniques. It is the realization of his **lifelong passion for mentoring**.

Tony and his family have lived in the Chicago area since 1985. Contact him at his website: www.tonysidio.com or email:tony@tonysidio.com.

tony sidio înc
Take ît To The Next Level™
www.tonysidio.com
630-202-6765

CHAPTER 42

DISCOVERING YOUR INNER COACH

BY TIM DIXON

We all go through life inspired and influenced by people in our inner circle. Parents, teachers, coaches, and friends are all influences we rely on for valuable life lessons. There comes a time in each of us when we need to start being influenced by our own values and inner voice. Too many of us seek validation from outside sources. Whether it is in school, a job, on a team, or in a relationship, we seek approval from others. As we look for that validation, we stop living life for ourselves. Who are you living your life for? Are your goals and dreams really yours? If you are guilty of falling into the trap of living for others, you're not alone. The majority of society is in your situation and subconsciously goes through their day numb to the choices they make. Without even knowing, we get stuck in mediocrity and settle for the hand we were dealt. It is time we put a stop to this and I am here to tell you that you don't have to settle! Go after your big dreams and stop letting people who never achieved their dreams discourage you from yours. We all have the passion and desire for greatness. We are wired for excellence, but sometimes we lose our way. The outside influences tend to steer us in the direction of mediocrity and the CHAMP inside us fades. Together we will awaken the CHAMP within and reveal purpose, passion, and desire to fight for what we want in life!

I was stuck in the trap of mediocrity, but I kept fighting until I got what I wanted. It was not easy and I was criticized, but when I look in the mirror I like what I see and am proud of the fact that I fought for my dreams. We are all capable of achieving more in life and I am excited to tell you how you can live a more productive existence. It all comes down to the choices you make, and when you become aware of those choices, life will never be the same. Get excited to live a more passionate life, filled with purpose and desire for the best. Learning to create your inner coach, you will break away from the norm and experience a more fulfilled life.

Winning a National Championship, playing six years of professional baseball, two minor league World Series championships, and 13 years of success as a baseball coach seems like I had a good life. I have no complaints, but my journey to where I am now was not on a straight and narrow path. Out of high school, I attended Long Beach State and thought I was on the fast track to fame and fortune as a Major League baseball player. In the summer of my freshman year, I was slapped with a reality check when my scholarship was taken from me. My coach indirectly told me I was not good enough to play at the Division One level.

Next stop was San Jose City College, where I would spend one year getting my degree and looking for the next opportunity to fulfill my dream of playing professional baseball. I did get my Associate's degree, but baseball once again fell short. Just an average year, I was left with few options of where to go next. University of Arkansas at Little Rock was where I would spend my junior year. Another year of mediocrity on the baseball field, yet I remained optimistic about my future.

That summer I was given the ultimate gift. I was presented an opportunity I knew in my heart and soul was the moment I had worked so hard for - the chance to play baseball for Cal State Fullerton, one of the best baseball programs in the country. With a powerhouse program like Fullerton, I had to prove myself on day one, or it could have meant the end to my dreams of playing at the next level. Knowing these risks, I signed my scholarship papers and began one of the most amazing journeys of my life. Before the first game in 1995, I was named the Saturday starter for the Titans and what a year we had. Our final record was 57-9. My pitching record was 13-0 and I still hold the record for most wins without a loss in Fullerton history. Our season ended on an eighteen game winning streak and we were crowned 1995 National Champions!

That magical year gave me so many amazing memories, but more importantly it gave me what I set my mind to several years prior - being drafted in the fourteenth round of the 1995 Major League Baseball Amateur Draft by the Montreal Expos. Talk about validation! So many times during the struggles and moves I could have given up on my dream. That was not an option and I was living my dream, making the most of every opportunity. I never made the fame and fortune, but I played six years of professional baseball, winning two Minor League Championships, making the All-Star team three times, and traveling the world as a professional athlete.

So how did this journeyman end up on one of the best college teams ever and play the game he loved till the age of thirty? Some say luck, others just good timing. For me, it was the ability to stick with a dream no matter the circumstances. There were some very influential people in my life that taught me about work ethic, caring for others, and the power of the mind. At Fullerton, we took a class taught by one of the best minds I have ever met, Ken Ravizza. We talked about controlling the controllables, learned about dealing with failure, and the power of choice. It was those skills that revealed a completely different person on the field and it was that difference that allowed me to have success. Eliminating the things I could not control, everything fell into place. I played with conscious clarity and that combined with my desire to be the best, I know I reached my maximum ability.

After my playing career was over, I immediately began coaching baseball and have spent the last thirteen years teaching the game that gave me so much. My career began to shift when I accepted a coaching position at the United States Air Force Academy. My mindset for coaching changed from winning games to inspiring my players. I was hired to make these future officers the best baseball players they could be while they learned the grueling details of defending our freedom. Baseball became less important and life lessons became priority. These kids took an oath and I had this amazing opportunity to influence their lives in a positive way. It was a responsibility I took very seriously, but I knew I had to work on myself before I could work on them. Listening to Jim Rohn, I learned that if I wanted things to get better, I had to get better. If I was to make these young men the best they could be, then I had to become the best I could be. I continued to ask myself - how do I get these kids to eventually become their own coach? To make the little choices on a daily basis that creates their best life. Not doing what everyone else was doing. Not settling for mediocrity. I went to work on myself and quickly began to see changes.

My first year was filled with constant teaching moments. Taking every opportunity to make my players aware of their choices and not allowing them to make excuses or blame others. Choices they were making every day were not drastic choices at the time, but made over a long period of time created magic! It was books like The Compound Effect by Darren Hardy and the Slight Edge by Jeff Olson that really opened my eyes to how the little choices made over time create who you are.

After several months with my players, I began to see a shift. What they talked about began to change. How they reacted to situations changed. They were taking more responsibility for their choices and were creating better attitudes towards things they once took for granted. I began to hear them talk about the things I talked about. Little sayings like controlling the controllables, stop pointing fingers and start pointing thumbs, and don't count the days, make the days count were becoming their vocabulary. At that moment, I got out of the way and watched them run with it. They took responsibility and ownership in their thoughts and actions. It was powerful and they were now listening to their inner coach. They had that inner voice telling them about making right decisions and not allowing the outside influences dictate who they became. I was still there for them, but it was apparent they were now in complete control of their lives.

What took several years for my players and me to discover can now be accomplished by taking action with five simple steps. Not only will these steps guide you to a more fulfilled life, but also you will see this person you were looking for was always within waiting to come out. Applying these steps will bring out your inner coach, revealing the true CHAMP in your life!

The purpose of your inner coach is to push you past mediocrity. That voice within has always been there, yet too many times you have ignored it, letting the outside voices and influences make your decisions for you. As you get in tune with your inner coach, you will quickly see a shift in your daily actions. Staying consistent with your choices will guide you to accomplishments you never thought possible. The five steps to discovering your inner coach are as follows:

C – Conscious Clarity in Choices

H – Honesty

A – Act of Gratitude

M – Maximizing every day

P – Pillow test

<u>CONSCIOUS CLARITY IN CHOICES</u> – Everything we become is due to the choices we make. Whether you want to believe it or not, you are where you are because of your choices. Conscious clarity in your choices can and will change who you become. Don't just show up for the choices that you make! Show up and participate in the choice with passion and purpose for a superior you. If each choice you make has that intent, the norm will no longer be enough. Your expectations for yourself will increase and once that momentum starts it will be impossible to stop. Listening to your inner coach will give you that clarity you need to stay on track. There will be outside influences trying to get you back to their world of mediocrity, but that world will no longer have appeal.

<u>HONESTY</u> – This is a big one. How many times have you consciously been dishonest with yourself? We have excuses why we can't get a promotion or why we can't keep a relationship. Your inner coach will demand honesty! When you look at yourself in the mirror you have to be honest with the person you are looking at. Stop blaming everyone for where you are! Stop pointing fingers and playing the role of victim! When you become honest with yourself it gives you freedom to explore a life of purpose. If we blame everyone for our mistakes, we can't move forward and we get stuck in the pit of excuses, victimhood, and mediocrity. Honesty gives you power and that power from within is what it takes to shatter expectations of what you think you are capable of accomplishing.

<u>ACT OF GRATITUDE</u> – Appreciation for life is something we often forget. We take for granted what we have. We expect things to be there for us. It usually takes a tragic event to make us take a step back and appreciate life. Your inner coach will help you appreciate and act on the little things. As you begin to act with gratitude, you fill your life with energy. That energy not only improves your life, but it improves the lives of those around you. Appreciate what you have. Be grateful for each day you are given and get everything you can out of those precious twenty- four hours. Here is the kicker. Put that appreciation in action! It is a MUST that you act. It is the act of appreciation that puts greatness in motion. Without action, we just have emotional moments that are temporary.

MAXIMIZE EVERY DAY – The old saying *live as if this was your last day* is a powerful statement. From the time you wake up until the time you go to sleep you should have purpose with everything you do. If what you are doing does not have purpose, stop doing it! No matter if you are driving to work or walking the dog, do it with passion, conviction, and desire. You cannot do more tomorrow to make up for what you didn't do today. It doesn't work that way. We are all given 24 hours in a day. What separates the mediocre from the great is what you do with those 24 hours. There will be failures, but when you fail, fail forward. Live life with conviction and when you get knocked down you get back up, learn from it, and get excited to try again! That inner coach will remind you to live everyday to the fullest.

PILLOW TEST – Your inner coach will ask you to take the pillow test at the end of every day. When you lay your head on your pillow each night, you need to ask yourself if you lived your best life for that day. If you answer yes, you will be able to sleep soundly. If you cannot answer yes, you will stare at the ceiling with regret. Your inner coach will keep you on track so you can have more peaceful nights of sleep as opposed to the feeling of regret.

So there you have it. The five steps above can be implemented at this very moment. You can literally stop reading right now and tell yourself that you will commit to these five steps and listen to your inner coach. If you do nothing after reading this chapter, nothing in your life will change, but if you commit to these five steps it could change your life forever. If you're looking for instant results, you won't get them here. But if you listen to your inner coach and make the right choices on a daily basis, you will become whatever you want to become. So what's it going to be? There should be no negotiating! You have a responsibility to see how far you can go in life. No more excuses and no more outside voices stealing your dreams from you. Hop on and get ready to take an amazing ride on this journey we call life.

About Tim

Tim Dixon is putting an end to mediocrity. With a background in psychology and 13 years of coaching experience, Tim is sought out by athletes at all levels, from high school to professionals. His expertise in visualization training delivers a true sense of clarity; allowing the athlete to perform at higher levels of play. Recognized for his presence and impact from the stage, Tim has been a featured speaker at Coaches Conventions, Baseball Camps, and several Business Events around the Country.

Although the majority of Tim's time is spent in the athletic arena, you can also find him coaching in a classroom or workshop. A Squadron Professional Ethics Advisor (SPEA) and Certified Character Coach with the United States Air Force Academy, Tim teaches honor lessons to 125 cadets each year as well as working one-on-one with future officers on building character and overcoming obstacles in everyday life. Tim's mental training workshops are not for those who seek comfort; he challenges the daily choices and forces you to push through current expectations.

Critically acclaimed for his slightly morbid talk "Your Final Word," an eye opening experience delivering your own eulogy. Tim exposes the ugly truth behind mediocrity and leaves you motivated for lasting change.

To learn more about Tim Dixon. visit: www.EndingMediocrity.com
or call: 719-297-1176.

www.EndingMediocrity.com

CHAPTER 43

DESIGNING A CUSTOM-FIT LIFE

BY DR. SUSAN TAPLE

I have always been interested in people and how they were living their lives. As soon as I understood I would have a career and lifestyle choices to make someday, I began observing people and collecting data on lifestyle choice and contentment. Similar to how you might survey a person's outfit, I have been surveying if people's selected lifestyle fit them. At first, my interest in lifestyle choice grew out of my need to design my own life someday and the hope that I would be happy into adulthood. As I grew up my curiosity expanded to include concern for others. While I knew of many success stories where people had accomplished a lifestyle that incorporated their strengths, had meaning and brought them pleasure, I also knew of people who experienced stress and disappointment over their chosen lifestyle – a lifestyle where they were underutilized, felt insignificant, and experienced on-going defeat. I sought to then understand how people could avoid poor choices, or recognize them, and make changes.

Curiosity has driven me to try on several different lifestyles for myself. I grew up in an apartment building in Chicago with doormen, but as an adult, bought a horse and hobby farm in rural Minnesota. Not being opposed to change, I have visited over 25 countries and lived in just under 10 cities including New Orleans, Los Angeles and Minneapolis. My work experiences grew out of an interest in fine art to gemology and personal property appraising. My formal study of education led to work in administration, training, human resources, and finally small business ownership. As a doctoral student, I conducted historical research on dressmakers and milliners. It was through these women that I realized a custom-fit life brings the most rewards. They were entrepreneurs that bucked the conventional role of homemaker and created a lifestyle for themselves where they used their artistry, had worth in society, and experienced gratitude. Through all of my formal and informal research, I have been looking for the ideal lifestyle that would bring success and happiness, but what I discovered was, as uniquely talented individuals, we all need to create the right lifestyle for ourselves.

Two early role models in my research were excellent examples of designing a custom-fit life. Ellen was slightly older than I was when she went off to attend college. She became an archeologist and found work in Egypt. She spent long days digging under the hot sun, sleeping in a tent, and loving every minute. Ellen has a lifestyle that makes the best use of her abilities, values, and brings her joy. Ellen's best friend Margaret knew that she wanted to be a nurse, but her family thought she should become a doctor instead. I witnessed Margaret walking straight down her chosen path despite the objection. Margaret is a model of determination and she understood no one else should choose her lifestyle for her.

People will try to influence the lifestyle choice of their friends and family. It behooves all of us to let people design their lifestyle and to create our own without influence. I worked with a physician who came to realize having children was everyone else's idea for him. He identified through leadership coaching his passion was for adult relationships and research. It is critical to do the work to know who we are as individuals and to only seek affirmation from ourselves.

There is no one right way to arrange your life, but at some point you will know if you have arranged it in a way that is holding you back. Tom is a talented communications director. He recently made a job change because he realized, through personality profile work, he only loved the idea of his job. In actuality he was experiencing political turmoil and marginalization. While he put his organization on a pedestal, he recognized the job did not allow him to use his best skills and add value.

What other people find acceptable or unacceptable is irrelevant to choosing our own lifestyle. We each need to discover what works and is healthy for us. We all need different things in jobs and relationships. I have consulted with people whose work atmosphere was so toxic they sought medical attention, but their colleagues fared better. A married couple I know agrees the husband can go out of town when the wife is pregnant. Others couples would not feel the same way. The only thing that matters it what matters to you, judge your lifestyle by your own measurements.

Often we focus on our career and family to gauge our lifestyle satisfaction, but it is broader than that. While many of us at times complain about the weather, traffic, or culture of the town we live in, some people are living in a region that meets few of their needs. When I moved to my hobby farm, I lost access to many of the services and activities I had grown accustomed to while living in larger cities. I had to find replacements, create my own, or acknowledge it was a need not being met. In designing a custom-fit life we need to consider all eight areas of life, what we want in regard to each area, and if we are having positive outcomes.

EIGHT AREAS OF LIFE AND POTENTIAL POSITIVE OUTCOMES

1. Career
Fulfillment from work through contributions leading to favorable results.

2. Financial
Access to the necessary funds in order to have a chosen lifestyle and the proper management of those funds.

3. Intellectual
Experiencing new concepts, improving skills, and seeking challenges in pursuit of learning.

4. Social
Rewarding connections with other people.

5. Emotional
Understanding and acknowledging emotions to cope with challenges.

6. Spiritual

Connecting with the deepest part of self to have feelings of peace and harmony, bringing meaning, and the knowledge that you have a purpose to fulfill.

7. Environmental

Having a positive impact on the environment; office, home, community, and planet.

8. Physical

Maintaining a healthy quality of life that allows for activity without fatigue or pain.

For the person who realizes they have unmet needs and their current lifestyle is not working, the critical next step is to do something about it. Philosopher Maxine Greene said that "Freedom is the capacity to surpass the given and look at things as if they could be otherwise." I support people in understanding they have the ability to design a custom-fit life. A lifestyle that incorporates their skills, values, and brings them joy. This is so important because it is only through a custom-fit life that we can become top performers in our chosen field, have successes, make valuable impacts on people, and spread knowledge and compassion.

I believe there is always a way to have the life you want, but it takes dedication to allow yourself to operate out of a place of confidence and optimism about your value and the future. For some people, it takes a great deal of preparation to get to this place of confidence and optimism and be ready to design a custom-fit life. Issues from the past such as prior hurts and trauma can interfere. It also takes time, time to focus on yourself, your needs, and future options. Current lifestyle design can be limiting in and of itself. I have talked with young leaders, raising children on their own, who feel overwhelmed just by doing the minimum at work and at home. Some people concede they have a life of few real choices and feel trapped. Like-minded people who also see scarcity everywhere surround them. Their thoughts, based on fears and limitations, keep them in the same place. Additionally the people in their life confirm and affirm these fears. It is essential to break away from this kind of thinking and the people who are not ready for risk because the longer people are in positions of failure the more resigned they become to feelings of having no control. Tools such as coaching, goal setting, and reading about positive behavioral change can help.

When working with people who want to make lifestyle changes, I remind them they can learn anything they need to learn. You can always gain content knowledge. Training you have not yet completed is simply an opportunity to grow. A friend of mine has taught herself four different languages. Reference materials are available on virtually very topic and there is a plethora of intelligent professionals who can help you make any kind of transition. Universities are full of non-traditional students going back to get a degree. There are many examples of successful career changes and relocations. Additionally, alterations can be made, even if we are not accustomed to making them. Houses, cars, and personal property can be bought or sold, children's schools can be changed, jobs can be left and others can be obtained, relationships can be started, ended or redefined. Financing the design of a custom-fit lifestyle is a worthy investment.

I encourage people not to let fear and doubt prevent them from creating a custom-fit life, a life that employs their best skills, incorporates their values, and is enjoyable. The real fear should be in living a life of lack, dishonesty, and sadness. Additionally, I point out that no action is an action. If someone determines they are unfulfilled in their current lifestyle but chooses to take no action, they need to take responsibility for remaining the same. There is always a way to the life you want but you must take action to have it. Feeling stuck is a self-created illusion and understanding this helps propel people forward. Additionally while other people want to influence us, no one cares as much about our life as we do. Therefore, it is important to recognize feelings of insecurity for what they are – a self-created illusion that can be exposed.

Steve Jobs summed it up well "Your time is limited, so don't waste it living someone else's life. Don't be trapped by dogma — which is living with the results of other people's thinking. Don't let the noise of others' opinions drown out your own inner voice. And most important, have the courage to follow your heart and intuition. They somehow already know what you truly want to become. Everything else is secondary."

EIGHT STEPS TO CREATING A CUSTOM-FIT LIFE

1. Get to Know Yourself.

Identify your strengths, understand what is meaningful to you, and identify what brings you joy. Coaching and tools such as the Myers Briggs Type Indicator®, mind mapping, and journaling can help you understand your needs in each of the eights areas of life. Look at your current lifestyle. Make a list of what is working and what is not working in each of the eight areas. Then determine the changes necessary to design a lifestyle that meets your needs based on what you have learned about yourself.

2. Goal Setting.

Become a master at goal setting and follow through. Read up on how this process can be most effective and use a complete system that includes daily review of goals and incorporates timelines. Goal Setting is a critical step in designing a custom-fit life and in working towards your full potential. You cannot hit a target that you cannot see.

3. Research.

Take the time to investigate new ideas. Information gathering is important when you are looking to take on a new venture or make a change. I became excellent at interviewing only by reading about it extensively and taking all the advice I read such as practicing my answers in a mirror. I did not even consider going into network marketing until I had read four books, cover to cover, on the business model.

4. Exploration.

Try on aspects of the lifestyle you are considering. Volunteer in a new industry, set up informational interviews, visit cities you have thought of relocating to, and talk to people who have what you want.

5. Network.

Get around successful, open-minded, healthy people. At the same time, weed out negative, narrow-minded people. When you need advice turn to the people who have accomplished what you want as the opposed to the people who have not. Find expertise through business and professional associations, universities, and networking groups.

6. Maximize your energy.

Activities that pertain to your health, physical fitness, hygiene, life extension, nutrition, sleep, and stress management are worthy activities. Value them, schedule them, and participate in them with no regrets. I have learned that it does not matter to me what I eat, it matters to me that I eat. So, eat defensively and without guilt. Plan to work out everyday except the days you just cannot. When traveling stay at hotels that provide workout facilities and even workout clothes.

7. Obtain multiple streams of revenue.

Especially for people looking to make a career change or be in some type of transition, adding a part-time job, paid project, network marketing, or home-based small business, can give you some options. Consider a portfolio career. Look to build residual income, income from investments, and at least one revenue stream of which you are in charge.

8. Minimize debt and financial worry.

Debt, lack of funds, and sometimes personal property, are burdens that hold people back. Become intimately aware of your financial picture: income, expenses, debt, and net worth. Work with a professional to plan for a secure future with little to no debt and ample revenue for your custom-fit lifestyle.

You owe it to yourself, and the world, to be a happy, successful, top performer. You obtain this by designing a custom-fit life. A lifestyle tailored to your strengths, that is meaningful, and brings you joy. It takes work to discover who you are and what you want, but it is the most important work we each will do.

You are where you are because of choices you have made up to now. Identify your fears and the obstacles that have prevented you so far from having a custom-fit life. Examine areas of stress or unhappiness. Consider how you are responsible for them. Blaming others is unproductive, so do not make excuses but instead create solutions. Recognize your negative reactions and spend time understanding yourself through them. Begin to free yourself from harmful emotions such as jealousy and anger. Practice having positive reactions. Something is only a problem if you decide it is a problem. Work towards being self-disciplined in your response to stress and feelings of disappointment.

Your thoughts control your reality. Fill your mind with positive images about life, your value and the future. At the same time, exclude negative thoughts, feelings of fear, doubt, and insecurity. You are what you think about, so think about what you want and how to get it. You have the power to forge and govern your own life. Once you internalize the understanding that you are responsible for everything in your life, you are better poised to design a custom-fit life. The only way to have the future you want is to create it.

About Dr. Susan

Dr. Susan Taple is passionate about developing leadership in others and helping organizations improve their relevance and viability. Her extensive professional background includes training and human resource development, administration, and personal property appraising. Susan focuses on teaching executives to how to best manage their careers to achieve success and genuinely engage others.

Susan believes we all have a responsibility to determine who we are, identify our strengths, and be top performers in our chosen field. Susan has found her success through her company Cultivation Conquest. Here, she uses her best skills to perform the work she considers to be both a privilege and a responsibility.

Susan is an advocate of lifelong learning for her clients and her own educational background includes a doctorate degree in educational leadership. Susan is known for being motivating, influential and organized.

To learn more about Dr. Susan Taple, visit: www.cultivationconquest.com